Pathways to Recovery
Group Facilitator's Guide

Lori Davidson
Diane McDiarmid
Jean M. Higbee

The University of Kansas School of Social Welfare
Office of Mental Health Research & Training

© Copyright 2006, Revised 2007, Revised 2012 University of Kansas School of Social Welfare

All rights reserved. No part of the material (except the accompanying handouts) may be reproduced in any form or by any means, electronic or mechanical, including photocopying, recording, or by any information storage and retrieval system without written permission from the authors.

The authors of this book do not receive any of the profits from sales of this publication. All profits go towards reprinting the guide for distribution and to provide scholarships for Kansas mental health consumers to return to post-secondary education.

This facilitator's guide to accompany *Pathways to Recovery: A Strengths Recovery Self-Help Workbook* is published by the University of Kansas School of Social Welfare, Lawrence, KS, through a contract with Kansas Social & Rehabilitation Services.

Other publication includes:
The Trail is the Thing: A Year of Daily Reflections Based on Pathways to Recovery. For more information, visit: pathwaystorerecoverybooks.com, or pathways@ku.edu.

Dedication

"If you are planning for a year, sow rice;
if you are planning for a decade, plant trees;
if you are planning for a lifetime, educate people."

~ Chinese Proverb

This facilitator's guide is dedicated to the many outstanding individuals who give daily of their talents, energy and passion to bring the message of recovery from mental illness out of the darkness into the glorious light of hope.

We're honored to join you on the *Pathway to Recovery!*

In Appreciation

"Sometimes our light goes out but is blown into flame by another human being. Each of us owes deepest thanks to those who have rekindled this light."
~ Albert Schweitzer

Although our names appear on the *Pathways to Recovery Group Facilitator's Guide*, this has truly been a collective project and team effort. We are particularly grateful to the dedicated group of professionals at the University of Kansas School of Social Welfare's Supported Education Group—Anna Collins, Karen Cook, Dinah Dykes and Susan Kobzar—and to our recent social work students, Christa Denzer, Vincent Starnino, Barb Torgerson and Ryan Veesart. These dedicated individuals have provided valuable expertise, insight and feedback. They have shared the Supported Education Group office as a repository for ideas, pilot projects and resources, all focused on helping people embrace, succeed and thrive on their recovery journey.

We also offer our appreciation to Charles A. Rapp, Ph.D., who serves as the Director of KU's Office of Mental Health Research and Training. Charlie serves as our mentor and provides us valuable support, suggestions and perspective along the way.

We are especially grateful to several talented individuals. Ty Scott, Janice Driscoll and Suzette Mack added their unique perspective and knowledge in the development and implementation of the original pilot group. Karen Cook, Liz Gowdy, Tonya Hinman, Matt Phillips, Joan Poss, Sarah Ratzlaff, Elizabeth Sheils, Mark Turner and Sherrie Watkins-Alvey shared valuable feedback and editing for the session agendas. The input of these creative and spirited individuals has made a significant impact on our decisions and the product that you have before you.

The State of Kansas, Social & Rehabilitation Services (SRS) is a strong partner and advocate for community support services, best practices and recovery-oriented services in our state. SRS has provided financial assistance for this project and we are deeply appreciative of their ongoing support of our efforts.

Johnson County Mental Health Center's Community Support Services (CSS) in Shawnee, Kansas, under the leadership of Tim DeWeese and Sandra Lyke, promoted the *Pathways to Recovery* pilot within their organization and the Kansas City community. Mike Higgins, Heather McKaig and Patrice Murphy with the Resource Development Team at Johnson County CSS, co-facilitated a pilot training of the *Pathways to Recovery Group Facilitator's Guide*. Their feedback and suggestions were particularly helpful.

Finally, we are most grateful to the individuals, students, families and practitioners who have shared their personal truth and experiences with us during this process. As *Pathways to Recovery* groups flourish, their willingness to partner with us reminds, inspires and keeps us focused on why we are so excited about this project and the multifaceted components of recovery.

We encourage and invite you to join us in our enthusiasm and passion towards supporting and promoting strengths-based recovery orientated practices. Enjoy the journey!

Lori Davidson, Diane McDiarmid & Jean M. Higbee
The University of Kansas, 2006

November, 2007
Since the first printing of *Pathways to Recovery*, we at the University of Kansas has been both honored and humbled at the response this recovery tool has had worldwide. We have heard from hundreds of individuals and organizations who have found this workbook helpful and life-altering. We sincerely thank you for your ideas and comments & stories and trust you will continue sharing these with us.

We are truly thankful to those individuals who became our initial "testers" for the guide. Simply by being the first to use the guide, you have provided honest feedback and exciting suggestions that support even more options for *Pathways to Recovery*. In addition, thanks also goes to Mark Holter, PhD, Susana Mariscal, Jon Hudson and Sadaaki Fukui, PhD who have joined our efforts since this guide was first published. It's an honor to work with you and to call you friends. Susan Murphy has also provided extensive feedback to us and our thanks to her for her honesty and feedback.

As we embark on examining *Pathways* from a research perspective, we are also thankful to individuals at our Kansas consumer-run organizations that are taking the information from this recovery tool and sharing it with their peers, their families, their providers – even with strangers who have crossed their paths. It is our honor to work together with you!

We'd also like to take this opportunity to remember the memory of at least four individuals who shared their stories in *Pathways to Recovery* - Crystal Dirks, Jan Hanson, Carrie Hunter & Shelly Scott. Each of these individuals shared their lives and their stories of hope and compassion within the pages of Pathways. We miss them dearly.

Lori Davidson
The University of Kansas School of Social Welfare, 2007

Forward

"Most of the important things in the world have been accomplished by people who have kept on trying when there seemed to be no hope at all."

~ Dale Carnegie

When *Pathways to Recovery: A Strengths Recovery Self-Help Workbook* was first printed, spontaneous groups sprung up around the globe. Some were held in formal settings; others were conducted with just two or three people in someone's living room. In most, participants found themselves completing the exercises, discussing the quotations and even arguing about whether certain topics should be in one chapter or another. One group in Minnesota spent a year meeting at their drop-in center, getting, as one of the members shared, "all the way through chapter five!" There's a group in rural Kansas who even created a float for a local community parade using *Pathways to Recovery* as the theme.

Facilitators have found a variety of ways to share the information from the book. The initial focus group in Shawnee, Kansas, was held for only twelve weeks. While participants liked the group, they quickly gave the feedback that this was much too short a time to take in all the material. Others have enjoyed covering a chapter a week.

As authors and educators, we truly believe in the power of recovery and self-help. We know the value that resources and tools can bring to individuals who are searching, especially when put in *their* hands and done in whatever way they find helpful.

But sometimes, it's easy to forget the impact you can have on individual lives. That's why we were so humbled by the following letter. In a synchronistic moment, we received these words — unsolicited — from an individual in Toronto. We share it as a reminder that our efforts in writing this guide and your efforts in sharing the material, *do* make a difference...

Dear Friends,

*I just completed the **Pathways To Recovery** group...At first, I had no idea what I was committing myself to, but I was drawn by the title to join. I have to say that I've attended many groups in the past 14 years that I've been in the mental health system. Yet, I absolutely feel that this is one of the best groups I have ever attended.*

Sure there are many self-help groups out there, but none other than this one relate, state, or include and allude to one being a consumer/survivor in the mental health system and the stigma that follows with it.

***Pathways to Recovery** gave me a deep sense of understanding myself and ways of coping in all aspects, or as the book refers to, the domains in one's life. (Domain in the dictionary states it as a territory or an area or section in your life.)*

In the book, it talks about "reclaiming a fuller life" and, in order to do that, we build on our strengths. It looks at 8 different domains such as our living situation, education, health and wellness, and so on.

I like the fact that it was a small group. I felt the link, the tie, the warmth as we got to know each other. I felt that I was accepted and understood just as I was, and I didn't need to use my mask. The support and encouragement from the group was great and I sensed a bond between us.

I highly recommend this group to anyone who is ready to move on to a better state of mind and spirit. You need to ask and look deep inside yourself and decide, "Do I want to stay like this forever or am I ready for change?"

By reading and viewing each chapter, answering each question honestly and truthfully, you come to know the real person you were meant to be. There might be something you didn't know about yourself – this could be positive or negative – either way it's a great feeling. It's great because at this point you will have the knowledge and ability to make the changes to better yourself, your life, and your relationships.

Trust me after many years in the darkness, I finally found the light, the hope and courage to move on. I no longer see myself as a victim, a loser, a failure or a burden on society [or one] that only deserves death. I finally found myself, my strength and I'm holding my own.

This is the first year in 10 years that I didn't spend my birthday...in the hospital feeling despair and wishing I was dead. This year I celebrated "me," a new beginning, a new chapter in my road to recovery. I am alive! I am free to be me!

You too can have this discovery called life. Live each and every day to the fullest. All you need is to have an open mind and the will to believe in yourself. Know that you have choices and can make changes within yourself and your community.

I wish you all the best on your own unique journey to recovery!

Just remember that each person's journey is different and each person moves forward at their own pace. There is no rush whatsoever. God Bless!

~ Anonymous

Table of Contents

Introduction to the Facilitator's Guide
Welcome to the Facilitator's Guide. 17
    The Concept of Self-Help 17
    The Story of *Pathways to Recovery*. 18
    Content of the Facilitator's Guides 21
    Format of the Group Sessions 23
    Guidelines for Creating Groups 25
    Guidelines for Facilitating a Group 30

Module One
Introduction to Module One 37
Session 1: *Welcome & Introductions* 39
Session 2: *The Strengths Approach to Recovery* 43
Session 3: *What is Recovery?* 46
Session 4: *Recovery & Resilience* 49
Session 5: *Foundations of Recovery* 52
Session 6: *Supercharging Strategy: Creativity* 55
Session 7: *Recovery & Creativity* 58
Session 8: *The ABCs that Get Us into Gear* 60
Session 9: *A=Attitudes: Hope* 63
Session 10: *A=Attitudes: Building Hope* 66
Session 11: *A=Attitudes: Building Courage* 69
Session 12: *B=Behavior: Risks & Wrong Turns* 72
Session 13: *C= Cognition: Ways of Thinking*. 75
Session 14: *Supercharging Strategy: Celebration!*. 78
Session 15: *Motivation: The Fuel for the Journey*. 81
Session 16: *Taking the Driver's Seat for Recovery*. 84
Session 17: *Motivation in Action*. 87
Session 18: *Reactions to the Movie*. 89

Table of Contents, cont.

Module One, cont.

Session 19: *Turnaround Toward Recovery*...91
Session 20: *Facilitator's Choice*...94
Session 21: *Small Group Project Presentations*......................................97
Session 22: *Small Group Project Presentations, cont.*...............................99
Session 23: *Module Evaluation & Looking Ahead*....................................101
Session 24: *Celebration!*...104

Module Two

Introduction to Module Two...109
Session 1: *Welcome & Introductions*...111
Session 2: *Detours & Roadblocks*..115
Session 3: *Driving Using the Rearview Mirror*.....................................118
Session 4: *Heading in Someone Else's Direction*...................................121
Session 5: *Driving Ourselves Day & Night*...124
Session 6: *Slowed Down by Low Expectations*.......................................127
Session 7: *Healing Self-Stigma*...129
Session 8: *Driving in Circles & Feeling Lost*.....................................133
Session 9: *Thrown Off-Track by Symptoms*..136
Session 10: *Riding the Brake Pedal*...139
Session 11: *When the Going Gets Boring*...142
Session 12: *Supercharging Strategies: Meditation & Visualization*.................145
Session 13: *Changing Our Course*..148
Session 14: *Getting Going*..151
Session 15: *Getting Going, cont.*...154
Session 16: *Making the Most of Our Strengths*.....................................157
Session 17: *Creating a Personal Vision*...160
Session 18: *Setting a Course to Succeed*..163
Session 19: *Bringing It All Together*...166

Table of Contents, cont.

Module Two, cont.

Session 20: *Facilitator's Choice* 169
Session 21: *Small Group Project Presentations* 172
Session 22: *Small Group Project Presentations, cont.* 174
Session 23: *Evaluation & Looking Ahead* 176
Session 24: *Celebration!* 179

Module Three

Introduction to Module Three 183
Session 1: *Welcome & Introductions* 185
Session 2: *Moving Forward on the Journey* 188
Session 3: *Heading Toward Home* 191
Session 4: *Learning as We Go* 194
Session 5: *Ticket to Ride* 197
Session 6: *Ticket to Ride, cont.* 200
Session 7: *Building a Career Path* 203
Session 8: *Building a Career Path, cont.* 206
Session 9: *Recharging Our Batteries* 209
Session 10: *Feeling Good Along the Way & Supercharging Strategy: Exercise* 212
Session 11: *Private Pleasures* 215
Session 12: *Private Pleasures, cont.* 219
Session 13: *Forging a Higher Path* 223
Session 14: *Forging a Higher Path, cont.* 226
Session 15: *Travel Companions & Social Support* 229
Session 16: *Writing the Personal Recovery Plan* 232
Session 17: *Bringing It All Together* 235
Session 18: *Bringing It All Together, cont.* 238
Session 19: *Supercharging Strategy: Humor* 241
Session 20: *Facilitator's Choice* 244

Table of Contents, cont.

Module Three, cont.

Session 21: *Small Group Project Presentations* 247
Session 22: *Small Group Project Presentations, cont.* 249
Session 23: *Module Evaluation & Looking Ahead* 251
Session 24: *Celebration!* 254

Module Four

Introduction to Module Four 259
Session 1: *Welcome & Introductions* 261
Session 2: *Assessing Your Circle of Support* 264
Session 3: *Roadblocks to Communication* 267
Session 4: *Expanding Our Circle of Support* 270
Session 5: *Exploring Our Relationships* 273
Session 6: *Exploring Our Relationships, cont.* 276
Session 7: *Exploring Our Relationships, cont.* 279
Session 8: *Nourishing Our Circle of Support* 282
Session 9: *Supercharging Strategy: Gratitude* 285
Session 10: *Reducing Stress* 288
Session 11: *Rebalancing* 291
Session 12: *Living "In the Moment"* 294
Session 13: *Travel Tips* 298
Session 14: *Supercharging Strategy: Affirmations* 301
Session 15: *Why Tell Your Story?* 304
Session 16: *Why Tell Your Story?, cont.* 307
Session 17: *Beginning the Process* 310
Session 18: *How & Where to Share Your Story* 312
Session 19: *Where Do We Go From Here?* 315
Session 20: *Facilitator's Choice* 318
Session 21: *Small Group Project Presentations* 321

Table of Contents, cont.

Module Four, cont.

Session 22: *Small Group Project Presentations, cont.* 323
Session 23: *Module Evaluation & Looking Ahead* 325
Session 24: *Celebration!* 328

Group Handouts

- Reasons to Participate in the *Pathways to Recovery* Group 333
- Questions to Ask Yourself about Participating in the *Pathways to Recovery* Group 334
- Handy Reminder for Group Members 335
- The Partnership Pact 336
- Icebreaker Questions: *Who Are You?* 337
- Identifying My Strengths Worksheet 338
- Module One Small Group Project Presentations: *Instruction Sheet* 339
- Great Movies that Inspire Hope 340
- Famous People with Mental Illness 341
- Mid-Session Satisfaction Survey 342
- Facilitator Self-Assessment 343
- "STOP" Those Negative Thoughts! 344
- Positive/Negative Self-Talk Worksheet 345
- 101 Ways to Celebrate! 346
- Questions to Think About During the Movie 347
- Final Satisfaction Survey 348
- Certificate of Achievement: *Module One* 349
- To Live! 350
- Be a STAR! 351
- Module Two Small Group Project Presentations: *Instruction Sheet* 354
- Arrivals & Departures 355
- "Re-Frame" Relapse 356
- Self-Nurture Calendar 357

Table of Contents, cont.

Handouts, cont.

- Strengths Encounters...358
- Strengths You See in Me...359
- Certificate of Achievement: *Module Two*...........................362
- My Favorite Things..363
- Module Three Small Group Project Presentations: *Instruction Sheet*...364
- The Benefits of Exercise..365
- 101 Things to Do to Create Humor...................................367
- Certificate of Achievement: *Module Three*..........................367
- This or That: Which Will You Choose?................................368
- Module Four Small Group Project Presentations: *Instruction Sheet*...369
- Mixed Up Messages...370
- 101 Things to Be Thankful For.......................................371
- Finding Balance...372
- These Things I Can..373
- The Road Leads Home...374
- Story Circles...375
- Writing Your Story..376
- Certificate of Achievement: *Module Four*...........................377
- A Recovery Pledge...378

Appendix

References...379
Resources..381
Meet the Authors...383

Introduction to the Pathways to Recovery Group Facilitator's Guide

"Good for the body is the work of the body,
and good for the soul is the work of the soul,
and good for either is the work of the other."
~ Henry David Thoreau

Welcome to the Facilitator's Guide

Pathways to Recovery: A Strengths Recovery Self-Help Workbook was designed, written and illustrated through a two-year collaboration with consumers, providers and recovery educators. The *Pathways to Recovery Group Facilitator's Guide* works in conjunction with the *Pathways* text as it informs, builds skills and delivers specific content for group facilitators. Through this process, group facilitators can be instrumental in helping to inspire and empower individuals as they learn, thrive and succeed in achieving their personal goals of recovery.

The Concept of Self-Help

Self-help is an ancient concept; people have always found means and methods of mutual support. Formalized self-help groups in the last century can be traced back to the establishment of Alcoholics Anonymous in the 1930s. In recent years, self-help has experienced a phenomenal and unbridled enthusiasm across all fields, ages, experiences and interests. In any bookstore, shelf after shelf contain books on the subject. Television shows focus on the concept of self-help and strategies for making positive life changes. People not only attend self-help groups, but also turn to the Internet in chat rooms and other forums to seek and provide self-help strategies. Self-help appears to be here to stay.

Typically, the concept of self-help is described as a process where individuals work to change their personal situation while gaining encouragement in a mutually supportive group setting. The centerpiece of self-help is to promote self-autonomy. Effective self-help groups are centered upon building hope; groups allow participants a place to alleviate loneliness and isolation while fostering healing. Beyond mutual support, effective self-help groups can provide understanding, encourage mutuality and ultimately, enhance positive personal change.

Self-help is a very individualized process of learning new strategies and perspectives to help one's self. This can be done through the use of books (like *Pathways to Recovery*), Internet sites, research, journaling or a variety of other tools and resources. Self-help can also be facilitated by other trained professionals who provide knowledge and/or skill building to recognize and develop specific skills needed to deal with a problematic situation.

"You have to leave the city of your comfort and go into the wilderness of your intuition. What you'll discover will be wonderful. What you'll discover is yourself."
~ Alan Alda

Self-help groups that have high participation, interest and the most positive outcomes have, as a core component, participants who are interested in active change for themselves *and* the group. While some self-help groups are not specifically goal driven, the overall purpose is to provide mutual support for positive change. The modules developed to accompany the *Pathways to Recovery* workbook will help you in the design and ultimate effectiveness of your self-help group.

The Story of Pathways to Recovery

Pathways to Recovery takes the evidence-based practice of a Strengths Approach—an approach developed in Kansas and that has been used effectively for 15 years worldwide—into a person-centered, self-help approach. The Strengths Approach has proven successful in reducing psychiatric hospitalization, allowing people to set and achieve personal goals and, in turn, increase one's quality of life. *Pathways to Recovery* puts the processes of setting goals and creating personal recovery plans into a self-guided format.

Pathways to Recovery translates important elements of the recovery paradigm and recovery research into terms that people find useful. Within *Pathways* are more than thirty first-person narratives of recovery as well as uplifting quotations to help people reframe their experience. Readers will find exercises and a variety of cognitive techniques that embody recovery and help break through internalized stigma.

The concept for *Pathways to Recovery* came forth in 1999 when Diane McDiarmid and Priscilla Ridgway traveled to Vermont to attend a Wellness Recovery Action Plan training taught by WRAP creator, Mary Ellen Copeland. The workshop offered attendees time to engage in deep and interesting discussions based on each participant's individual experiences, knowledge and values.

During these discussions, we described the passion we had for our work at The University of Kansas and the vision we had to expand recovery based on the Strengths Approach. The more we listened to others, the more we became convinced that a large gap existed in helping people move past just the management of psychiatric symptoms. People were wanting a tool to help them embrace and reclaim their life and expand their individual horizons. On

"History paints the human heart."

~ Napoleon I

a crisp autumn day, along the shores of the Connecticut River in Vermont, Diane & Priscilla conceptualized the idea for *Pathways to Recovery*.

We returned to Kansas with a different and fresh perspective. We became even more excited to put our ideas into a workable plan for writing a self-help text.

We spent a day developing a comprehensive outline of what should be included in *Pathways to Recovery*. As the initial plan was finished, we felt quite satisfied with our work until we realized the outline didn't include anything about psychiatric symptoms or barriers! This insight was profound for us, for what we had outlined was a tool designed to help *all* people reclaim their life.

With a clear plan and outline, the next step was to convene an expert panel of individuals who had direct experience with the impact of psychiatric symptoms, along with state mental health officials, case managers and local community support service staff. This strong and vocal panel provided us with guidance, feedback and many helpful suggestions.

We met with the panel regularly to seek their feedback for each chapter. Initially, we planned for *Pathways to Recovery* to be a total of 200 pages. However, the panel kept requesting more information, more stories and additional resources be added to the manuscript. As you can see by thumbing through the *Pathways* text, the expert panel had a significant impact as we doubled the amount of information in the text.

After the introduction of *Pathways to Recovery*, self-help groups sprang up spontaneously. At the same time, a formalized *Pathways to Recovery* pilot curriculum was being developed, conducted and analyzed. From this first pilot, group participants provided us with specific and extensive feedback. Building upon this and other information from the field, the facilitator's guide that you have in front of you was designed and written.

People are truly excited about the *Pathways to Recovery* workbook. The text is heralded by the Center for Psychiatric Rehabilitation as one of the top three resources on recovery in the United States. The Substance Abuse and Mental Health Services Administration (SAMHSA) and the National Association of State Mental Health Program Directors (NASMHPD) have both promoted *Pathways to Recovery* as an important resource for recovery. The workbook is

"When you do things from your soul, you feel a river moving in you, a joy."
~ Rumi

in use by individuals and self-help groups across the nation, as well as many countries throughout the world.

Numerous individuals who have successfully self-managed their mental health symptoms (many with Mary Ellen Copeland's WRAP resources) have said *Pathways to Recovery* helped them enter a new phase of recovery. Group members from both self-help and psychosocial groups have told us about individuals who have not responded to other types of recovery education courses that have had a very positive reaction to *Pathways*. As a result, they have become involved and active in their own recovery journey. This may be true because *Pathways to Recovery* gives people the opportunity to explore more than just what they shouldn't be doing; it gives readers positive, strengths-based ways of developing their own personal vision of recovery.

"In the time we have, it is surely our duty to do all the good we can to all the people we can in all the ways we can."
~ William Barclay

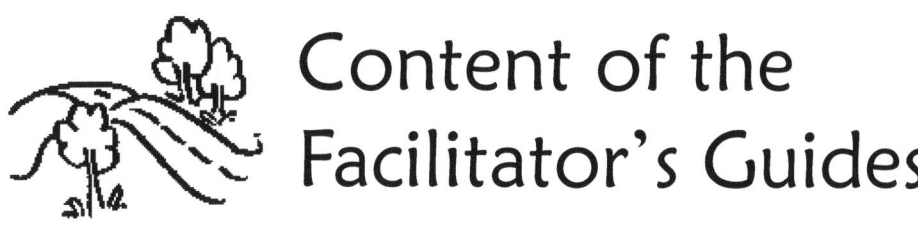

Content of the Facilitator's Guides

The *Pathways to Recovery Facilitator's Guide* was designed to be easy to navigate and use. Each module of the guide is created in the same format so that, as the facilitator, you can become familiar with the general layout. Each module includes an introduction and twenty-four planned group sessions.

As you review each module, you will see that the material covered does *not* always follow the sequential order of the text. The *Pathways* text was designed for readers to start with any chapter or section of interest and proceed from there.

From our experience and from feedback we have received from readers, it is clear that each person has a different place in which they start their recovery journey. As such, they tend to read and use *Pathways to Recovery* in a variety of ways. Because of this, you will find certain sections earlier or scattered throughout the modules. For example, many people shared that Chapter 9 on "Making it Past Detours and Roadblocks" came much too late in the text. They suggested examining the roadblocks earlier so group members could "let go" of these barriers and move on to more positive recovery planning (the chapter *is* included in Module Two.) In addition, the "supercharging" strategies in Chapter 11 have been scattered throughout the sessions to better incorporate this material into one's recovery journey.

The four modules ARE designed to be used in sequential order although each one builds upon the skills and knowledge learned in previous modules. However, if necessary, each module can stand on its own. Facilitators who choose to take this approach should plan sessions to prepare the group with any information needed.

Here is a summary of the material covered in each module:

Module One: Preface & Chapters 1, 2 & 3
The purpose of Module One is to build group unity and provide a foundation of knowledge from which to launch recovery.

"It's what you learn after you know it all that counts."
~ Harry Truman

21

Here, the group is introduced to *Pathways to Recovery* and learn about the concept of recovery, the strengths perspective and the foundations of the recovery movement. Participants explore motivation, self-responsibility, the "turnaround" toward recovery and the attitudes and behaviors that enhance a personal recovery journey. The supercharging strategies of creativity and celebration are included.

Module Two: Chapters 9, 4 & 5

Module Two builds on information learned in the first module. This module begins with the discussion of the common detours and roadblocks found on the journey and participants will brainstorm ways to overcome these common barriers. Next, the group will begin the process of creating or enhancing their recovery journey through the exploration of personal strengths and goal setting. Group members will identify and explore their unique personal strengths and create a personal recovery vision. Finally, the supercharging strategies of meditation and visualization are examined.

Module Three: Chapter 6, 7 & 8

Using their identified strengths and the goal setting skills learned in Module Two, this module helps participants explore and set goals within each life domain. These include housing, education, financial assets, vocation, leisure and recreation, health and wellness, intimacy and sexuality and spirituality. Participants will be introduced to the "Personal Recovery Plan" which they can use to reach their personal goals in each life domain. Humor and exercise are the supercharging strategies included in this module.

Module Four: Chapters 7, 10 & 12

Module Four builds on all the information learned in the previous three modules. Group members will further explore the importance of personal support as well as how to use common "rest stops" and "travel tips" to enhance the recovery journey. Participants will also take a look at creatively developing their own recovery story. This module examines the supercharging strategies of affirmations and gratitude.

> "The larger the island of knowledge, the longer the shoreline of wonder."
> ~ Ralph Sockman

Format of the Group Sessions

The content of each module provides a clear and specific outline to help facilitators be effective and feel confident in presenting information, guiding exercises, sparking discussion and offering additional resources. Each session guide will help you lead and facilitate a supportive and well-received session.

Feel free to adapt the agenda to meet your unique needs. While we believe we have created a format that will fit most groups, each facilitator should consider their own participants, the time available and their own individual creativity. Adapting this format to meet your own needs is critical to the success of the group and the ability of the participants to apply the concepts learned to their own lives.

Each session contains the basic information you will need as a facilitator to prepare and conduct each group. Specific facilitator's tips are also included, many corresponding to the topic for that session. Additional resources can be found at the end of the guide. The following sections are included in each session:

Overview
The overview includes a "snapshot" of the session that defines the content to be covered.

Goals
This section provides at least two clear, specific and measurable goals to be learned during the session.

Readings
This section includes the pages in *Pathways to Recovery* that correspond to the session. As the facilitator, it is important for you to read the passages *before* each session. Many of the readings are also included as part of the agenda or you may want to assign the pages as homework.

Quote
We have selected a quote for each session from the *Pathways* text. Some sessions include scheduled time to discuss one or more

> "If you would thoroughly know anything, teach it to others."
> ~ Tryon Edwards

quotes. For those that don't, you can use this quotation for added discussion.

Materials
The materials section provides you with a list of items to help organize and gather resources before group sessions.

Handouts
This section includes a list of recommended supplemental handouts that can be used for group sessions. Remember that you may also have other resources that can be helpful to group members.

Facilitator's Tip
This area provides specific tips to help you be more effective as a group facilitator. Many will also follow the topic discussed for that session.

Notes
The information included in the notes section gives you extra ideas and suggestions that are specific to the session content.

Agenda
Each agenda provides a timed and detailed outline of each session, including activities and discussion questions. The agenda will help you plan more effectively in order to cover all the material. Please remember these are recommendations; some of the best learning experiences come from unplanned discussions. Don't be afraid to adjust the agenda in order to facilitate a lively and interesting group that will help participants begin to actively apply the concepts learned to their own lives.

Personal Notes
This is an area for you to record your thoughts and reactions *before* and *after* the session. You can include suggestions for improvement or other ideas for the next time you facilitate the group. Each facilitator's approach to leading a group is different; keeping track of your ideas and observations in writing will be helpful as you continue to grow in this role.

> "Though no one can go back and make a brand new start, anyone can start from now and make a brand new ending."
> ~ Carl Bard

Guidelines for Creating Groups

The process of recovery can be a scary and strange time for some. *Pathways to Recovery* group participants may be flooded with strong emotions and have a hard time changing or incorporating new thoughts and ideas. Establishing a supportive and understanding environment during each session will allow for the greatest amount of learning. Here are some guidelines that will help you create a meaningful environment.

Structure of Groups

In learning about how *Pathways to Recovery* groups have spontaneously developed, we have come across different formats for each group. Some groups have simply read the text aloud before discussing the topics and completing the exercises. Others have preferred to read the workbook on their own and discuss it as a group. You can adapt the group modules to fit your style and the specific needs of the group.

Some groups have been conducted in a very formal manner with participants being very committed; others have been much less formal with group members attending sporadically. In general, it is our experience that groups with more committed members will learn more from the *Pathways* text and the group will provide a higher level of peer support. You will need to identify and understand the level of commitment intended for your group.

One way to determine this is to ask potential participants to complete the form, "Questions to Ask Yourself about Participating in the *Pathways to Recovery* Group." This form (p. 336) could be completed prior to beginning a group or at the first session. Either way, it will give you an idea of how to better meet the needs and learning styles of individual participants.

Getting People Interested in Attending the Sessions

One of the most effective ways of promoting any group is to use a variety of methods at the same time to recruit potential members. Some promotional ideas include:

"You explore concepts and things that interest you, but you are also exploring inside of yourself."
~ Ed Paschke

1. Hanging flyers advertising the group.
2. Personally inviting individuals who you think might be interested (use both a verbal and written invitation). It might also be helpful to use the "Reasons to Participate in a *Pathways to Recovery* Group" (p. 335).
3. Hold an orientation meeting to introduce the *Pathways* workbook and the details of the upcoming group.
4. Encourage previous group members to invite their peers to share their personal experiences with the group. They could also attend *with* a peer to provide them support during the session.
5. Include a description of the group in your regular schedule of classes or agency newsletter.
6. Develop a brochure about *Pathways to Recovery*, including the details about how your group will be conducted.

We have seen a variety of creative and unique ways to promote *Pathways to Recovery* groups. One agency hung flyers around their building a few weeks prior to the group. The flyers simply said, "Are you ready for the journey?" This created mystery and a keen sense of interest. On the week before the group, the facilitators replaced the flyers with ones that said, "Come join us for *Pathways to Recovery*," listing the times, location and contact information.

Another group developed a variety of activities to encourage participation at many different levels. They hung flyers and announcements throughout their site. They took pictures of prior group participants, added their comments on what they had learned in the group and posted these around their organization. They created a display board with pictures and short highlights from the book and placed it in the lobby where everyone entered.

When it came time for the group, they chose to hold the sessions in their main gathering space. They included a small, circular group of tables for those choosing to attend but they believed the information in *Pathways to Recovery* was so important they wanted to see the positive and hopeful messages reach *all* their members.

What happened turned out to be an unexpected and overwhelming success. By holding the group in a "public" area, they found some individuals who had been reluctant to participate in other activities began listening and contributing. Some people eventually moved to join the others at the table; still others would only hear bits and pieces of the discussions as they

"It's what you learn after you know it all that counts."
~ Harry Truman

walked through the room. Each person attending was given the opportunity to participate at their own comfort level and pace.

Over time, the group facilitators continued to provide enthusiasm for the sessions and developed several creative ways to encourage further participation. They started an open journal, allowing anyone to comment about their experience in the group (the journal was also available for anyone to read). One member even used her creativity and helped other members develop a large painting to represent their journey of recovery. Whatever promotional methods you choose to encourage attendance at *Pathways to Recovery* groups, be creative and include multiple ways to "spread the word." Always remember to personalize your efforts, keeping in mind the potential participants, the group location and your own personal style.

Format & Size of Your Group

We have found it effective to offer each *Pathways to Recovery* module in a twice-a-week format for 12 weeks. The typical group lasts two hours with a 10-15 minute break. In the interest of building strong group unity and continuity, you may want to consider "closing" the group sessions to new participants after the second or third session.

The size used for *Pathways to Recovery* groups has typically been 6-15 participants. A group can still be effective if it is smaller or larger. However, the experiences we have had with running groups would suggest no fewer than five and no more than twenty participants. Groups that are too small or too large may hinder group discussion and the ability of all group members to actively participate. Larger groups may feel overwhelming for some participants while others feel "lost in a crowd." Groups with over 8-10 participants should have a co-facilitator.

Many sites experience a strong outcry for more groups once participants start talking about their experiences. To meet this need, some agencies offer co-occurring or "staggered" groups or place interested individuals on a waiting list for the next scheduled group.

Suggested Locations to Conduct a Group

Pathways to Recovery groups can be held in a variety of locations. Some of the places in which groups have occurred include:
1. Consumer-run or peer-to-peer organizations
2. Community mental health agencies (such as

"All truths are easy to understand once they are discovered; the point is to discover them."
~ Galileo

community support programs or therapy groups)
3. Family or community support groups (like NAMI)
4. In the community utilizing naturally occurring community resources with closed-door meeting rooms (like local colleges or libraries that offer comfort, accessibility and confidentiality)
5. Specialized service areas (such as with individuals experiencing homelessness or those in forensic groups)
6. Psychiatric hospitals (especially prior to discharge)
7. Veteran's Administration programs

Psychosocial Groups vs. Peer-Run Groups

Many individuals who have the experience of psychiatric disability have been required to attend groups as a part of their clinical treatment. For some, these groups were experienced as boring, demeaning and, for many, attendance was mandated in order to receive other services.

With the advent of consumer-centered, strengths and recovery-based practice, psychosocial and other types of self-help groups have positively and dramatically changed the complexion of group work. Consumer-providers often lead or co-facilitate groups within mental health agencies. Most consumer-run organizations routinely provide self-help groups as a core component of their activities.

Within these two different types of organizations, there is often a vast difference in how groups are structured and conducted. However, it is our belief that *Pathways to Recovery* can work for either group.

Mental health agencies may offer a *Pathways to Recovery* group as a choice in their psychosocial programs. Typically, such groups meet as part of a structured weekly or twice-a-week offering. Center staff typically recruit and co-facilitate the groups within a 1-to-2 hour time period. The staff provide documentation in the individual's treatment chart, indicating group attendance, personal observations and individual progress toward goals.

Consumer-run organizations are typically much less formal in their offerings of *Pathways to Recovery* groups. These groups often focus heavily upon peer support and are offered in the true sense of self-help. Groups are facilitated by peers and place strong emphasis on each member feeling they are an important part of the process.

"Dare to reach out your hand into the darkness, to pull another hand into the light."
~ Norman B. Rice

Core Values & Guidelines

Regardless of where the group is conducted, we do believe there are several core values and elements of recovery that *must* be present. It is vital that, as the facilitator, you embrace and uphold these critical guidelines whenever you are conducting a *Pathways to Recovery* or other recovery-based curriculum. These values include:

1. **The group should NOT be required or mandated by or for anyone.** All participants should be able to choose their own attendance and participation levels.

2. **There are no limits to anyone's recovery journey.** It must be understood that people can and do recover; it is not up to us as facilitators to force recovery on anyone.

3. **Always encourage and provide a message of hope.** This should be present in every thing you do and say. Harsh words, criticisms or "spirit-breaking" behaviors are not welcome.

4. **Recovery is a process and not a result.** It is driven by the hope that an individual can create the life they want.

5. **Always promote motivation, self-responsibility and personal achievement.** Celebrate and reward accomplishments. Participating in a *Pathways to Recovery* group can be hard work. Recognize and encourage personal participation and leadership.

6. **Provide as many options and choices as possible.** Remember that what works for one person may not work for another. Your ability to provide a variety of activities will best meet the learning needs of all group members.

7. **Always foster a sense of dignity and respect for each individual.** Each person's life has value and meaning to the things they have experienced.

8. **Each person is their own expert.** Reinforce the skills, abilities and talents of all as equal and important. Encourage group members to seek out and use their inner power and strength.

> "You cannot help but learn more as you take the world into your hands. Take it up reverently, for it is an old piece of clay, with millions of thumbprints on it."
> ~ John Updike

Guidelines for Facilitating a Group

Your role as a *Pathways to Recovery* group facilitator is to provide ongoing guidance and support. The following guidelines will help you develop a positive environment for all group members.

Before the Sessions

As the facilitator, you will want to complete the following activities before each group session:

1. Read the pages in the *Pathways* text that correspond to the session.
2. Review the facilitator notes and agenda for the session.
3. Make copies of the handouts.
4. Collect the suggested supplies.

Beginning the Sessions

At the beginning of the first sessions, explain any situations that may occur in which a session could be cancelled (for example, illness or bad weather). Be sure participants know how to contact you if they are going to miss a session or have questions between them. You may want to start a phone tree (each person signs up to call one other person in case of cancellation). Also, make sure you have basic information for all group members so you can contact them with any changes.

Books

It is our belief that each participant should receive their own copy of *Pathways to Recovery* at the first session. Explain the book is theirs to keep and encourage them to write in and use the workbook as much as possible.

Pathways to Recovery is the centerpiece of each session; group members will be reading, writing and completing exercises in the book during the sessions. Since much of the group is focused on the workbook, ask participants to bring their own copy to each session. If a participant loses their workbook, it should be their responsibility to replace it. It is also recommended that each participant have a notebook, folder or 3-ring binder to keep extra handouts or personal notes.

"Dreams are journeys that take one far from familiar shores, strengthening the heart, empowering the soul."
~ Author Unknown

It's also important for participants to have the book in *their* possession. This will give them an opportunity to explore and read it on their own. Storing the books in a centralized location compromises confidentiality and can limit the freedom to use the book to its greatest advantage. (Besides, when was the last time you had an instructor who kept *your* class text or notebook for you?)

Housekeeping
Go over all housekeeping details at the start of the first sessions. Do all you can to make sure each participant feels safe, comfortable and has firsthand knowledge of the physical space. Everyone should know where to find the restrooms, water fountains, vending machines and break areas. Also ask participants to turn off all electronic devices (cell phones, radio headsets, etc.).

Breaks
Offer at least one ten-minute break each session. Depending on the needs and desires of the group members, you may want to schedule longer &/or more frequent breaks.

Accommodations
Since some group members may need special accommodations or assistance in order to fully participate in the group, be sure to let them know they can request these. Ask them to contact you individually at the break or after the session to discuss options in a confidential setting. If you need additional information or ideas, talk with others who are knowledgable about accommodations, search the Internet or check out resources from your local library.

Reading the Text
Many of the groups that sprang up after the publication of *Pathways to Recovery* simply spent time in the group by reading and discussing what they read. Because of this positive feedback, we have included the reading of the text in most of the agendas. There are several ways for you to include this as part of the group. These can include:

1. You can read sections of the text.
2. Ask for group volunteers to read all or part of the scheduled pages.
3. Assign the readings as homework so group members can be prepared to discuss the readings prior to the sessions.

Which method you choose will depend on the desires of your group, time available for group discussion and/or your own

> "He who would learn to fly one day must first learn to stand and walk and run and climb and dance; one cannot fly into flying."
> ~ Friedrich Nietzsche

comfort level and facilitation skills. However, it will probably work best to use a combination of all three methods.

Discussions

Many *Pathways to Recovery* facilitators have shared that the discussion of the material is extremely important. You will find opportunities in each session for the group to talk about the readings and activities and to share their ideas or suggestions.

Remember that each person works at their own pace; don't force group members to share if they are not comfortable or let one or two people dominate the conversations. While there are suggested questions to lead discussions, don't hesitate to expand on these to create more interaction and heighten the discussions.

Small Group Activities & Projects

There will be many opportunities for participants to work together in a small group format. Be sure to vary how you divide the groups so participants have a chance to work with everyone and encourage them to share the reporting activities. If your group is already a small one, most of the activities can still be completed together.

Each module also provides time during several sessions for small groups to develop their own special project which they will share with the larger group during Sessions #21 & 22.

Sharing Our Stories

Throughout the *Pathways* text, there are numerous first-person accounts of recovery. Since personal stories are some of the strongest learning opportunities, these are included for discussion, encouragement and motivation.

The "Recovery Pledge"

Some groups have found that using the "Recovery Pledge" (p. 20 in *Pathways to Recovery*) is a good way to build peer support and keep the participants connected. You may want to use it occasionally to help the group stay focused or weekly to start or end the session.

Group Support

In a group environment, everyone attending has something to offer and each participant *can* learn from one another. Strongly encourage group members to share their experiences, reactions and insights. Once these experiences are shared and stories told, life lessons can be learned. Remember, however, that sharing

"The moments of happiness we enjoy take us by surprise. It is not that we seize them, but that they seize us."
~ Ashley Montagu

will only take place in a group environment that feels safe, comfortable and nurturing.

Sometimes group members may seek advice. However, in order to support someone else, the most effective groups have members who help each other by being strong listeners, providing constructive feedback and offering realistic assessments of the here and now. Encourage group members to supply helpful suggestions, brainstorm different ways of tackling a problem and share ideas for resources. Positive group member support will help the person develop strategies and behaviors that will allow them to take risks, feel accepted and move forward.

Identify Your Limitations

Each one of us has strengths—things we excel at, have talent with or in which we have great interest. But in spite of our strengths, we all experience different types of limitations. Some people may feel scared at the prospect of getting up in front of a group of peers. Others may have a hard time arguing their point of view in a helpful and convincing way. Everyone struggles with something.

As a facilitator, it's also important to reflect upon and recognize the limitations that you have. If you are uncomfortable with a certain topic, consider inviting someone to present that session. If you are unfamiliar with specific material, conduct an open discussion with the group rather than sharing facts.

As you facilitate the group, you may also recognize that a participant is struggling or they need more support than you can provide at the time. If it appears the person is headed for a crisis, you also need to understand your limitations. In this situation, encourage the person to talk with a mental health provider (like a case manager or therapist) or other qualified individual. You may find it necessary to accompany them or that it's helpful for a peer to support them.

Final Thoughts

Above all, take pleasure in what you are doing! You truly are helping to make a difference in the lives of the participants in *Pathways to Recovery* groups. Not only do you have the opportunity to help others, you will also have the opportunity to learn from the group participants and learn more about yourself. Have fun and enjoy the process!

"Unless someone like you cares a whole awful lot, nothing is going to get better. It's not."
~ Dr. Seuss

"Tell me and I'll forget; show me and I may remember; involve me and I'll understand."
~ Chinese Proverb

Module One

"The aim of education should be
to teach us rather how to think,
than what to think — rather to improve our minds,
so as to enable us to think for ourselves,
than to load the memory with thoughts of other men."
~ Bill Beattie

Introduction to Module One

"If we would have new knowledge, we must get a whole world of new questions."

~ *Susanne K. Langer*

Module One begins the first of four modules to provide twenty-four, 2-hour group sessions on the material found in the *Pathways to Recovery* workbook. The information covered will help you build group consensus and unity, explore the basic history and concepts of recovery and examine the ABCs (Attitudes, Behaviors and Cognitions) essential to "set the course" for a successful recovery journey.

Module One includes the following chapters from *Pathways to Recovery*:

- Preface: Is this Workbook for You?
- Chapter 1: Introduction to a Strengths Recovery Approach
- Chapter 2: Gearing Up for the Journey
- Chapter 3: Setting Ourselves in Motion

In addition, Module One covers two of the supercharging strategies from Chapter 11 — creativity and celebration.

REMEMBER...

If you have not already done so, it is important for you to read the introduction to this guide. In it you will find key elements and guidelines for facilitating a successful, recovery-focused and positive experience for all.

Don't hesitate to add your own ideas, activities, resources and energy. Your ability to be creative will enhance the positive nature of the group and help to build a safe, supportive and fun environment for all participants. Examine your own creative style as you prepare for each session. The important point is to include the activities and exercises that will best help group members understand and apply the concepts learned.

Session #1
Welcome & Introductions

Overview
Session #1 introduces participants to the *Pathways to Recovery* workbook and establishes basic guidelines for the group process. Participants will meet each other and together determine the structure and function of future sessions.

Goals
During this session, participants will:
1. Introduce themselves to each member of the group and start the process of building group unity.
2. Discuss how the *Pathways to Recovery* group will be conducted.
3. Discuss the basic group function, commitment and develop clear expectations of the group process.
4. Identify items to include in the "Partnership Pact."

Readings
Pathways to Recovery, Preface, pp. iii-viii (begin at "How to Use This Workbook")

Quote
"The trail is the thing, not the end of the trail. Travel too fast and you miss all you are traveling for." (Louis L'Amour, *Pathways to Recovery*, p. iii)

Materials
- An individual copy of the *Pathways to Recovery* text for each person in the group
- A binder or folder for each participant (for handouts and other materials)
- Flip chart or white board with markers
- Pens/pencils
- A roll of toilet paper, bag of candy or any similar item containing multiple amounts

Handouts
- Reasons to Participate in the *Pathways to Recovery* Group, p. 335
- Questions to Ask Yourself about Participating in the *Pathways to Recovery* Group, p. 336
- Handy Reminder for Group Members, p. 337
- The Partnership Pact, p. 338

Facilitator's Tip

Your role as group facilitator is to establish a warm, caring and comfortable environment from the very beginning. A smile and a friendly greeting go a long way toward helping each person feel welcome and look forward to returning to the next session.

Notes

The "Partnership Pact" can be a very helpful document for the entire group. Since all members develop it—including you—it provides specific written guidelines in which every member of the group has participated and approved. The pact can be one of your best resources to maintain a safe and comfortable environment, especially when faced with group challenges. Don't forget to use one! Some common items are:

- Whatever is said in the group, stays with the group.
- Encourage—don't discourage.
- Respect each other (be sure to define how the group defines "respect").
- Practice good listening skills—everyone's input is valuable.
- You are responsible for your own learning.
- Don't interrupt others.
- If you need help or support, ask for it.
- Everyone has a right to "pass" in discussions or readings.
- Be on time and prepared for the session.

There will also be times during the sessions that the group will be making a variety of creative projects. Ask for donations of old magazines or art supplies as needed.

Agenda

15 minutes — **Introduction & Icebreaker Activity: *Toilet Paper Tales***
1. Begin on time and welcome all participants.
2. Briefly introduce yourself.
3. Review the agenda for today's session.
4. Conduct the icebreaker exercise.
   a. Pass around a roll of toilet paper (or other item found in multiples) and ask participants to "take some."
   b. When everyone has some of the item, ask them to share their name and one fact about themselves for each item (sheet of paper, piece of candy, etc.) they have taken.

15 minutes — **Why participate in the *Pathways to Recovery* group?**
1. Hand out "Questions to Ask Yourself about Participating in the *Pathways to Recovery* Group."
2. Have participants complete the form and discuss their ideas together as a group.
3. Hand out "Reasons to Participate in the *Pathways to Recovery* Group."
4. Review each guideline and ask for questions.

10 minutes	**Is this Workbook for You?**

1. Hand out a copy of *Pathways to Recovery* to each participant and give them a few minutes to look through it.
2. Read or explain pp. iii in the *Pathways* text.
3. Lead a discussion using the following questions:
   a. What is your first impression of this workbook?
   b. How do you think *Pathways to Recovery* can be a helpful tool or resource to you?

20 minutes	**How to Use this Workbook**

This will give group members an idea of how to individually use the workbook.

1. Read pp. iv-viii in the *Pathways* text.
2. Ask for and answer any questions.

10 minutes	**Break**

Remind participants to return at the scheduled time.

20 minutes	**Group Guidelines, Process & Commitment**

1. Go over each item found on pp. 32-35 of the facilitator's guide (start at "Beginning the Session" and end at "Group Support") and explain how the sessions will be conducted.
2. Discuss the benefits of making a commitment to the group.
   a. Remind participants that group dynamics takes hard work and commitment from each member.
   b. Encourage a supportive and recovery-focused environment.
   c. The group can be successful if everyone is consistent with their attendance and participates actively.
   d. Remind group members that sharing is more likely to occur when a positive connection is developed.

20 minutes	**The "Partnership Pact"**

The pact is the agreement made between group members to insure a safe, supportive and strengths-focused group based on the individual's unique values and needs.

1. Review the concept of the "Partnership Pact."
2. Develop or review a list of items to include in the pact (see suggestions on p. 42) that will serve as ground rules and expectations. These include:
   a. Everyone in the group should agree with the items.
   b. Write all the remarks on the flip chart or white board.
   c. Participants can add remarks at any time.
   d. Development of the pact will continue during the next session and everyone will receive a copy of it.

10 minutes **Review the Day's Session**
1. Review the day's session and ask participants if they have any final questions about the group.
2. Provide the reading assignment for the next session.
3. Remind the group of the next session and thank them for coming.

Personal Notes

_____
_____
_____
_____
_____
_____
_____
_____
_____
_____
_____
_____
_____
_____

Session #2
The Strengths Approach to Recovery

Overview
Session #2 continues the process of group building. It allows participants to examine what *Pathways to Recovery* is and how it can be used to further one's recovery journey. The group will also define and begin to use the strengths approach to recovery.

Goals
During this session, participants will:
1. Continue the process of building group unity.
2. Identify the key elements in the process of recovery.
3. Discuss the "Strengths Approach" to recovery.
4. Continue development of the "Partnership Pact."
5. Recognize the important and relevant parts of the "Recovery Pledge."

Readings
Chapter 1, pp. 3-5 (end at "What is Recovery?"), p. 20 (The "Recovery Pledge")

Quote
"We have no choice of what color we're born or who our parents are or whether we're rich or poor. What we do have is some choice over what we make of our lives once we're here." (Mildred Taylor, *Pathways to Recovery*, p. 3)

Materials
- *Pathways to Recovery* text
- *Pathways to Recovery* books for new participants
- Flip chart or white board with markers
- Pen/pencils
- A hat, basket or bag
- A rough draft of the "Partnership Pact"

Handouts
- Icebreaker Questions: *"Who Are You?,"* p. 339

Facilitator's Tip
What are your strengths as a facilitator? Do you feel comfortable working with people? Are you creative and energetic? Do you find yourself helping others learn? Take time to develop your own list of strengths that you bring to your role as facilitator. Always remember that a good facilitator is constantly learning from themselves and others.

Notes
Prior to the group, copy the "Icebreaker Questions." Cut each question in an individual strip and fold the strip in half. Place all the questions in a hat, basket or bag and have ready for the group activity.

Agenda

20 minutes — **Introduction & Icebreaker Activity: *Who are You?***
1. Begin on time and warmly welcome all participants.
2. Ask if anyone has questions or comments to add.
3. Review the agenda.
4. Conduct the icebreaker activity.
   a. Pass the container with questions around the room, asking each person to take one slip of paper.
   b. Have each participant share their name, read the question out loud and share their answer.

20 minutes — **The "Partnership Pact"**
1. Review the list of items that were collected during Session #1.
2. Ask for and add any new ideas.
3. Let group members know you will finalize the pact during the next session.

20 minutes — **The "Recovery Pledge"**
1. Have the group read the "Recovery Pledge" on p. 20 of the *Pathways* text.
2. Lead a discussion using the following questions:
   a. Why is this pledge important?
   b. What does the pledge mean to you?
   c. What do you need to make the pledge work for you?
   d. What can we do as a group to uphold this pledge?

10 minutes — **Break**
Remind participants to return at the scheduled time.

20 minutes — **What is the Strengths Approach to Recovery?**
1. Read pp. 3-4 (end at "What Will You Get?).
2. Lead a discussion using the following questions:
   a. Have you had any experience with the Strengths Approach?
   b. Why is it important to focus on our strengths instead of our deficits?
   c. How do you feel about starting this journey?

20 minutes | **<u>What Will You Get Out of the Strengths Recovery Process?</u>**
1. Read pp. 4-5 (begin at "What Will You Get" and end at "What is Recovery?").
2. Lead a discussion using the following questions:
   a. What do you think about what we have just read?
   b. How do you feel about learning these things?
   c. Have you tried to do any of these things before? Were you successful?
   d. What barriers did you encounter?

10 minutes | **<u>Review the Day's Session</u>**
1. Provide the reading assignment for the next session.
2. Remind the group of the next session and thank them for coming.

Personal Notes

Session #3
What is Recovery?

Overview
Session #3 examines the concept and definition of recovery. Participants will complete a personal assessment of where they are on the journey of recovery and finalize the "Partnership Pact."

Goals
During this session, participants will:
1. Complete and sign the "Partnership Pact."
2. Define recovery.
3. Identify the personal progress they have made on their personal journey.

Readings
Chapter 1, pp. 5-7, 13-15

Quote
"Where you are is where you start from." (Anonymous, *Pathways to Recovery*, p. 13)

Materials
- *Pathways to Recovery* text
- Flip chart or white board with markers
- Pens/pencils
- One copy of the "Partnership Pact" for everyone to sign

Facilitator's Tip
What is facilitation? The word is derived from the French "*facile*," meaning "easy." Good facilitation then, is the ability to make the group process easier. A good facilitator doesn't lecture and may not even be an expert in the subject discussed. Instead, they help the group gain new information, express ideas and build on personal experiences.

Notes
Some *Pathways to Recovery* groups have developed either group or personal recovery journals to document their journey through the workbook. It can be a great way for participants to see the growth they have made.

Group journals can be very be powerful. Participants add their own thoughts, comments, drawings, etc. as well as view what others have expressed. If the group decides to do this, you may need to help keep it going by adding questions (such as "What would you tell

Notes, cont.

someone starting a recovery journey?") or comments for others to respond. If you choose to create personal journals, remind participants of the need for privacy.

Agenda

10 minutes   **Introduction**
1. Begin on time and welcome all participants.
2. Review the agenda for today's session.

10 minutes   **The "Partnership Pact"**
Remind the group members they are making a commitment to conduct themselves according to the agreed upon items.
1. Review the "Partnership Pact."
    a. Ask for and add any new items.
    b. Pass out one copy and have participants sign the form.
    c. If possible, at break, make individual copies for everyone; if not, have copies ready for the next session.

30 minutes   **What is Recovery?**
Defining recovery is instrumental in having a shared vision throughout the modules.
1. Read pp. 5-7.
2. Lead a discussion using the following questions:
    a. What do you think recovery is?
    b. What concepts do you think are common to most recovery journeys?
    c. What things have been helpful to you in your recovery?
3. Write the responses on the flip chart or white board.
4. If helpful, you can categorize the responses (for example, things that are hope-building, supports used, etc.).

10 minutes   **Break**
Remind participants to return at the scheduled time.

30 minutes   **Where am I on My Journey of Recovery?**
Remind the group that it is important for each person to create and live the journey at their own pace and in their own way. Wherever they find themselves on this self-assessment is important.
1. Have group members complete the self-assessment on p. 13.
2. Lead a discussion using the following questions:
    a. Where did you find yourself on your recovery journey?
    b. Were you surprised at where you were? Why? Why not?
    c. Why is it important to understand each person works their recovery in their own way and at their own pace?

20 minutes · **Sharing Our Stories: *Cherie***
  1. Read Cherie's story on pp. 14-15.
  2. Lead a discussion using the following questions:
     a. Can you relate to Cherie's story? How?
     b. What does she mean by "believable hope"?
     c. How have you seen recovery be "contagious"?
     d. Do you know of others who, like Cherie, have created their own definition of recovery? What can we learn from these role models?

10 minutes · **Review the Day's Session**
  1. Provide the reading assignment for the next session.
  2. Remind the group of the next session and thank them for coming.

Personal Notes

Session #4
Recovery & Resilience

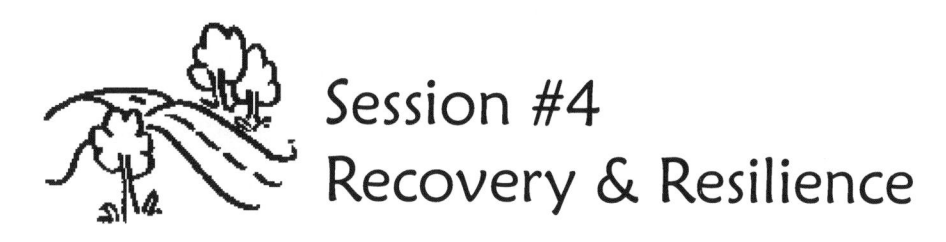

Overview
Session #4 begins to examine the role resilience plays within a recovery journey. Group members will start the process of identifying their own strengths and that of other participants. Recovery "whiplash" will be clearly defined and discussed.

Goals
During this session, participants will:
1. Discover the connection between recovery and resilience.
2. Identify at least one personal strength.
3. Identify at least one strength for each group member.
3. Describe the concept of "recovery whiplash."

Readings
Chapter 1, pp. 10-11, 18-19

Quote
"You gain strength, courage and confidence by every experience in which you really stop to look fear in the face. You must do the thing which you think you cannot do." (Eleanor Roosevelt, *Pathways to Recovery*, p. 18)

Materials
- *Pathways to Recovery* text
- Flip chart or white board with markers
- Pens/pencils

Handouts
- Identifying My Strengths Worksheet, p. 340

Facilitator's Tip
Resilience is a good skill for you to further develop as a facilitator. Give yourself the opportunity to learn from your experiences within the group and seek out and use new resources or ideas to enhance your skills. Don't forget that support is also important for *you* to have; find others with whom you can co-facilitate or who will provide you with constructive feedback to help build your confidence and abilities.

Notes

This session is a good time to encourage the use of mutual support. Participants may find it helpful to share their contact information so they can further discuss ideas from the group or other sections of the *Pathways* text. Give group members a choice as some will find it beneficial to have the extra support from a peer who has been through similar experiences; others may not be comfortable sharing their personal information.

This session also sets the foundation for group members to identify their personal strengths and those of others within the group. However, some may find it difficult to see the resilience they have developed because of their experiences and struggles. Resiliency requires learning specific coping skills, finding resources and using support. Even though group members may have had many challenges, these are important learning experiences that will help them form coping skills and enhance their personal values and beliefs.

Agenda

10 minutes **Introduction**
1. Begin on time and welcome all participants.
2. Review the agenda for today's session.

30 minutes **Recovery & Resilience**
1. Read pp. 10-11 in the text.
2. Have participants complete the two questions on p. 11.
3. Lead a discussion using the following questions:
   a. How would you define resilience?
   b. What resources have you used to "keep on going"?
   c. What other resources might be helpful to you?

20 minutes **Recovery Whiplash**
Many individuals who have actively pursued a recovery path talk about the "whiplash" that occurs (for example, two steps forward, three steps back, four steps forward, etc.). While embracing a strengths-based journey is possible, it doesn't mean the path is straight or without bumps and detours. In fact, the power of the recovery journey is in recognizing – and accepting – ALL the experiences along the way as meaningful. Mixed emotions are very common.
1. Explain the concept of "recovery whiplash."
2. Lead a discussion using the following questions:
   a. How are you feeling about the idea of recovery?
   b. Have you ever experienced "recovery whiplash" before? What was it like for you?
   c. What are some ways we can support others who may be experiencing this "whiplash"?

10 minutes **Break**
Remind participants to return at the scheduled time.

15 minutes **<u>Identifying Personal Strengths</u>**
This discussion begins to set the foundation for helping group members identify their own personal strengths and those of others in the group.
1. How do you define a strength?
2. Write the responses on the flip chart or white board.
3. Ask each group member for one strength which they can identify in themselves (give the opportunity to pass as needed).

15 minutes **<u>Group Activity:</u>** *<u>Identifying My Strengths</u>*
1. Pass out the "Identifying My Strengths" worksheet and have group members add their name to the top of the form.
2. Ask group members to pass their form to the left. Each person will write one strength they have observed about each participant (they should only share *positive* and *affirming* comments).
3. The group will continue passing the form and add comments until the person receives their own list.
4. Allow time to read what the others have listed as their strengths.
5. Lead a discussion using the following questions:
    a. How does it feel to read this list of strengths?
    b. Did you learn anything new about yourself?
    c. Do you think it is important to identify your strengths as part of your recovery journey? Why?

10 minutes **<u>Sharing Our Stories:</u>** *<u>Jay</u>*
1. Read Jay's story on p. 18.
2. Lead a short discussion using the following questions:
    a. What are the "inner and outer resources" that Jay talks about? Can you give an example of each?

10 minutes **<u>Review the Day's Session</u>**
1. Provide the reading assignment for the next session.
2. Remind the group of the next session and thank them for coming.

Personal Notes

_____
_____
_____
_____
_____
_____

Session #5
Foundations of Recovery

Overview
Session #5 looks at the history and foundation of the recovery movement as well as current research findings.

Goals
During this session, participants will:
1. Describe what they were told about their chances for recovery.
2. Examine at least two factors of the positive and negative aspects of their illness.
3. Identify three historical factors influencing the recovery movement.
4. Describe what research says about an individual's chances for recovery.

Readings
Chapter 1, pp. 8-9, 12-18

Quote
"New opportunities await and abound. Never stagnate and settle." (Katherine Negermajian, *Pathways to Recovery*, p. 9)

Materials
- *Pathways to Recovery* text
- Flip chart or white board and markers
- Pens/pencils

Handouts
- Small Group Project Presentation: *Instruction Sheet*, p. 341

Facilitator's Tips
Planning and preparation are the foundation for good facilitation. Do your best to spend time prior to each session getting everything ready (familiarize yourself with the agenda, gather materials, copy handouts, arrange for room setup, etc.). The more prepared you are, the more comfortable you will be and the more effective the learning experience for group participants.

Notes
During this session, participants will be introduced to the small group project. As part of this assignment, group members will design their own project and are free to be creative in

Notes. cont.
developing a 10-15 minute presentation on a topic of recovery from Module One. Some examples might include:

- Examining further ideas on how to use creativity in recovery.
- Creating a brochure for family and community members describing recovery.
- Developing a skit to express the positive way to present the symptoms of mental illness in the media.
- Reading poetry or writings from famous individuals who have also had symptoms of mental illness (such as William Styron, Virginia Wolff, Edgar Allan Poe, Emily Dickinson, etc. or see examples on p. 343).

Encourage participants to be creative in developing their group project. Brainstorm with the groups if they have a hard time beginning.

Agenda

10 minutes   **Introduction**
1. Begin on time and welcome all participants.
2. Review the agenda for today's session.

20 minutes   **Is Recovery Something New?**
It is important for participants to realize people have always recovered from mental illness. These readings will help the group begin to establish a hopeful attitude about their own experiences.
1. Read pp. 8-9.
2. Have the group discuss their answers to each question.
3. Record the answers on the flip chart or white board.

30 minutes   **Foundations Toward Recovery**
There are three distinct factors that have contributed to the beginning of the recovery movement and it is helpful to understand the historical changes that occurred as part of its development. In fact, participants may be surprised to learn that recovery is NOT something new or created by researchers or providers; rather, it is one that is grounded in the consumer roots of advocacy.
1. Read each section of pp. 15-18 separately (begin at "What are the Foundations" and end at "Recovery and a Strengths").
2. After each section, discuss that movement using the following questions:
    a. What do you think about this section? Were you aware of its existence?
    b. Do you think it is important to examine these historical perspectives? Why or why not?
    c. How has this historical change has impacted your recovery journey? (This could include mental health services, their wellness, personal advocacy efforts, etc.)

10 minutes   **Break**
Remind participants to return at the scheduled time.

20 minutes   **What Does the Research Say about Recovery?**
1. Read pp. 12-13 (end at the "Self-Assessment").
2. Lead a discussion using the following questions:
   a. How is research confirming the positive elements of people's recovery?
   b. Why is it important to conduct research on recovery?
   c. Have you been involved in a research study? What was that like for you?
   d. Are you aware of any new research on recovery?

20 minutes   **Small Group Project Presentations**
Having small groups develop and present on a topic of interest provides a wonderful experience for learning. Groups will create their own project and share a 10-15 minute presentation during Sessions #21 & 22.
1. Hand out the "Small Group Project Presentation: *Instruction Sheet*" for this module.
2. Review the project instructions, helping participants brainstorm ideas for a topic.
3. Divide the class into groups of 3-5 people.
4. Give the groups time to meet and brainstorm ideas.
5. Since the presentations will be done during two separate sessions, have them decide the order in which they will present.

10 minutes   **Review the Day's Session**
1. Provide the reading assignment for the next session.
2. Remind the group of the next session and thank them for coming.

Personal Notes

_____
_____
_____
_____
_____
_____
_____
_____

Session #6
Supercharging Strategy: Creativity

Overview
This session will explore creativity and provide some practical ideas that participants can use to develop and enhance their recovery process.

Goals
During this session, participants will:
1. Describe at least two reasons why creativity is important in recovery.
2. Identify at least four different ways to bring creativity into their lives.
3. Practice what it is like to "play."

Readings
Chapter 11, pp. 337-346

Quote
"The artist is not a different kind of person, but every person is a different kind of artist." (Eric Gill, *Pathways to Recovery*, p. 339)

Materials
- *Pathways to Recovery* text
- Flip chart or white board and markers
- Pens/pencils
- Examples of creative projects
- Art supplies as needed (paper, old greeting cards or magazines, ribbon, stickers, scissors, glue sticks, tape, etc.)
- Supplies for "play time"
- Index cards or colored note paper

Facilitator's Tip
Using your own creativity is vital to your effectiveness as a facilitator. Try different methods for sharing information. Include activities based on your ideas and experiences. Don't be afraid to adjust or change material to better fit the needs of your group's participants or to more completely explain a particular concept. Your enthusiasm for creativity will set a positive example for the group.

Notes
Today's session will help build a base of expressing creativity that individuals can use to supercharge their recovery journey. This session is a FUN day! Participants may be

Notes, cont.

hesitant at first to participate (many people don't believe they are "creative") but typically, participants really get into the spirit of the topic. You may want to go to the library, search the Internet or get ideas from friends and colleagues about the various methods to express creativity.

Some ideas for this time could include:

- <u>"Be a Kid" Time</u>: This is time spent blowing bubbles, working with clay or play-doh, playing children's games (like *Go Fish, Candyland*, etc.), finger painting, reading comics, coloring, etc.
- <u>Nature Collage</u>: A collage made of things found in nature and/or a person's idea about nature (participants could go outside and collect items to use).
- <u>An "Open Mike" Time</u>: Each person develops something to share with the group. It could include a poem, drawing, painting, song, etc.

You will want to point out several times during the session how much fun using creativity is and how it benefits wellness and recovery. Enjoy the session!

Agenda

10 minutes   **Introduction**
1. Begin on time and welcome all participants.
2. Review the agenda for today's session.

30 minutes   **Using Creative Potentials to Explore New Paths**
1. Read pp. 337-340 (end at "How Can We Nurture").
2. Using the questions in the workbook, ask participants to share their responses with the group. Other questions might include:
   a. How do you define creativity?
   b. Does being creative only mean you are artistic (see today's "Quote" section)?
   c. What are other reasons for developing your creativity?
   d. How do you see creativity contributing to your recovery?

20 minutes   **From a Child's Perspective: *"Trying Creativity"***
Children are some of the "best" at being creative. They have a natural sense of exploration and inquisitiveness that often leads to being imaginative and having fun. This exercise gives participants a chance to "try" creativity. There are many activities that can occur simultaneously to help group members explore their creativity but all are meant to encourage the sense of freedom that creative activity can bring forth.
1. Give group members an opportunity to explore their creativity, either alone or with a few other participants.
2. Strongly encourage "play" time and help those who may be hesitant to join in the fun!

10 minutes	**Break**
	Remind participants to return at the scheduled time.
40 minutes	**How Can We Nurture and Develop Our Creativity?**
	1. Read pp. 340-343 (begin at "How Can We Nurture").
	2. Have participants answer the questions as you go, either verbally or by writing their answers.
	3. If time permits, have group members complete the questions on p. 344. If not, encourage them to do the section as homework.
	4. Finally, pass out index cards or colored note paper to everyone. Have the participants complete the exercise at the bottom of p. 40. Encourage them to keep this note in a place where they can see it.
10 minutes	**Review the Day's Session**
	1. Provide the reading assignment for the next session.
	2. Let the group know they will be doing a creative activity at the next session. Ask them to bring supplies as needed.
	3. Remind the group of the next session and thank them for coming.

Personal Notes

_____
_____
_____
_____
_____
_____
_____
_____
_____
_____
_____
_____
_____

Session #7
Recovery & Creativity

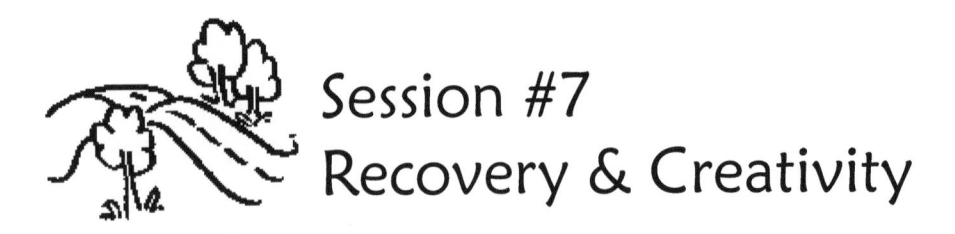

Overview
This session gives participants a way to explore their creativity by developing a recovery collage.

Goals
During this session, participants will:
1. Create a collage incorporating their personal meaning of recovery.
2. Describe at least three behavioral signs of recovery.

Readings
Chapter 11, p. 346

Quote
"If your heart is pulling you in a direction that has mystery and wonder, trust it and follow it." (David Wilcox, *Pathways to Recovery*, p. 341)

Materials
- *Pathways to Recovery* text
- Several poster boards or other large pieces of paper for each small group
- Art supplies (paper, old greeting cards or magazines, ribbon, stickers, scissors, glue sticks, tape, etc.)

Facilitator's Tip
Always remember that the experiences and knowledge of group members is one of your greatest resources. Whenever you can, get them to tell *you* what *they* know instead of you telling them. Respect their ideas and input and give credit for what they already know.

Notes
This session can be a very enjoyable one. It is an excellent exercise to build group cohesion and further the understanding of both the individual and the group's personal vision of recovery. Depending on the size of your entire group, you may want to consider one group collage or have individuals complete their own.

Provide a large poster board for each small group. Participants will cut images and words from magazines and create or embellish the piece with other art supplies. Remind group members that there is no right or wrong way to complete the collage; everyone is creative. Visit each group while they are working to provide encouragement to continue.

Agenda

10 minutes — **Introduction**
1. Begin on time and welcome all participants.
2. Review the agenda for today's session.

40 minutes — **The Recovery Collage**
1. Read the directions for the exercise on p. 346.
2. Divide the participants into small groups of 3-4 people.
3. Have all the supplies ready and answer any questions.
4. Let group members know you will spend the second half of the session presenting their work to the larger group. These will not be "formal" presentations, just an opportunity for the small groups to explain what they have created.

10 minutes — **Break**
Remind participants to return at the scheduled time.

40 minutes — **The Recovery Collage, cont.**
1. Have groups share their collage and their definition of recovery.
2. Give everyone an opportunity to ask questions about the work.
3. As a group, you may want to decide what to do with the collages or how to display them (for example, they could be hung in a public area as a way to encourage others).

10 minutes — **The Next Session: *What to Expect***
1. Briefly discuss the topic and activity for the next session (the "Release Ceremony").
2. Depending on what activity you choose, you may want to ask participants to help and/or bring materials with them.

10 minutes — **Review the Day's Session**
1. Provide the reading assignment for the next session.
2. Remind the group of the next session and thank them for coming.

Personal Notes

___
___
___
___
___

Session #8
The ABCs that Get Us into Gear

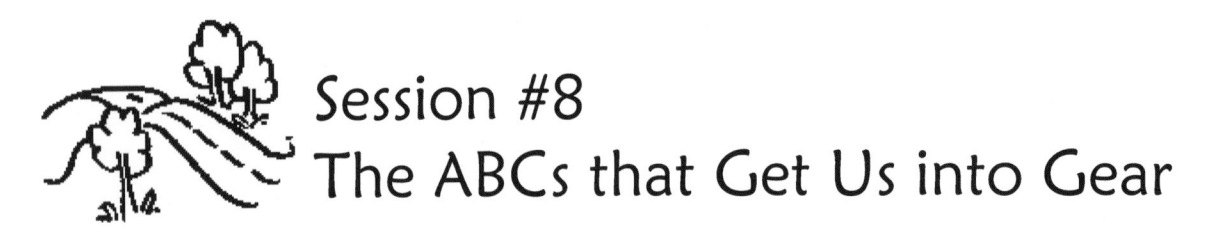

Overview
This session will introduce participants to the ABCs of recovery—attitude, behaviors and cognition. In addition, the group will participate in a "Release Ceremony" as a way to "let go" of old ABCs.

Goals
During this session, participants will:
1. Identify the three elements that make up the ABCs of recovery.
2. Identify at least two behavioral signs of the barriers to recovery.
3. Describe at least three ways to move past personal barriers to recovery.
4. Participate in the "Release Ceremony."

Readings
Chapter 2, p. 27

Quote
"Every intention is a trigger for transformation." (Deepak Chopra, *Pathways* text, p. 27)

Materials
- *Pathways to Recovery* text
- Flip chart or white board with markers
- Pens/pencils
- Materials for the "Release Ceremony"
- Positive word cards

Facilitator's Tip
What barriers do you face as a facilitator? Are you worried someone may ask you a question for which you don't know the answer? Are you afraid of group conflict? Do you feel as though you don't have enough knowledge about the topic? These—and probably any other barriers you can identify—are common to *both* new and experienced facilitators. Learning everything you can about how to facilitate and allowing yourself the freedom to make mistakes will help you relax and feel more comfortable.

Notes
In order to have a clear understanding of the factors which make up the ABCs, you may want to take time prior to the group to read Chapter 2. The group will be discussing each section at length during the following sessions.

Notes, cont.

Emotions can also be high during this session and some people can be triggered by the discussion. While most individuals on a journey of recovery have experienced multiple barriers and setbacks, this discussion allows group members to more closely examine specific challenges and look at ways they have found to overcome these difficulties. It is important that you guide the discussions in a positive and uplifting manner.

The "Release Ceremony" is held to provide group members the chance to "let go" of past ABCs that have been hurtful or are no longer wanted or needed. This ceremony brings *all* participants together in a safe, supportive and healing environment and will hopefully provide an opportunity for individuals to move forward. It is important to take time before today's session to plan this ceremony (you could ask for group volunteers to help). Share a poem, music or reading to start and explain what will happen during the activity.

The ceremony can be held in a variety of ways, depending on the place, time and members of the group. This list provides ideas on ways the ceremony can be conducted:

- Use a "burning bowl." This is based on a popular New Year's Eve ceremony in which participants write on a piece of paper the things in their lives they would like to get rid of or that no longer work. One by one, each individual throws their writings into the fire, essentially "letting go" of what they have written.
- Use a shredding machine. This is the same ceremony as #1 but you can use a shredder instead of the burning bowl.
- Ripping the writing and throwing it away. Again, the same ceremony as #1 but you have people throw away their past hurts in a trash can or sack.

Agenda

10 minutes	**Introduction**
	1. Begin on time and welcome all participants.
	2. Review the agenda for today's session.

10 minutes **The ABCs of Recovery**
1. Read the first paragraph on p. 27.
2. Define the ABCs (A=Attitudes, B=Behaviors, C=Cognition or ways of thinking).

30 minutes **Barriers to Recovery**
1. Remind participants that, while we want to focus most on our strengths, we ARE often faced with many barriers.
2. Using each ABC as the category, have participants name common barriers that occur in each area (write the responses on the flip chart or white board). Some examples might include:
    a. Being told you "can't" because of your illness can lead to a lack of hope.
    b. Dependence on others can make us unable to take risks.
    c. Negative thoughts keep us from seeing a brighter future.

10 minutes   **Break**
Remind participants to return at the scheduled time.

30 minutes   **The "Release Ceremony"**
For some, participating in this activity could be a trigger point; for others, it can be a powerful healing experience. Recognize the mixed emotions that may be present and provide positive support to all.
1. Explain how the ceremony will take place so everyone feels safe and comfortable with the activity.
2. Lead the ceremony using the suggestions in today's "Notes."
3. End the ceremony by giving each person a card with a positive, hopeful word (such as courage, thankful, loving, compassion, etc.) or a quotation to reflect upon.

20 minutes   **Group Discussion**
1. Lead a discussion using the following questions:
   a. What did you think about the ceremony? Has it been helpful to you?
   b. Is there anything you would like to change as we explore the ABCs?
   c. What is one step you will take to change the way you view your barriers?

10 minutes   **Review the Day's Session**
1. Provide the reading assignment for the next session.
2. Remind the group of the next session and thank them for coming.

Personal Notes

Session #9
A=Attitudes: Hope

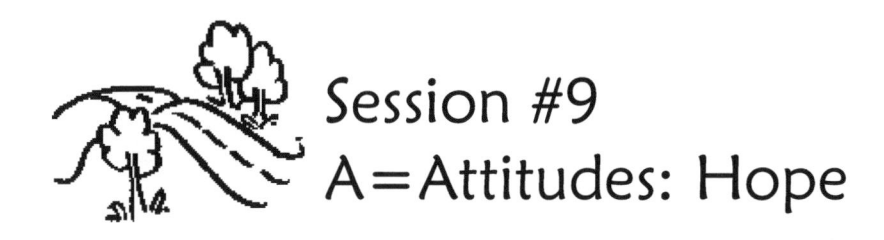

Overview
Session #9 gives participants the opportunity to define hope, complete a personal self-assessment and examine the level of hope they currently have in their life. Participants will also meet in their small groups to continue planning their presentations.

Goals
During this session, participants will:
1. Describe at least four indicators of the importance of hope in recovery.
2. Assess their current level of hope.
3. Describe three activities and/or people that give them hope.
4. Meet with their small groups to continue planning their presentation.

Readings
Chapter 2, pp. 27-31

Quote
"Don't be afraid of the space between your dreams and reality. If you can dream it, you can make it so." (Belva Davis, *Pathways to Recovery*, p. 28)

Materials
- *Pathways to Recovery* text
- Flip chart or white board and markers
- Pens/pencils

Handouts
- Great Movies that Inspire Hope, p. 342
- Famous People with Mental Illness, p. 343

Facilitator's Tip
As the facilitator, your goal is to do all you can to create a vision of hope for everyone. Hope can be inspired in others when they see you or their peers as role models, by being one who sees and acknowledges the possibilities in others or by letting each person know they are a worthwhile person. Make sure this message is consistent and real.

Notes
Having hope means that we have something to look forward to and a reasonable assurance that these things will happen. For many people with psychiatric symptoms, hope is

Notes, cont.
something that has often been lacking or was even taken away with a disparaging diagnosis. It can also be hard to hold on to when symptoms and life experiences interfere. Be sure to do all you can in this session to provide a sense of hopefulness and possibility. If you have a concern about any of the participants, speak to them privately.

Agenda

10 minutes **Introduction**
1. Begin on time and welcome all participants.
2. Review the agenda for today's session.

20 minutes **What is Hope?**
1. Read pp. 27-29 (begin at "A=Attitudes" and end before the question on p. 29).
2. As a group, define "hope." Record ideas on the flip chart or white board.
3. Lead a discussion using the following questions:
   a. How can developing an attitude of hope help people get "in gear" and move toward recovery?
   b. Donna Orrin (p. 28) states that "a lack of hope has the danger of almost paralyzing a person, preventing them from going after their dreams." Do you agree or disagree with this comment? Why?

20 minutes **How Hopeful are You?**
The questions and self-assessment can be difficult to complete if one is not feeling very hopeful. Let group members know that the purpose of this exercise is not only to learn where they are currently, but to give them an opportunity to learn how to increase their level of hope.
1. Read p. 29 and have group members answer the questions.
2. Have participants complete the self-assessment exercise on p. 30.
3. Lead a discussion using the following questions:
   a. What are some things that may cause our hope to go up or down?
   b. What things help you feel more hopeful?

10 minutes **Break**
Remind participants to return at the scheduled time.

20 minutes **How Hopeful are You, cont.**
1. Read the paragraph at the bottom of p. 30.
2. Lead a discussion using the questions on p. 31. Other questions you might use include:
   a. What do you think about the quote by Lin Yutang (at the bottom of p. 37)?

How Hopeful are You, cont.
    b. After hearing everything in this session, do you agree that, without hope, recovery will not happen? Why?
    c. What is the most important thing for you to remember about hope?
 4. Hand out the list of "Great Movies that Inspire Hope" and the list of "Famous People with Mental Illness."

10 minutes   **Sharing Our Story: *Chris***
 1. Read Chris's story on the top of p. 31.
 2. Encourage participants to consider trying the activity Chris describes. Remind them that they are not alone in their journey of recovery.

20 minutes   **Small Group Project Planning**
 1. Provide time for the small groups to work on their project.
 2. If they have not already done so, help the groups decide on the topic or activity they will present.

10 minutes   **Review the Day's Session**
 1. Provide the reading assignment for the next session.
 2. Remind the group of the next session and thank them for coming.

Personal Notes

Session #10
A=Attitude: Building Hope

Overview
Session# 10 continues the examination of hope and helps participants to build on and enhance their own level of hopefulness.

Goals
During this session, participants will:
1. Identify at least three ways to build or renew hope.
2. Discover at least two indicators that lead to positive change.
3. Describe three ways to connect with successful role models.

Readings
Chapter 2, pp. 32-36

Quote
"And the day came when the risk to remain tight in a bud was more painful than the risk it took to bloom." (Anais Nin, *Pathways to Recovery*, p. 35)

Materials
- *Pathways to Recovery* text
- Flip chart or white board and markers
- Pens/pencils

Facilitator's Tip
People are motivated by their own hopes and dreams. They want to do more and be more. As the facilitator, it is important to remember that you can help participants find – and build on – the hope they have in their life. With your guidance, individuals can – and will – begin to take risks and make positive changes to reach their dreams.

Notes
After reading and reviewing the exercises in the text, this session lends itself to much discussion. Keep the group positive and moving. Always be sure that you are prepared and comfortable with the material that you will be presenting. If not, consider asking someone to present the information for you or invite a special speaker to the session. If you do invite someone, be sure to inform the group ahead of time that the person will be joining the group for the session.

Agenda

10 minutes — **Introduction**
1. Begin on time and welcome all participants.
2. Review the agenda for today's session.

20 minutes — **How Can We Renew or Build Hope?**
1. Read each section on pp. 32-35 (do not include the "Hope Exercise" at this time).
2. After each section is read, have group members complete the questions in the workbook.

20 minutes — **Exercise:** *Proving Positive Change is Possible*

Hope is one of the crucial elements found in any recovery journey. When you engage the group in a positive discussion, it will help participants find where their hope lies. This is also a discussion that provides an opportunity for group members to help each other.
1. Have participants read the "Hope Exercise" on p. 33.
2. Either as a group or individually, have members brainstorm ideas of small goals they can accomplish during the next week that will help to increase their level of hope.

10 minutes — **Break**

Remind participants to return at the scheduled time.

20 minutes — **Small Group Activity:** *Hope Exercise*
1. Divide participants into small groups of 3-4 people and ask them to choose one person to record their ideas.
2. Read the instructions for the exercise on p. 36 and assign (or have each group choose) one hope-building strategy to discuss.

30 minutes — **Group Discussion**
1. Ask each reporter to share highlights from their discussion.
2. Record each group's comments on the flip chart or white board.
3. Challenge each group member to choose one of the ideas and try to use it before the next session.

10 minutes — **Review the Day's Session**
1. Provide the reading assignment for the next session.
2. Remind the group of the next session and thank them for coming.

Personal Notes

Session #11
A=Attitude: Building Courage

Overview
Session #11 offers participants a look at incorporating an attitude of courage in their recovery journey. Group members will also explore the importance of taking risks.

Goals
During this session, participants will:
1. Identify at least two behavioral indicators of courage that support recovery.
2. Discover two ways to build courage.
3. Describe three behaviors that support recovery.
4. Describe at least four reasons why taking risks supports recovery.

Readings
Chapter 2, pp. 37-44

Quote
"To dream anything that you want to dream. That is the beauty of the human mind. To do anything that you want to do. That is the strength of the human will. To trust yourself to test your limits. That is the courage to succeed." (Bernard Edmonds, *Pathways to Recovery*, p. 41)

Materials
- *Pathways to Recovery* text
- Flip chart or white board and markers
- Pens/pencils

Facilitator's Tip
Working in small groups is a very effective method of learning. Be sure you use different methods for creating the groups. There are lots of different ways for doing this. Use your creativity but here are some ideas:

- Divide the group by their month of birth (you might need to combine months);
- Group according to specific characteristics (for example, color of shirt, height, favorite animal, etc.);
- Count off by the number of groups you want to create;
- Use a deck of cards, different kinds of candy or other item to divide the group randomly.

Notes
Session #11 tends to be very thought provoking for participants. It may be easy for participants to shift into a negative space and carry a great deal of guilt and sometimes anger with the questions posed. Call for questions and encourage the group to provide a lot of mutual support for each other.

Agenda

10 minutes **Introduction**
1. Begin on time and welcome all participants.
2. Review the agenda for today's session.

30 minutes **What is Courage?**
1. Read p. 37.
2. Lead a discussion using the following questions:
   a. How would you define courage?
   b. In what ways are cou age and fear are the same thing?
   c. Can you share an example of how you used your courage to help you overcome a challenge and move forward?

10 minutes **Sharing Our Stories:** *Kathy*
1. Read Kathy's poem on p. 38.
2. Lead a short discussion using the following question:
   a. How does this poem inspire your courage?

10 minutes **Break**
Remind participants to return at the scheduled time.

20 minutes **Small Group Activity:** *Building Courage*
1. Divide participants into small groups of 3-4 people and ask them to choose one person to record their ideas.
2. Assign (or have groups choose) one of the four courage-building strategies (pp. 38-41) to discuss.

20 minutes **Group Discussion**
1. Ask each reporter to share highlights from their discussion.
2. List the responses on the flip chart or white board.

10 minutes **Sharing Our Story:** *Stormie*
1. Read Stormie's story on p. 39.
2. Lead a short discussion using the following question:
   a. How does this story help you "look deeper" into yourself for strength and courage?

10 minutes   **Review the Day's Session**
1. Provide the reading assignment for the next session.
2. Remind the group of the next session and thank them for coming.

Personal Notes

Session #12
B=Behaviors: Risks & Wrong Turns

Overview
Session #12 examines the importance of taking risks and learning from the mistakes we make. In addition, participants will have an opportunity to evaluate their experience in the group up to this point.

Goals
During this session, participants will:
1. Examine the importance of taking risks to make positive changes.
2. Identify at least two things learned from making a "wrong turn."
3. Share their personal experience about using *Pathways to Recovery*.

Readings
Chapter 2, pp. 42-44

Quote
"Only those who will risk going too far can possibly find out how far one can go."
(T.S. Eliot, *Pathways to Recovery*, p. 42)

Materials
- *Pathways to Recovery* text
- Flip chart or white board and markers
- Pens/pencils

Handouts
- Mid-Session Satisfaction Survey, p. 344
- Facilitator Self-Assessment, p. 345

Facilitator's Tip
Don't expect that participants will always finish homework assignments. In spite of our best efforts, there are times when things just don't go smoothly. If this happens, be prepared. You can still include these individuals in the discussion by asking questions such as, "How would this have been helpful to you?" or "Why do you think this could be useful?" Encourage participants to still complete the assignment after the session.

Notes
Evaluation is vital to becoming a better facilitator. Be prepared for compliments and criticisms. This is an opportunity for you to make changes to provide a greater learning experience for all group members. You may also want to invite someone to take notes or record participant's answers on the flip chart or white board. If you are uncomfortable or you would like to give the group an opportunity to be completely honest, consider asking someone who is not part of the group to conduct the evaluation. Finally, be sure to complete your own self-assessment.

Agenda

10 minutes   **Introduction**
1. Begin on time and welcome all participants.
2. Review the agenda for today's session.

15 minutes   **Moving Out of Our Comfort Zone: *The Dignity of Risk***
1. Read the quote by David Viscott on p. 42.
2. Lead a discussion using the following questions:
    a. What have you been told about taking risks?
    b. What can happen in our lives if we don't take risks?
    c. What fears do you have that keep you from t aking risks?

15 minutes   **The "Protective Bubble"**
1. Read the passage by Charlene Syx on pp. 42-43 (begin at "At times" and end at the question).
2. Lead a short discussion using the question on p. 43.

20 minutes   **Learning from "Wrong Turns"**
1. Read p. 44.
2. Lead a discussion using the following questions:
    a. Can you give us an example of a time when you took a "wrong turn"? What happened and how did you get through it?
    b. What can be learned from this experience?
    c. What can keep you from learning from these kinds of experiences?

10 minutes   **Break**
Remind participants to return at the scheduled time.

30 minutes   **Mid-Session Evaluation**
Evaluation can be a powerful tool in giving voice to participants. Encourage and respect open and honest comments.

Cont. **Mid-Session Evaluation, cont.**
1. Lead a discussion focusing on how the participants view the success of the sessions thus far. Use all or part of these questions:
    a. How has the experience of attending the sessions benefited your recovery?
    b. What is your favorite part of the group? Why?
    c. What is your least favorite part of the group? Why?
    d. What do I (the facilitator or co-facilitators) do to help you learn?
    e. What suggestions can you offer to make the group better?
    f. What could I (the facilitator or co-facilitators) do to improve the group?
    g. As a group, do you feel we are staying true to the "Partnership Pact"?
    h. Do you feel you are able to uphold the "Recovery Pledge"? Why or why not?
    i. Does anyone have a need for support around his or her recovery efforts?

10 minutes **Written Evaluation**
Be sure to let participants know their comments are anonymous and that their comments will only be used to make positive changes to the group as needed.
1. Pass out the "Mid-Session Satisfaction Survey."
2. Ask the group to complete the form and leave it with you.

10 minutes **Review the Day's Session**
1. Provide the reading assignment for the next session.
2. Remind the group of the next session and thank them for coming.

Personal Notes

_____
_____
_____
_____
_____
_____

Session #13
C=Cognition: Ways of Thinking

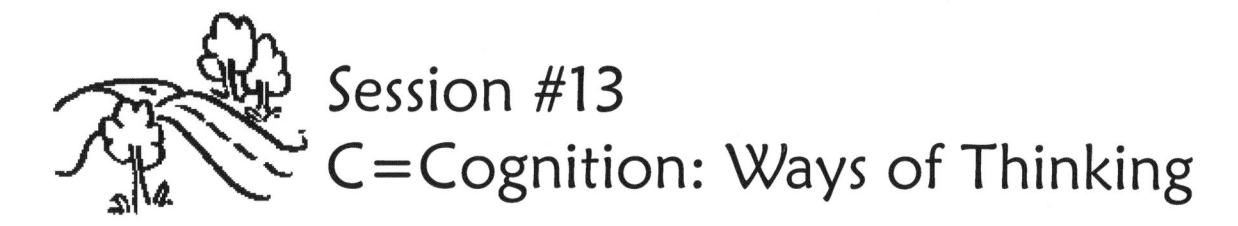

Overview
Session #13 looks at how our thinking can interfere with the recovery journey. Participants will examine ways to think more positively and learn how to substitute positive thoughts when the negative ones appear.

Goals
During this session, participants will:
1. Examine why negative thought patterns occur.
2. Describe at least two ways to use positive self-talk to reduce negative self-talk.
3. Learn how to use the negative self-talk "stop sign."
4. Identify how to move past the "shoulda-woulda-coulda cul-de-sac."

Readings
Chapter 2, pp. 45-52

Quote
"I cannot say whether things will get better if we change; what I can say is they must change if they are to get better." (Georg Christoph Lichtenbert, *Pathways to Recovery*, p. 48)

Materials
- *Pathways to Recovery* text
- Flip chart or white board and markers
- Pens/pencils

Handouts
- STOP Those Negative Thoughts!, p. 346
- Positive/Negative Self-Talk Worksheet, p. 347

Facilitator's Tip
"Brainstorming" can be a quick and fun way for the group members to develop new ideas without restrictions on what is said. There are several guidelines that should always be shared with the group before brainstorming. These include:

- All ideas are welcome, without criticism or discussion;
- Anyone can pass if they don't have a new idea;
- Write ideas *exactly* as they are shared (try not to paraphrase)

Facilitator's Tip, cont.
Continue as long as possible until there are no new ideas. True brainstorming will also include an opportunity for participants to rate &/or categorize the ideas, followed by a discussion on how to incorporate the suggestions.

Notes
In addition to personal positive self-talk, it is also important to think about what we say or do to others who are being negative. These exercises can also be helpful for participants to practice how they can be supportive of people who are using negative self-talk.

Agenda

10 minutes — **Introduction**
1. Begin on time and welcome all participants.
2. Review the agenda for today's session.

20 minutes — **The Importance of Positive Self-Talk**
1. Have the group read pp. 45-47 (end at "Shifting to Positive").
2. Ask participants to complete the self-assessment on p. 46.
3. Lead a discussion using the following questions:
    a. Do you think it is easy for negative self-talk to occur? If so, why do you think this is true?
    b. How has negative self-talk sidetracked your recovery?

20 minutes — **Shifting to Positive Self-Talk**
1. Read p. 47 (begin at "Shifting to Positive").
2. Lead a discussion using the following questions:
    a. Why is it important to shift our thinking?
    b. How do you think you can "tune out" negative thoughts?
3. Introduce the exercise on p. 48.
4. Encourage group members to use this self-talk inventory during the next several days, reminding them this is the first step in changing their thought patterns to ones that are more positive.

10 minutes — **Break**
Remind participants to return at the scheduled time.

15 minutes — **Stop Sign Worksheet**
Using this worksheet is one way for participants to begin the process of change. Encourage them to use the sign to replace negative thoughts with the ones they have written.

Cont.   **Stop Sign Worksheet, cont.**
1. Hand out the "Stop Sign Worksheet."
2. Have the group write positive words or phrases on the sign. Some suggestions include:
    a. "I am a good person."
    b. "I am welcome everywhere I go."
    c. "The past is behind me and today I am okay."

15 minutes   **Positive/Negative Self-Talk Worksheet**
1. Pass out the "Positive/Negative Self-Talk Worksheet."
2. Read the instructions on the worksheet.
3. As a group, examine the first column of comments and ask for responses.
4. Write the responses on the flip chart or white board while the participants complete their own form.

10 minutes   **Sharing Our Stories: *Beth***
1. Read Beth's story on p. 50.
2. Encourage the group to take the time to develop their own positive thought book (instructions are found on p. 51).

10 minutes   **Getting Out of the Shoulda-Woulda-Coulda Cul-de-Sac**
1. Read p. 52.
2. Lead a discussion using the questions in the workbook.

10 minutes   **Review the Day's Session**
1. Provide the reading assignment for the next session.
2. Remind the group of the next session and thank them for coming.

Personal Notes

Session #14
Supercharging Strategy: Celebration!

Overview
This session will focus on learning how to celebrate—not just the big things—but also the everyday and ordinary that life presents. Participants will also meet in their small groups to continue planning their presentations.

Goals
During this session, participants will:
1. Identify two reasons why incorporating regular celebration is important to recovery.
2. Describe at least three ways to celebrate individual progress toward recovery.
3. Meet with their small groups to continue planning their presentation.

Readings
Chapter 11, pp. 367-370

Quote
"Stop worrying about the potholes in the road and celebrate the journey!" (Fitzhugh Mullan, *Pathways to Recovery*, p. 367)

Materials
- *Pathways to Recovery* text
- Flip chart or white board and markers
- Pens/pencils

Handouts
- 101 Ways to Celebrate!, p. 348

Facilitator's Tip
Take some time to list your own accomplishments and celebrate your successes! Make your own plans to do something special for yourself to recognize the efforts you have made toward becoming a better facilitator.

Notes
Get an update on the progress of the small group project assignments. If barriers or problems are present, schedule a brainstorming time to help. Also be sure to take a minute to celebrate the progress participants have made so far on their small group projects.

Agenda

10 minutes **Introduction**
1. Begin on time and welcome all participants.
2. Review the agenda for today's session.

10 minutes **Celebrate Every Accomplishment!**
Listing one's accomplishments can be a difficult exercise for some. You may want to walk among the group to help and provide suggestions for those individuals who may be having trouble.
1. Read p. 367.
2. Have participants answer the questions in their workbook.

15 minutes **Small Group Activity:** *Keeping it in Overdrive*
1. Divide participants into small groups of 3-4 people and ask them to choose one person to record their ideas.
2. Ask the small groups to do the following:
    a. Discuss the questions on p. 367 which they just completed, looking for common themes as well as their reaction to the exercise.

15 minutes **Group Discussion**
1. Ask each reporter to share highlights from their discussion.
2. What are some of the common themes you found?
3. What were some of the reactions group participants had to the questions?

10 minutes **Break**
Remind participants to return at the scheduled time.

20 minutes **"101 Ways to Celebrate"**
This is a great exercise that allows participants to have fun and be creative. Remind participants that celebrations can be both large and public (like an award ceremony) but also the "ordinary" – daily accomplishments such as completing a task or sending a thank you note.
1. Explain to the group that you are going to create a list of "101 Ways to Celebrate."
2. Pass out the form.
3. Using the flip chart or white board, write down all the ideas that are offered.
4. If the group is unable to come up with 101 ideas, encourage them to add to the list as they think of more celebrations.

Module One

10 minutes · **Celebration Action Plan**
1. Using the question on p. 369, have group members develop an action plan of how they will begin to use celebration in their recovery journey.
2. If a group member is having trouble deciding what they would like to do, suggest one of the activities listed in *Pathways* on pp. 368-369).

20 minutes · **Small Group Project Planning**
1. Provide time for the small groups to work on their project.
2. Assist them with planning as needed.

10 minutes · **Review the Day's Session**
1. Provide the reading assignment for the next session.
2. Remind the group of the next session and thank them for coming.

Personal Notes

Session #15
Motivation: Fuel for the Journey

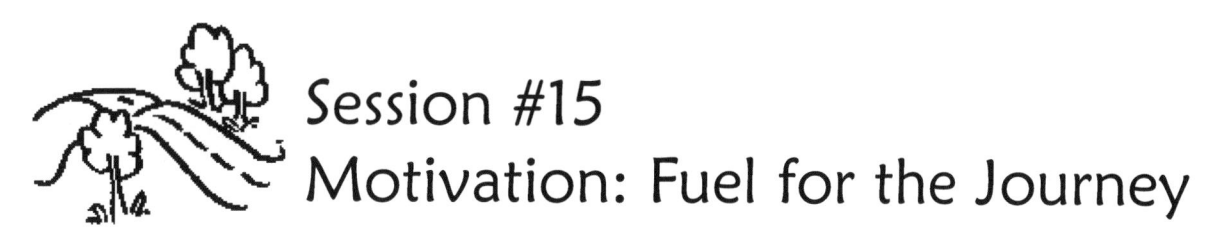

Overview
Session #15 examines the importance of motivation within the recovery journey. Group members will define the concept and evaluate their own level of motivation.

Goals
During this session, participants will:
1. Define three behaviors that are commonly found with motivation.
2. Describe at least two indicators of personal motivation.
3. Develop a motivational slogan.

Readings
Chapter 3, pp. 57-60 (ending with "Taking the Driver's Seat")

Quote
"Your distress about life might mean you have been living for the wrong reason, not that you have no reason for living." (Tom O'Connor, *Pathways to Recovery*, p. 58)

Materials
- *Pathways to Recovery* text
- Flip chart or white board and marker
- Pens/pencil
- Words or phrases cut from magazines

Facilitator's Tip
Always make sure you end the sessions on time. Respect the fact that group members may have other appointments or activities planned. It can also be helpful for you to plan and be available after each session in case one of the group members needs additional support or has further questions.

Notes
Group members might want to spend some time after the session to think about the things, people and places that motivate them. Is their motivation for themselves or for others they are caring for? Remind participants that motivation needs to be for themselves in order for them to live *their* journey.

Agenda

10 minutes — **Introduction**
1. Begin on time and welcome all participants.
2. Review the agenda for today's session.

10 minutes — **The Definition of Motivation**
1. Read pp. 57-58, 60 (end at "Taking the Driver's Seat").
2. Discuss the group's definition of motivation.
3. Write the participant's responses on the flip chart or white board.

40 minutes — **Understanding Motivation**
1. Have the group members complete the exercises on pp. 58 & 60.
2. Lead a discussion using the questions from the text. You can also include the following questions:
   a. What motivates you? Why?
   b. What doesn't motivate you? Why?
   c. How is your definition of motivation different from what we read in the *Pathways* text?
3. Have group members complete the self-assessment on p. 59.

10 minutes — **Break**
Remind participants to return at the scheduled time.

20 minutes — **Small Group Activity: *Motivational Slogan***
This exercise is similar to the refrigerator magnets many people use to create poetry or stories on their fridge. When completed, these slogans can be serious, funny or purely inspirational.
1. Divide the participants into small groups of 3-4 people.
2. Have each person select one motivational word from the basket or box.
3. Each member will share their word with the group.
4. Groups will then take the words and make a group slogan or motivational sentence (they can add extra words as needed).

20 minutes — **Group Discussion**
1. Have each small group share their slogan.
2. Encourage participants to write down their slogan and try to use it during the coming week.

10 minutes — **Review the Day's Session**
1. Provide the reading assignment for the next session.
2. Remind the group of the next session and thank them for coming.

Personal Notes

Session #16
Taking the Driver's Seat for

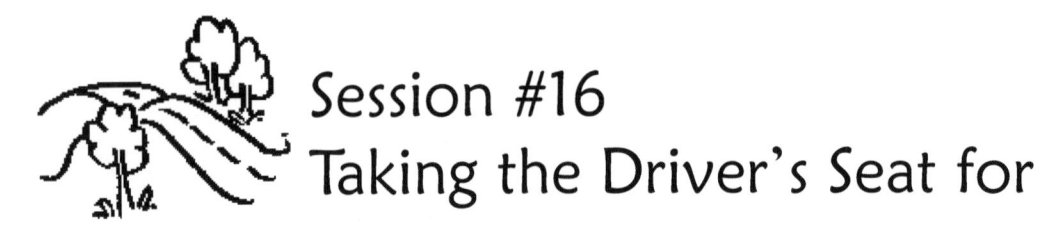

Overview
Session #16 continues the examination of motivation by exploring the importance of self-responsibility as part of the recovery journey.

Goals
During this session, participants will:
1. Identify obstacles that become a barrier for motivation.
2. Complete a self-assessment on motivation.
3. Describe at least two reasons why taking self-responsibility is important in one's recovery journey.

Readings
Chapter 3, pp. 60-63 (beginning at "Taking the Driver's Seat")

Quote
"The only things you regret are the things you didn't do." (Michael Curting, *Pathways to Recovery*, p. 62)

Materials
- *Pathways to Recovery* text
- Flip chart or white board and markers
- Pens/pencils

Facilitator's Tip
As the facilitator, your expectations can have a big impact on the potential learning of group members. If you act as though you expect participants to be involved, excited and knowledgeable, they are more likely to be so. But make sure your expectations *are* realistic—high enough to motivate and encourage but not so high they become frustrated.

Notes
You will need to discuss next session's movie and agree on what the group will watch. You may find it difficult to get group members to agree on one movie. In fact, choosing the film may cause quite a debate. Do your best to engage all members in the decision-making. You may need to pay special attention to body language or remind participants of the purpose of viewing the movie. Don't allow one person to dominate the discussion. If the group is unable to reach consensus, suggest they take a vote.

Agenda

10 minutes — **Introduction**
1. Begin on time and welcome all participants.
2. Review the agenda for today's session.

30 minutes — **The Importance of Self-Responsibility**
1. Lead a discussion using the following questions:
    a. What is self-responsibility?
    b. Can you give an example of using self-responsibility that helped you reach a goal or get something you wanted?
    c. What happens if we don't accept self-responsibility?
    d. In what ways does avoiding self-responsibility feel good?
    e. In what ways can others see you being responsible?

20 minutes — **What Motivates Me?**
1. Read p. 62 (end at the question).
2. Have participants complete the self-assessment on p. 61.
2. As a group, add other sources of motivation that are not listed.

10 minutes — **Break**
Remind participants to return at the scheduled time.

25 minutes — **Small Group Activity: *Barriers to Motivation***
1. Divide the participants into small groups of 2-3 people.
2. Using the obstacles to motivation on pp. 61-63, assign one obstacle to each group.
3. Have the small groups quickly brainstorm 1-2 ideas of how to overcome these barriers.
4. When everyone is done, have the groups list their ideas on separate sheets of the flip chart or on the white board.

15 minutes — **What to Expect: *Next Session***
Session #17 will give participants an opportunity to watch a motivational movie. Even though some people may have seen the film, they will be watching it to look specifically for the themes of recovery and motivation.
1. Explain that one way to understand motivation is to see it in action. Let them know the group will be watching a movie during the next session
2. Help the group decide on the film. Ask for suggestions from the group. Some movie ideas include:
    a. Benny and Joon
    b. Seabiscuit
    c. A Beautiful Mind
    d. Milagro Bean Field War
    e. Stand & Deliver

Module One

Cont. **What to Expect: *Next Session*, cont.**
3. Provide the details needed for the next session (for example, you may be meeting in a different location, you may want to have popcorn or other treats, the movie may last longer than your regular session).

10 minutes **Review the Day's Session**
1. Provide the reading assignment for the next session.
2. Remind the group of the next session and thank them for coming.

Personal Notes

_____
_____
_____
_____
_____
_____
_____
_____
_____
_____
_____
_____
_____
_____
_____
_____

Session #17
Motivation in Action

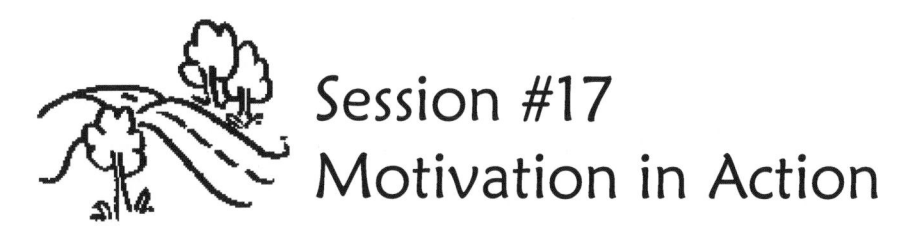

Overview
Session #17 provides participants the opportunity to watch a major motion picture, reviewing and examining it for their reactions to its portrayal of motivation and recovery.

Goals
During this session, participants will:
1. View a movie to look for examples and themes of motivation.
2. Begin to develop questions and ideas about the movie that will be discussed during the next session.

Readings
None

Quote
"One starts an action because one must do something." (T.S. Eliot, *Pathways to Recovery*, p. 61)

Materials
- Television and a VCR or DVD player (this could be supplied by the organization where your group is being held or you could meet at someone's home for this session)
- Movie of the group's choice
- Popcorn or other snack (if available)

Handouts
- Questions to Think About During the Movie, p. 349

Facilitator's Tip
Don't hesitate to use the stories and experiences of others to help motivate participants. Sometimes our greatest learning comes by examining the challenges others have overcome. By using stories—like today's movie—you can provide powerful examples of motivation and give group members ideas they can try in order to feel more confident.

Notes
Participants may have many different reactions to the film. Remind them they will discuss the movie during the next session but you should be prepared to talk with individuals after the movie as needed. Having the participants complete the study guide before the next

Notes, cont.
session also gives them an opportunity to examine their own feelings about what they have watched prior to the group discussion.

Agenda

10 minutes — **Introduction**
1. Begin on time and welcome all participants.
2. Review the agenda for today's session.

Length of movie — **Watching the Movie**
Group members will only watch the movie today. A discussion about their reactions will be held during the next session.
1. Pass out "Questions to Think about During the Movie." Encourage group members to think about the questions as they are watching the film.
2. Ask for and answer any questions.
3. Watch the movie.

10 minutes — **Review the Day's Session**
1. Provide the reading assignment for the next session.
2. Remind the group of the next session and thank them for coming.

Personal Notes

Session #18
Reactions to the Movie

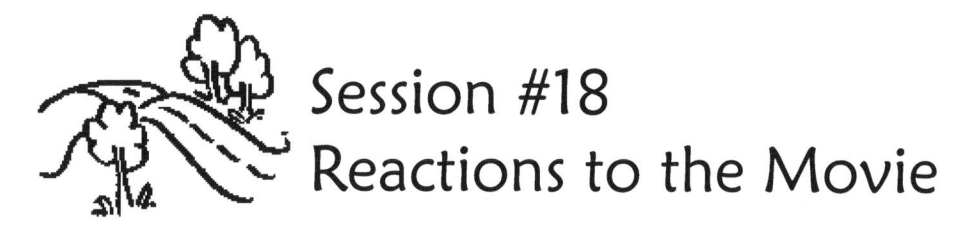

Overview
Session #18 gives participants an opportunity to discuss their reactions to the movie that was seen during the previous session. Participants will also meet in their small groups to finalize their presentations.

Goals
During this session, participants will:
1. Discuss their reactions to last session's movie.
2. Identify at least four motivational films that embrace the aspects of recovery.
3. Meet with their small groups to finalize planning their presentation.

Readings
None

Quote
"If you just set people in motion, they'll heal themselves." (Gabrielle Roth, *Pathways to Recovery*, p. 66)

Materials
- *Pathways to Recovery* text
- Flip chart or white board and markers
- Pens/pencils

Handouts
- Questions to Think About During the Movie (extra copies as needed), p. 349

Facilitator's Tip
One way to make handouts effective is to build in tasks and activities that are clear and simple enough so participants will remember and be able to relive using them once the session is over.

Notes
This is a time to focus on the participants reactions to the movie, not whether they liked or disliked it. Keep the group focused on the discussion questions.

Agenda

10 minutes — **Introduction**
1. Begin on time and welcome all participants.
2. Review the agenda for today's session.

40 minutes — **Reactions to the Movie**
1. Have extra copies of the discussion questions as needed.
2. Lead a discussion using these questions as your guide.

10 minutes — **Break**
Remind participants to return at the scheduled time.

10 minutes — **Other Motivational Movies**
1. Ask the group to name other movies with a motivational or inspirational theme (see the list of movies from Session #9).
2. List the names of the films on the flip chart or white board.

20 minutes — **Sharing Our Stories:** *Anonymous*
1. On p. 58, read the story and the quote at the bottom of the page.
2. Lead a discussion using the following questions:
   a. How does what these writers say relate to what we have been talking about regarding motivation?
   b. What is one thing you will make a commitment to do that will help you increase your motivation?

20 minutes — **Small Group Project Planning**
This may be the last time the small groups have time to work together before their presentations.
1. Provide time for the small groups to finalize their project.
2. Assist them with planning as needed.

10 minutes — **Review the Day's Session**
1. Provide the reading assignment for the next session.
2. Remind the group of the next session and thank them for coming.

Personal Notes

_____

_____

_____

_____

Session #19
Turnaround Toward Recovery

Overview
Session #19 looks at the concept of "turnaround" in recovery. Participants will get the opportunity to examine what recovery turnaround is and how they can make their own personal turnaround toward recovery.

Goals
During this session, participants will:
1. Describe two concepts of a turnaround toward recovery.
2. Learn about the idea of making a "you" turn.
3. Identify at least three behaviors that describe the personal experience of turnaround.

Readings
Chapter 3, pp. 64-69

Quote
"The task is not to become normal. The task is to take up your journey of recovery and to become who you are called to be." (Pat Deegan, *Pathways to Recovery*, p. 65)

Materials
- *Pathways to Recovery* text
- Flip chart or white board and markers
- Pens/pencils

Facilitator's Tip
When small groups are meeting together, make sure you check in with each group. You may need to help participants who are hesitant to speak up or get the group back on topic. It they appear to be working well together, simply provide your encouragement and be available to them if needed.

Notes
In many ways, telling our stories is how we communicate with others. Reading personal stories is a powerful way for participants to understand that others have gone through similar experiences. These stories are powerful reminders of recovery and can help participants gain perspective on their lives, connect them with others, and ultimately, provide healing. As the facilitator, be sure to help participants see how the stories shared

Notes, cont.
in this session can be used as motivation and encouragement on their journey of recovery. Also remind them to be respectful of others and limit details of their own stories.

Agenda

10 minutes   **Introduction**
1. Begin on time and welcome all participants.
2. Review the agenda for today's session.

10 minutes   **Making a "You" Turn**
1. Read p. 64 in the text.
2. Ask for questions about the definition of "turnaround." Make sure everyone understands the concept.

40 minutes   **What Do We Know about Turnaround?**
One of the best ways to learn how a "you" turn occurs is to hear from those who have gone through it before.
1. Review the different types of turnaround experiences listed on pp. 65-69). These include:
   a. The "eureka" or "aha" moment.*
   b. Deciding to do whatever it takes to make a change.*
   c. Accepting help, getting good treatment and acknowledging our barriers.
   d. Hitting bottom.*
   e. Getting angry about how we are treated.*
   f. Having others depend upon us.*
   g. Learning that we can and do recover.*
   h. Finding a role model.
   i. Being in a safe and stable environment.
   j. Hearing hopeful message from others.
   k. A slow, subtle change in lifestyle.
2. For those experiences listed with a (*), read the stories included in the *Pathways* text.
3. For the other types of turnaround, ask group members to share their personal stories (or stories of other individuals they may know) in order to illustrate how turnaround can begin.
4. Group members may also be familiar with other ways to make a "you" turn. Have them share their ideas and comments.

10 minutes   **Break**
Remind participants to return at the scheduled time.

20 minutes	**Small Group Activity:** *Your Experience of Turnaround* 1. Divide participants into small groups of 3-4 people and ask them to choose one person to record their ideas. 2. Ask the small groups to discuss the questions on pp. 68-69.

20 minutes	**Group Discussion**
	1. Ask each reporter to share highlights from their small group discussion.
	2. Record each group's ideas on the flip chart or white board.
	3. Lead a discussion using the following questions:
	   a. Do you see any similarities among the groups?
	   b. Why is it important to think about turnaround?
	   c. Are there alternative ways of looking at the experience of turnaround?

10 minutes	**Review the Day's Session** 1. Provide the reading assignment for the next session. 2. Remind the group of the next session and thank them for coming.

Personal Notes

_____
_____
_____
_____
_____
_____
_____
_____
_____
_____
_____
_____
_____

Session #20
Facilitator's Choice

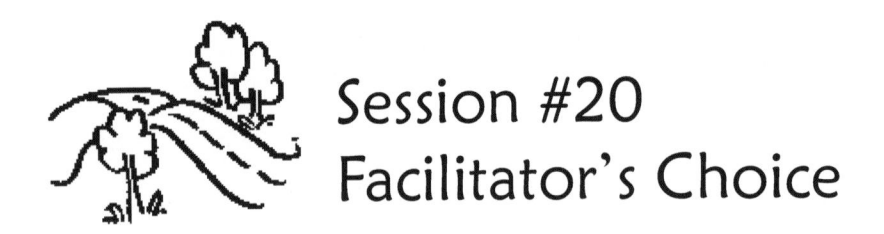

Overview
This session allows the group to further explore subjects of interest or to examine sections of the *Pathways to Recovery* text not covered during Module One.

Goals
During this session, participants will (*to be determined by the group &/or the subject chosen*). List your goals below:

1.

2.

3.

Readings
To be determined by the group &/or the subject chosen

Quote
"We are not permitted to choose the frame of our destiny. But what we put into it is ours." (Dag Hammerskjold, *Pathways to Recovery*, p. 352)

Materials
- *Pathways to Recovery* text
- Flip chart or white board and markers
- Pens/pencils

Handouts
To be determined by the group &/or the subject chosen

Facilitator's Tip
Here's some suggestions for the effective use of flip charts or white boards:

- Don't write too much. Write big and use wide markers so everyone can see.
- Printing is more readable than typical handwriting.
- Use "bullet points" instead of long sentences.
- A single color marker is monotonous and difficult to read. Instead, alternate colors for each new idea. Also, use darker colors.
- Use the right pens or markers. For white boards, use ones made specifically for them. For flip charts, watercolor markers are best as they don't bleed through the paper.

Notes

There are a variety of options for this session, including:

1. Covering previous topics in which the group needed more time.
2. The group may choose a topic in which they would like more information. However remember that, as the facilitator, you may need to spend time preparing materials.
3. Arrange for a special speaker to share with the group. This might include a peer role model or a panel of individuals who can talk about their recovery.
4. You may have local sites or museums that the group would like to visit.

At the end of the session, talk with the group about the upcoming end of Module One. Discuss how they would like to celebrate the completion of the sessions. Each group is different and they will come up with unique ideas that will fit the members of the group. Here are some of the ways other *Pathways to Recovery* groups have celebrated:

- Have a pizza party or potluck dinner
- Coordinate a craft or activity day
- Get a movie and a pizza
- Have lunch or dinner at a restaurant
- Spend the day at the park (with a picnic, nature walk or other park activities)
- Attend a free concert
- Take a special hike
- Volunteer in the community together

If the group is planning on working through all four modules, you might want to consider an activity that can be built on after each session like a time capsule, scrapbook or other creative effort.

You will also want to make some decisions on activities to recognize the progress and outcomes of this group. Recognition and validation is extremely important! Be creative and have fun!

Agenda

10 minutes **Introduction**
1. Begin on time and welcome all participants.
2. Review the agenda for today's session.

40 minutes **Group Activity**
To be determined by the group &/or the subject chosen.

10 minutes **Break**
Remind participants to return at the scheduled time.

30 minutes	**Group Activity** *To be determined by the group &/or the subject chosen.*
20 minutes	**Celebration Planning** 1. Talk with the group about the celebration during Session #24. 2. Provide a list of possible activities (see "Notes" section). 3. Decide what activity most represents the group. 4. If possible, ask the group members to share in the planning and preparation of the celebration.
10 minutes	**Review the Day's Session** 1. Provide the reading assignment for the next session. 2. Remind the group of the next session and thank them for coming.

Personal Notes

Session #21
Small Group Project Presentations

Overview
Session #21 allows participants—within a small group format—to share more in-depth information on a topic of recovery.

Goals
During this session, participants will:
1. Present recovery-oriented information to the other group members.
2. Identify at least four aspects of recovery from the small group assignment presentations.

Readings
Small group participants will provide their own readings if needed

Quote
"Life is an immense mural that requires each of us to pick up the brush and paint a bold stroke." (Holly Near, *Pathways to Recovery*, p. 49)

Materials
Small group participants will provide their own materials as needed

Handouts
Small group participants will provide their own handouts if needed

Facilitator's Tip
Be prepared to negotiate with the group. Some tasks or activities may not be relevant to them or they might have done it before. Ask for their suggestions on how to make changes; don't be surprised if what they develop is actually better than what was planned.

Notes
Your role as facilitator is to keep the presentations moving and on time. Don't allow one group to take more time than allotted. Keeping the groups on time shows respect for the other groups who have spent time planning and preparing for their presentation.

Take time to review the presentations with the group. Be sure to celebrate and recognize the accomplishments of each group. Encourage members to talk with their peers if they are interested in learning more about a specific topic.

Agenda

10 minutes — **Introduction**
1. Begin on time and welcome all participants.
2. Review the agenda for today's session.

40 minutes — **Small Group Project Presentations**
1. Allow a few extra minutes if a group needs to do any set up for their presentation.
2. Introduce each small group, their members and their project.
3. Validate each group's efforts in presenting information to the larger group.

10 minutes — **Break**
Remind participants to return at the scheduled time.

40 minutes — **Small Group Project Presentations, cont.**
1. Continue the presentations.

10 minutes — **Discussion and Thanks**
1. Briefly discuss what group members have learned from their peers in today's session.
2. Thank each group and acknowledge them for their efforts and courage in presenting to their peers.

10 minutes — **Review the Day's Session**
1. Provide the reading assignment for the next session.
2. Remind the group of the next session and thank them for coming.

Personal Notes

_____
_____
_____
_____
_____
_____
_____

Session #22
Small Group Project Presentations

Overview
Session #22 continues the small group presentations, allowing participants—within a small group format—to share more in-depth information on a topic of recovery.

Goals
During this session, participants will:
1. Present recovery-oriented information to the other group members.
2. Identify at least four aspects of recovery from the small group assignment presentations.

Readings
Small group participants will provide their own readings if needed

Quote
"Having the world's best idea will do you no good unless you act on it. People who want milk shouldn't sit on a stool in the middle of a field in hopes that a cow will back up to them." (Curtis Grant, *Pathways to Recovery*, p. 268)

Materials
Small group participants will provide their own materials as needed

Handouts
Small group participants will provide their own handouts if needed

Facilitator's Tip
Every facilitator needs to learn to be forgetful! It's easy to remember negative feedback or the details of mistakes made. Instead, focus on the positive comments that have been shared, revel in the progress participants have made and learn from what has gone wrong. You'll feel better and be able to move on more effectively.

Notes
Remember, your role as facilitator is to keep the presentations moving and on time. Don't allow one group to take more time than allotted. Keeping the groups on time shows respect for the other groups who have spent time planning and preparing for their presentation.

Notes, cont.
Take time to review the presentations with the group. Be sure to celebrate and recognize the accomplishments of each group. Encourage members to talk with their peers if they are interested in learning more about a specific topic.

Agenda

10 minutes — **Introduction**
1. Begin on time and welcome all participants.
2. Review the agenda for today's session.

40 minutes — **Small Group Project Presentations**
1. Allow a few extra minutes if a group needs to do any set up for their presentation.
2. Introduce each small group, their members and their project.
3. Validate each group's efforts in presenting information to the larger group.

10 minutes — **Break**
Remind participants to return at the scheduled time.

40 minutes — **Small Group Project Presentations, cont.**
1. Continue the presentations.

10 minutes — **Discussion and Thanks**
1. Briefly discuss what group members have learned from their peers in today's session.
2. Thank each group and acknowledge them for their efforts and courage in presenting to their peers.

10 minutes — **Review the Day's Session**
1. Provide the reading assignment for the next session.
2. Remind the group of the next session and thank them for coming.

Personal Notes

Session #23
Module Evaluation & Looking

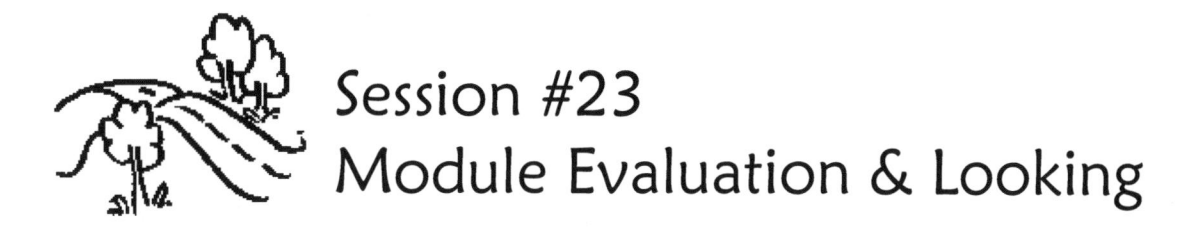

Overview
Session #23 will allow participants to reflect on the past sessions and share any ideas or comments about what they have learned. It will also allow group members to formally evaluate their experience and begin planning for future sessions.

Goals
During this session, participants will:
1. State at least three learning experiences from participating in Module One.
2. State what they liked and disliked about the sessions.
3. Identify their personal readiness to continue with the *Pathways to Recovery* series.

Readings
None

Quote
"Our own life is the instrument with which we experiment with the truth." (Thich Nhat Hanh, *Pathways to Recovery*, p. 7)

Materials
- *Pathways to Recovery* text
- Flip chart or white board and marker
- Pens/pencils

Handouts
- Final Session Satisfaction Survey, p. 350
- Facilitator Self-Assessment, p. 345

Facilitator's Tip
Remember, evaluation is vital to becoming a better facilitator. Be prepared for both compliments and criticisms. Build on the positives and take steps to improve your skills. And remember, every facilitator struggles with negative comments. Take them as an opportunity to make changes that will provide a greater learning experience for all group members.

Notes
You may want to invite someone to take notes or record participant's answers on the flip chart or white board. If you are uncomfortable or you would like to give the group an opportunity to be completely honest, consider asking someone who is not part of the group to conduct the evaluation. Finally, be sure to complete your own self-assessment.

Agenda

10 minutes — **Introduction**
1. Begin on time and welcome all participants.
2. Review the agenda for today's session.

15 minutes — **Small Group Activity: *Review of Module One***
1. Divide participants into small groups of 3-4 people and ask them to choose one person to record their ideas.
2. Ask the small groups to make a list of the things they have learned in the group.

25 minutes — **Group Discussion**
1. Ask each reporter to share highlights from their discussion.
2. On the flip chart or white board, list the ideas given in categories for the different topics discussed (for example, recovery, identifying strengths, things needed for the journey, etc.).
3. If possible, record the responses and make copies for everyone.

10 minutes — **Break**
Remind participants to return at the scheduled time.

30 minutes — **Final Session Evaluation**
While some may feel sad the sessions are ending, remind them of all the things they have learned. Encourage participants to share and support each other in this stage of change. Allow ample time to share their feelings about the group.
1. Explain the importance of evaluating the participant's experiences during Module One.
2. Lead a discussion using the following questions:
    a. What did you like about this module? Not like?
    b. What was your favorite session?
    c. What was your least favorite session?
    d. What would you change about the group?
    e. Have any of you had problems or experienced anything negative around your recovery so far? If so, how have you dealt with it or how do you plan to make changes?
    f. Does anyone need help with anything related to recovery or with what anything from previous sessions?
    g. Are you ready to start Module Two? Why or why not?

10 minutes	**Written Satisfaction Survey**
	Let participants know that the written forms are anonymous and will be used only to improve the next sessions. Share your appreciation for their honesty.
	    1. Hand out the "Final Session Satisfaction Survey."
	    2. Have participants complete the evaluation.

10 minutes	**Celebration Planning**
	    1. Take this time to finalize plans for the celebration activities during Session #24.
	    2. If needed, remind participants of any details for the celebration (for example, change of location, time, things to bring, etc.).

10 minutes	**Review the Day's Session**
	    1. Provide the reading assignment for the next session.
	    2. Remind the group of the next session and thank them for coming.

Personal Notes

Session #24
Celebration!

Overview
Session #24 reviews Module One, with participants reflecting on their experience and learning. It also provides all group members the opportunity to celebrate individual and group accomplishments.

Goals
During this session, participants will:
1. Identify accomplishments, individually and for each member.
2. Celebrate the completion of Module One.

Readings
To be decided by the facilitator or the group

Quote
"Celebration of passages provides an opportunity for people to remember stories of the experience being observed and to draw new insights from them." (The *United Church of Christ Book of Worship*, Pathways to Recovery, p. 367).

Materials
Materials for today's session will depend on what the group decides to do

Handouts
- Certificate of Achievement (or similar recognition), p. 351

Facilitator's Tip
Understanding that most learning comes *after* the session is important for facilitators to know. Group members will need time to try new tools, practice different behaviors or attempt alternative activities. While *learning* to do things is different than being *competent* in them, for most people, it will take time to feel comfortable with the new learning.

Notes
The activities for this final session should be predetermined by the participants. Let them know there will be much more to learn in the following modules and encourage them to continue in the group. Also let them know that, if they have any doubts or are simply not ready for this journey, you and the group members will understand.

Notes, cont.

The main goal for today is to celebrate the accomplishments of coming together as a group to work on the journey of recovery. Getting to know one another better in a social setting will reinforce the peer support needed for work that will be done in future modules.

You should also recognize individual accomplishments made during the sessions. Some suggestions include:

- Certificates of attendance or accomplishment
- Small gifts individualized for each person
- The same gift for each person
- A card or note with your personal thanks

Above all, make sure that *each* person is recognized and celebrated.

Agenda

10 minutes **Introduction**
1. Begin on time and welcome all participants.
2. Review the agenda for today's session.

10 minutes **Highlights of Module One**
1. Start by having the group recite the "Recovery Pledge" (p. 20).
2. Using the flip chart or white board, make a list of the highlights and outcomes for Module One.

90 minutes **Celebration!**
1. Conduct the celebration activities.
2. Be sure to recognize each individual and their accomplishments during the session.

10 minutes **Review the Day's Session**
1. Invite participants to join in attending Module Two.
2. Thank each group member for participating.

Personal Notes

_____

_____

_____

_____

_____

Module Two

"Learning is finding out what we already know.
Doing is demonstrating that you know it.
Teaching is reminding others that
they know just as well as you.
You are all learners, doers and teachers."

~ Richard Bach

Introduction to Module Two

"Start by doing what's necessary, then what's possible and suddenly, you're doing the impossible."

~ *St. Francis of Assisi*

Module Two continues the exploration of *Pathways to Recovery* and provides twenty-four, 2-hour sessions. This section includes the following chapters:

- Chapter 9: Making it Past Detours & Roadblocks
- Chapter 4: Recovery is Self-Discovery
- Chapter 5: Setting a Course for the Recovery Journey

In addition, two supercharging strategies — meditation and visualization — will also be explored.

You will note the inclusion of Chapter 9 in Module 2. Many individuals and group leaders reported how important it is for individuals on a recovery journey to examine the roadblocks early on, thus allowing individuals to identify barriers and hopefully, move on to more effective planning. Chapters 4 and 5 continue the exploration of the recovery journey by examining personal strengths and will allow participants to develop their own personal vision of recovery.

REMEMBER...

If you have not already done so, it is important for you to read the introduction to this guide. In it you will find key elements and guidelines for facilitating a successful, recovery-focused and positive experience for all.

Building on your experiences from Module One, don't hesitate to add your own ideas,
activities, resources and energy. Your ability to be creative will enhance the positive nature of the group and help to build a safe, supportive and fun environment for all participants. Examine your own creative style as you prepare for each session. The important point is to include the activities and exercises that will best help group members understand and apply the concepts learned.

Session #1
Welcome & Introductions

Overview
Session #1 allows participants to get to know each other better and to determine the structure and function of the group. It will also introduce group members to the information that will be covered in Module Two, including the common detours and roadblocks to recovery and identification of their personal strengths.

Goals
During this session, participants will:
1. Introduce/reintroduce themselves to each member of the group and continue the process of building group unity.
2. Discuss how the *Pathways to Recovery* group will be conducted.
3. Discuss the basic group process, commitment and expectations.
4. Identify items to include or expand upon in the "Partnership Pact."

Readings
Pathways to Recovery, Preface, pp. iii-viii (begin at "How to Use This Workbook")

Quote
"It takes courage to push yourself to places that you have never been before...to test your limits...to break through barriers." (Anais Nin, *Pathways to Recovery*, p. viii)

Materials
- An individual copy of the *Pathways to Recovery* text for each person in the group
- A binder or notebook for each participant (for handouts and other materials)
- Flip chart or white board and markers
- Pens/pencils

Handouts
- Reasons to Participate in the *Pathways to Recovery* Group, p. 335
- Questions to Ask Yourself About Participating in the *Pathways* Group, 336
- Handy Reminder for Group Members, 337
- The Partnership Pact, p. 338

Facilitator's Tip
If you don't already know everyone in the group, get to know their name as soon as possible. Use name tags (write the names large enough for everyone to see) or table top cards (fold a piece of heavy paper in half and write participant's names on one

Facilitator's Tip, cont.

side). Be sure to also use their *preferred* name with correct spelling (don't assume someone uses a nickname). It's also important for group members to learn each other's names; the nametags or place cards will be helpful to them as well.

Notes

The addition of any new member will change the complexion of the group and will provide both benefits and challenges. They can bring new energy, new ideas and a different perspective. At the same time, new members may be fearful about disrupting the group or experience the pressure of fitting in. Individuals who have already been attending can also be worried about the changes new members bring. They may be concerned about the comfort levels in the group or how relationships may change.

It will be important for you to welcome all group members and do your best to help them feel supported. Watch for specific levels of discomfort and address them with the group. Find ways that each group member can participate. Remind the group that, while you are working on common goals together, you do want them to enjoy each other and the activities. By establishing group guidelines early on, you can better incorporate new members who will feel supported and willing to participate.

Agenda

20 minutes — **Introduction**
1. Begin on time and welcome all participants.
2. Review the agenda for today's session.
3. Conduct the icebreaker activity.
   This exercise will encourage participants to not only think positively but begin to identify personal strengths which will be important during future sessions. If the name is too long (like Elizabeth or Benjamin), consider using a nickname or other word that describes the person).
   a. Ask participants to share their first name.
   b. Using each letter of their name, have them state a personal strength or skill that begins with each letter of their name (for example, "My name is Joy. I'm **J**ovial, **O**riginal and **Y**oung.").
   c. If you list each quality on the flip chart or white board, you will have created a long list of group strengths.

20 minutes — **Why participate in the *Pathways to Recovery* group?**
1. Hand out "Questions to Ask Yourself about Participating in the *Pathways to Recovery* Group."
2. Have participants complete the form and discuss their ideas as a group.
3. Hand out "Reasons to Participate in the *Pathways to Recovery* Group."
4. Review each guideline and ask for questions.

20 minutes | **Group Guidelines, Process & Commitment**
If you are just starting the Modules with this session, hand out personal copies of Pathways to Recovery to each participant; give them a few minutes to look over the workbook.
  1. Go over each item found on pp. 32-35 of the facilitator's guide (start at "Beginning the Session" and end at "Group Support") and explain or remind the group how the sessions will be conducted.
  2. Discuss the benefits of making a commitment to the group.
     a. Remind participants that group dynamics takes hard work and commitment from each member.
     b. Encourage a supportive and recovery-focused environment.
     c. The group can be successful if everyone is consistent with their attendance and participates actively.
     d. Remind group members that sharing is more likely to occur when a positive connection is developed.

10 minutes | **Break**
Remind participants to return at the scheduled time.

20 minutes | **Group Expectations**
  1. Hand out "*Pathways to Recovery* Handy Reminder for Group Members."
  2. Discuss these items as they will serve as the group expectations.

20 minutes | **The "Partnership Pact"**
The pact is the agreement made between group members to insure a safe, supportive and strengths-focused group based on the individual's unique values and needs.
  1. Review the concept of the "Partnership Pact."
  2. Develop or review a list of items to include in the pact (see suggestions on p. 42 of Module One) that will serve as ground rules and expectations. These include:
     a. Everyone in the group should agree with the items.
     b. Write all the remarks on the flip chart or white board.
     c. Participants can add remarks at any time.
     d. Development of the pact will continue during the next session and everyone will receive a copy of it.

10 minutes | **Review the Day's Session**
  1. Review the day's session and ask participants if they have any final questions about the group.
  2. Provide the reading assignment for the next session.
  3. Remind the group of the next session and thank them for coming.

Personal Notes

Personal Notes

Session #2
Detours & Roadblocks

Overview
Session #2 continues the process of building the group by adding to the "Partnership Pact" and discussing the "Recovery Pledge." Participants will also start the process of examining the common detours and roadblocks that can exist on the recovery journey.

Goals
During this session, participants will:
1. Continue the process of building group unity.
2. Review the key elements of the "Recovery Pledge."
3. Describe the concept of detours and roadblocks.

Readings
The "Recovery Pledge," p. 20, Chapter 9, pp. 281-282

Quote
"A gem cannot be polished without friction, nor people perfected without trials." (Chinese Proverb, *Pathways to Recovery*, p. 283)

Materials
- *Pathways to Recovery* text
- *Pathways to Recovery* text for new participants
- Flip chart or white board and markers
- Pens/pencils
- Rocks for each participant
- A bag to hold all the rocks (canvas, etc.)

Facilitator's Tip
Be ready for the unexpected as it will definitely happen! Do your best to cope with anything that might come up. Seek help from the group and always have alternate plans ready. But don't worry if you have difficulty coping—every facilitator faces these challenges. Use the unexpected events as a learning experience for the entire group.

Notes
This session begins the look at common detours and roadblocks. As discussed earlier, Chapter 9 is being included now so participants can address these challenges and move on to the true work of recovery.

Notes, cont.

As you work through each roadblock over the next several sessions, keep in mind that participants will likely find the material difficult and emotional. Do your best to let the group know how common these roadblocks are to *everyone*, not just those individuals who happen to be diagnosed with symptoms of mental illness. Make sure that supports are available as needed.

The final exercise for today, "Bag of Burdens," is a physical activity to help participants understand the "heaviness" of carrying around all the emotions and behaviors that are commonly found as part of the detours and roadblocks. You will need to collect enough rocks for each person and a bag strong enough to hold them all.

Agenda

10 minutes — **Introduction**
1. Begin on time and welcome all participants.
2. Review the agenda for today's session.

15 minutes — **The "Partnership Pact"**
1. Building on the work done in Session #1, add any new ideas to the list (especially from individuals new to the group).
2. Remind participants they will finalize the pact during Session #3.

15 minutes — **The "Recovery Pledge"**
1. Read or review the "Recovery Pledge" (p. 20).
2. Lead a discussion using the following questions (for groups only doing Module Two, use the discussion questions on p. 46):
   a. Is this pledge still important to you?
   b. Does it mean anything different to you now?
   c. Do you believe the group is upholding the pledge?
   d. How can we work together to make the pledge real and be more effective?

20 minutes — **Introduction to the Common Pitfalls, Detours & Roadblocks**
1. Explain why this chapter is being included now (see "Notes.").
2. Read p. 281-282 (begin after the poem; end at "Driving Using").
3. Have the group name some of the common roadblocks they have found on their journey. List on the flip chart or white board.

10 minutes — **Break**
Remind participants to return at the scheduled time.

20 minutes — **"The Hole in the Sidewalk"**
Most individuals make a very distinct connection with this poem. An effective way to present it is, as you read the poem, take a step each time you begin with "I walk down the street." This simple action creates movement and is an example of how things are constantly changing.

Cont. **"The Hole in the Sidewalk", cont.**
1. Read the poem on p. 281.
2. Lead a discussion using the following questions:
    a. Do you connect with this poem? Why or why not?
    b. What is it like when we "fall in the hole?"
    c. What does the author mean by "It isn't my fault?"
    d. How would/does it feel to find a new street?
    e. Given what you have learned in previous sessions, can you name one or two things that would help you find or create a new street?

20 minutes **Group Exercise: *"Bag of Burdens"***
1. Give each person a rock and ask them to think about one "burden" they have been carrying with them.
2. Using the stone as the "burden," pass the bag around, having them share their "burden" and add it to the bag.
3. When each stone has been added, pass the bag around so everyone has a chance to see how heavy it is with all the stones.
4. Next, take out each stone one by one as if you are removing the burdens (this is the goal of examining the detours and roadblocks). Explain to the group that, while the next several sessions may be difficult, they also offer the opportunity to let go of difficult or painful roadblocks or burdens, replacing them with *lighter*, more positive ways to make their recovery journey more fulfilling.
3. Lead a short discussion using the following questions:
    a. How did it feel to hold all the "heavy burdens?"
    b. What would it be like to carry an empty bag?

10 minutes **Review the Day's Session**
1. Provide the reading assignment for the next session.
2. Remind the group of the next session and thank them for coming.

Personal Notes

_____
_____
_____
_____
_____
_____

Session #3
Driving Using the Rearview Mirror

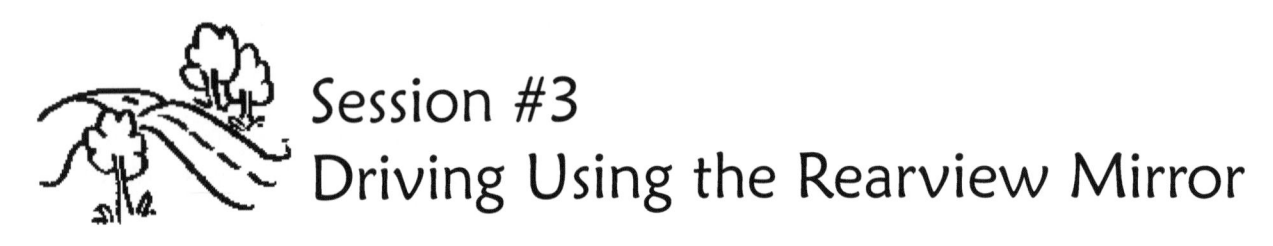

Overview
During Session #3, participants will explore the impact of trying to "head back to the past," including a discussion of how to handle one's psychiatric history.

Goals
During this session, participants will:
1. Finalize the "Partnership Pact."
2. Describe what it means to "drive using the rearview mirror."
3. Examine their own psychiatric history in order to embrace, integrate or "seal over" their past.
4. List at least two positive elements from their past which they would like to reclaim &/or hold on to for the future.

Readings
Chapter 9, pp. 282-284

Quote
"Fall seven times, stand up eight." (Japanese Proverb, *Pathways to Recovery*, p. 282)

Materials
- *Pathways to Recovery* text
- Flip chart or white board and markers
- Pens/pencils
- One copy of the "Partnership Pact" for everyone to sign
- One piece of ribbon, 10-12" long, for each participant
- One copy of "To Live!," p. 352, cut in strips

Handouts
- Be a STAR!, p. 353

Facilitator's Tip
Most groups will include people who are quiet. They may be simply shy or feel insecure. Others may be bored, feel they know more than others or be distracted by other things. They may also be having trouble understanding the discussion or be disinterested. Try to encourage these individuals to share their opinion, perhaps in a small group discussion. If/when they do contribute, recognize their contribution in an encouraging manner. It may be helpful to talk with them privately, assuring them that their voice is important.

Notes

"To Live!," gives the group an opportunity to work together and complete a short and simple task. Using a copy of the handout, cut the page into strips equal to the number of people in the group (some people could get two pieces if needed). You can also create your own activity with a picture or a different quote or verse.

Beginning today, each session of the roadblocks will end with a positive and uplifting activity, "Be a STAR!" You will find several "stars" in the handouts and you will also need some ribbon or other item to attach each session's star together. At the end of the group, participants will add a new star. Be creative! You could also hand out another positive quote, a personal challenge or an uplifting word.

Agenda

10 minutes **Introduction**
1. Begin on time and welcome all participants.
2. Review the agenda for today's session.

10 minutes **Partnership Pact**
Remind the group members they are making a commitment to conduct themselves according to the agreed upon terms.
1. Review the "Partnership Pact."
   a. Ask for and add any new items
   b. Pass out one copy and have participants sign the form.
   c. If possible, at break, make individual copies for everyone; if not, have copies ready for the next session.

20 minutes **Heading "Back to the Past"**
1. Read p. 282-283 (begin at "Driving Using" and end at the question on p. 283).
2. Lead a discussion using the following questions:
   a. How does "using the rearview mirror" impact your life?
   b. What do you think causes us to spend more time on our past than our future?
   c. What might you be able to do if you began focusing more on the future and less on the past?

20 minutes **Group Activity: *"To Live!"***
1. Give each participant one piece of the handout (if the group is smaller, give some individuals more pieces).
2. Explain the activity; let the group assemble the quotation.
3. Once the quotation is completed, lead a discussion using the following questions:
   a. What is the main message of this quotation?
   b. In what ways can you "not merely survive," but live?

10 minutes **Break**
Remind participants to return at the scheduled time.

30 minutes **How do We Handle Our Psychiatric History?**
1. Read p. 283 (begin at "How do We Handle").
2. Lead a discussion using the following questions:
   a. How have you chosen to view your psychiatric history? Do you embrace it, have you integrated it or do you prefer to "seal over" your experience?
   b. Does your psychiatric history keep you in the past? Why or why not?
   c. Are there alternative ways to view one's psychiatric history?

10 minutes **"Be a STAR!"**
1. Hand out the front cover, the 1st star and a piece of ribbon.
2. Read the quotation and have participants attach the pieces together with the ribbon.

10 minutes **Review the Day's Session**
1. Provide the reading assignment for the next session.
2. Remind the group of the next session and thank them for coming.

Personal Notes

_____
_____
_____
_____
_____
_____
_____
_____
_____
_____
_____

Session #4
Heading in Someone Else's

Overview
Session #4 looks at the roadblock of heading in someone else's direction. Participants will examine expectations (their own and others) and how to successfully develop their own self-direction.

Goals
During this session, participants will:
1. Define what it means to "head in someone else's direction."
2. List at least two past and/or present expectations that other's may have of them.
3. Read and discuss a story of someone who found their own personal path.
4. Complete a self-assessment to help determine their own course or direction.
5. List at least one past and one present expectation of themselves.

Readings
Chapter 9, pp. 284-288

Quote
"You must know for which harbour you are headed if you are to catch the right winds to take you there." (Seneca, *Pathways to Recovery*, p. 284)

Materials
- *Pathways to Recovery* text
- Flip chart or white board and markers
- Pens/pencils
- One piece of flip chart or other large size paper per person
- Colored markers or pens

Handouts
- Be a STAR!, p. 353

Facilitator's Tip
Another challenging person in a group is the one that rambles off topic. These individuals use unlikely examples or comparisons or simply go on and on with unrelated comments. Facilitators often have difficulty refocusing these individuals. Try asking them to restate their most important point or how what they are saying relates to the current topic. You might be able to rephrase what they are saying or you could have them summarize their ideas. Often other group members will help bring the discussion back on topic.

Notes
As you discuss expectations and roadblocks, be sure the conversation steers away from blaming others. This session can also be difficult for people who have been caregivers throughout their life. Because of their circumstances, they may have little idea what it means to be an individual or to have a life of their own.

Agenda

10 minutes   **Introduction**
   1. Begin on time and welcome all participants.
   2. Review the agenda for today's session.

20 minutes   **Common Expectations**
   1. Read p. 284-285 (end at Julie's story).
   2. As a group, develop a list of common expectations. Using the following categories, list these on the flip chart or white board.
      a. Family & friends
      b. Our culture or society
      c. The environment
      d. Mental health providers
      e. Peers
      f. Ourselves

20 minutes   **Sharing Our Stories:** *Julie*
This story is a good example of someone who took many of the expectations in her life and turned them into a motivator for change.
   1. Read Julie's story on p. 285.
   2. Lead a discussion using the following questions:
      a. What is Julie saying about her past?
      b. What did she learn?
      c. What was the "deep seeded voice" that Julie heard? Why was it different?
      d. What can we learn from Julie's story?

10 minutes   **Break**
Remind participants to return at the scheduled time.

20 minutes   **Self-Assessment**
Explain how answering these questions can provide a good beginning toward deciding the course of **their** *life. If participants are uncomfortable with completing this on their own, the exercise can be done as a group.*
   1. Have group members complete the self-assessment on p. 286.
   2. Using the list of expectations just created as a guide, have participants complete the questions on pp. 287-288.
   3. End by reading p. 288 (begin at "What We Want"). Remind the group that they do have the right to direct their own journey.

20 minutes · **Write Your Own Story**

This exercise can provide a fun and creative way for group members to move past the expectations of others and develop their own story.

1. Give each individual one piece of flip chart paper (if you don't have this available, you can use several blank pieces of 8½ x 11" paper & staple them on the side like a book).
2. Have participants fold the paper in half and then fold it in half again so it looks like a book.
3. Ask the group to choose the title of "their book." This can be their own title or perhaps the name of a favorite song or poem.
4. On the inside, participants can "write their own story." This might include:
    a. A few paragraphs about how they learned, like Julie, to take back their own journey
    b. A self-portrait
    c. Answering the question, "What I Want Most for My Recovery Journey"
5. If time permits and individuals are comfortable sharing, have them show their "book" to the larger group.

10 minutes · **"Be a STAR!"**

1. Hand out the next star.
2. Read the quotation and have participants attach the pieces together with the ribbon.

10 minutes · **Review the Day's Session**

1. Provide the reading assignment for the next session.
2. Remind the group of the next session and thank them for coming.

Personal Notes

_____
_____
_____
_____
_____
_____
_____
_____
_____

Session #5
Driving Ourselves Day & Night

Overview
Session #5 examines what happens when we speed up the journey—driving ourselves day and night. Participants will complete a self-assessment and learn new skills to pace the journey. In addition, the small group project will be introduced.

Goals
During this session, participants will:
1. Identify the signs of "moving too fast."
2. Complete a self-assessment to determine one's personal pace in life.
3. Identify at least two ways to pace their recovery journey.
4. Develop groups for the small group project.

Readings
Chapter 9, pp. 289-291

Quote
"Asking me to 'accept my limitations' is like asking me to stand in an open field and imagine high brick walls all around me with no way out. If I had 'accepted my limitations' there is no way I would be where I am now." (Randy Johnson, *Pathways to Recovery*, p. 291)

Materials
- *Pathways to Recovery* text
- Flip chart or white board and markers
- Pens/pencils

Handouts
- Be a STAR!, p. 353
- Small Group Project Presentations: *Instruction Sheet*, p. 356

Facilitator's Tip
What about a participant who talks too much? This person typically rambles and tries to dominate the conversation. This behavior can occur because an individual has a need for attention, they might want to share their own knowledge or they could be over or under prepared for the session. While it might seem logical to discourage this person from talking, it's better to encourage others to participate more. Ask for different opinions or give limited time for responses. You could also enlist the person's help in getting others to speak up.

Notes
During this session, participants will be introduced to the small group project. As part of this assignment, group members will design their own project and are free to be creative in developing a 10-15 minute presentation on a topic of interest from Module Two. Some examples for this module might include:

- Examining the life of someone famous who has overcame roadblocks
- Other ways of doing meditation
- Creating a positive quotation booklet for everyone in the group
- Developing a handbook of local community resources
- Creating a game to play (like *bingo, Jeopardy, Life*, etc.) focusing on the group members' strengths

Encourage participants to be creative in developing their group project. Brainstorm with the groups if they have a hard time beginning.

Agenda

10 minutes — **Introduction**
1. Begin on time and welcome all participants.
2. Review the agenda for today's session.

20 minutes — **Small Group Activity:** *Falling Into the Speed Trap*
1. Read pp. 289-290 (end at the self-assessment).
2. Divide participants into small groups of 3-4 people and ask them to choose one person to record their ideas.
3. Ask the small groups to discuss the following questions:
    a. In what ways do you (or have you) "fallen into the speed trap"?
    b. What kind of things can derail you when you're moving too fast?
    c. What are some things you can do to "pace yourself" better?

15 minutes — **Group Discussion**
1. Ask each reporter to share highlights from their discussion.
2. Are there common themes? List these on the flip chart or white board.

15 minutes — **Self-Assessment**
1. Have participants complete the self-assessment on p. 290.
2. Have the group complete the questions on p. 291.

10 minutes — **Break**
Remind participants to return at the scheduled time.

30 minutes	**Small Group Project Presentations** *Having small groups develop and present on a topic of interest provides a wonderful experience for learning. Groups will create their own project and develop a 10-15 minute presentation to be given during Sessions #21 & 22.* 1. Hand out the "Small Group Project Presentations: *Instruction Sheet*" for this module. 2. Review the project instructions, helping participants brainstorm ideas for a topic. 3. Divide the class into groups of 3-5 people. 4. Give the groups time to meet and brainstorm ideas. 5. Since the presentations will be done during two separate sessions, have them decide the order in which they will present.
10 minutes	**"Be a STAR!"** 1. Hand out the next star. 2. Read the quotation and have participants attach the pieces together with the ribbon.
10 minutes	**Review the Day's Session** 1. Provide the reading assignment for the next session. 2. Remind the group of the next session and thank them for coming.

Personal Notes

Session #6
Slowed Down by Low Expectations

Overview
This session examines the effects we feel from the negative messages and expectations we get not only from others, but from ourselves.

Goals
During this session, participants will:
1. Discuss how the expectations of others impacts the recovery journey.
2. Complete a self-assessment of how self-stigma has impacted thoughts and behaviors.
3. Describe how common barriers can be or are caused by self-stigma.

Readings
Chapter 9, pp. 291-296

Quote
"It's not who you are that holds you back, it's who you think you're not."
(Unknown, *Pathways to Recovery*, p. 293)

Materials
- *Pathways to Recovery* text
- Flip chart or white board and markers
- Pens/pencils

Handouts
- Be a STAR!, p. 354

Facilitator's Tip
Participants who participate in side conversations do so for several reasons. They may be trying to "catch up" or further understand a point that was made. They could be bored or have a comment to share which they don't feel comfortable making to the larger group. They may have a point to make or something to say about the topic but feel they would not be heard. While side conversations can be distracting, there are several options for trying to minimize this behavior. First, try not to embarrass them but ask if they would like to share their ideas or opinions on the topic. Making eye contact or casually walking toward them will often stop the talking. You could also try asking a question of another participant sitting nearby. If all else fails, you may need to stop and wait.

Notes
This session can be one of the most difficult for participants. Consistently give the message that examining the barriers of self-stigma and low expectations is the first step in healing from these negative experiences. Offer support and encourage group members to seek additional help after the group if needed.

Agenda

10 minutes

Introduction
1. Begin on time and welcome all participants.
2. Review the agenda for today's session.

20 minutes

Slowed by the Drag of Low Expectations
*Discussions of expectations and self-stigma will be difficult for the group. Many people hold on to the "shoulda-woulda-coulda" view of life and may talk of feelings of guilt, shame or loss. Encourage a frank discussion but try to stay focused on how identifying difficult life experiences can be used to learn how **not** to continue negative patterns.*
1. Read pp. 291-292 (begin at "Slowed by the Drag" and end at "Self-Stigma").
2. Lead a discussion using the following questions:
   a. What do you think about what we have just read?
   b. How do low expectations affect you?
   c. What do you think about "mentalism"? Does this term make sense to you given your experiences?

20 minutes

Self-Assessment
1. Have participants complete the self-assessment on pp. 293-294.
2. As an alternative to having group members answer the questions on their own, complete the questions as a large group discussion.

10 minutes

Break
Remind participants to return at the scheduled time.

20 minutes

Small Group Activity: *Exploring the Impact of Self-Stigma*
1. Ask the group to define self-stigma. Write responses on the flip chart or white board.
2. Have participants pair up with one other person in the group.
3. Using the seven factors listed on pp. 295-296, assign 1-2 sections to each pair.
4. Have them read over the factors and develop 1-2 possible solutions.

20 minutes   **Group Discussion**
1. Ask each pair to share highlights from their discussion. For each of the factors, list the ideas created on the flip chart or white board.
2. If time permits, let the larger group add to the list.

10 minutes   **Be a "STAR!"**
1. Hand out the next star.
2. Read the quotation and have participants attach the pieces together with the ribbon.

10 minutes   **Review the Day's Session**
1. Provide the reading assignment for the next session.
2. Remind the group of the next session and thank them for coming.

Personal Notes

_____
_____
_____
_____
_____
_____
_____
_____
_____
_____
_____
_____
_____
_____
_____
_____

Session #7
Healing Self-Stigma

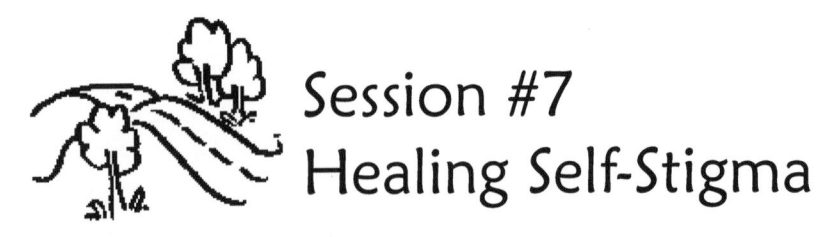

Overview
Session #7 will take the concepts learned in the previous session and give participants an opportunity to learn how to heal self-stigma.

Goals
During this session, participants will:
1. Identify five ways to help them heal from self-stigma.
2. Choose one healing idea to incorporate into their life.

Readings
Chapter 9, pp. 297-299

Quote
"No one can make you feel inferior without your consent." (Eleanor Roosevelt, *Pathways to Recovery*, p. 297)

Materials
- *Pathways to Recovery* text
- Flip chart or white board and markers
- Pens/pencils

Handouts
Arrivals & Departures, p. 357
Be a STAR!, p. 354

Facilitator's Tip
As a facilitator, it's important to let group members know it is all right to have "feelings." Our feelings are ours and, although not always rational, they are real. Help group members to share their feelings and talk about them. Asking, "How do you feel about this?" is a good way to start.

Notes
Some participants may find it hard to deal with self-stigma. Often, this type of stigma is related to low self-esteem. It's easy to look down on yourself or blame others for your illness, especially when others have also put you down. Be positive and respect the feelings and emotions of group members.

Agenda

10 minutes   **Introduction**
1. Begin on time and welcome all participants.
2. Review the agenda for today's session.

20 minutes   **Sharing Our Stories:** *Michael*
1. Read Michael's quote at the top of p. 297.
2. Lead a discussion using the following questions:
    a. What do you think about Michael's comment?
    b. Why is this comment important?
    c. Of all we have discussed about self-stigma, what seems most important to you?

20 minutes   **"Arrivals & Departures"**
This activity will give individuals the opportunity to decide what actions and behaviors they would like to keep and those they would like to get rid of.
1. Hand out "Arrivals and Departures" and provide the following explanation:
    a. Under the "Arrivals" section, have participants list the behaviors &/or thoughts they would like to keep to use on their recovery journey.
    b. Under the "Departures" section, have participants list the behaviors &/or thoughts they would like to get rid of to make their journey easier.
2. As a group, discuss the answers and encourage participants to continue adding to their lists as needed.

10 minutes   **Break**
Remind participants to return at the scheduled time.

25 minutes   **Small Group Activity:** *Overcoming Self-Stigma*
Explain that to heal self-stigma, it will take time and some effort.
1. Divide the participants into 5 groups (if the group is smaller, this can be done individually).
2. Hang five sheets of flip chart paper around the room. At the top of each sheet, list the suggestions for overcoming stigma found on pp. 297-299.
3. Give each group a different color marker. Assign the groups to each of the flip chart pages. (Using a different color marker keeps the activity flowing and will represent each group's ideas.)
4. Give each group five minutes to list ideas on "how" to use the ideas in the workbook. Encourage them to make their ideas specific and action-oriented, including any local resources.
5. Have the groups rotate to each flip chart every 5 minutes and add any new ideas they may have.

15 minutes   **Group Discussion**
1. For each section, ask the following questions:
   a. How easy/difficult was it to come up with specific examples?
   b. Which section was the most difficult to complete? Why?
   c. Are you surprised by any of the suggestions?
   d. Is there one suggestion that you think you can incorporate into your life to help you overcome self-stigma?

10 minutes   **"Be a STAR!"**
1. Hand out the next star.
2. Read the quotation and have participants attach the pieces together with the ribbon.

10 minutes   **Review the Day's Session**
1. Provide the reading assignment for the next session.
2. Remind the group of the next session and thank them for coming.

Personal Notes

Session #8
Driving in Circles & Feeling Lost

Overview
Session #8 examines combines two roadblocks—driving in circles and feeling lost. The group will examine what occurs when there is an unclear destination or few clear goals while also looking at how to adjust and make changes to the journey.

Goals
During this session, participants will:
1. Explore the roadblock of "driving in circles."
2. Examine what it is like to "feel lost."
3. Identify at least two ways to learn how to change a habit.

Readings
Chapter 9, pp. 299-300, 307

Quote
"Be patient toward all that is unresolved in your heart and try to love the questions themselves...Live the questions now. Perhaps you will then gradually, without noticing it, live your way some distant day into the answers." (Rainer Maria Rilke, *Pathways*, p. 300)

Materials
- *Pathways to Recovery* text
- Flip chart or white board and markers
- Pens/pencils
- Art supplies (paper, old greeting cards or magazines, ribbon, stickers, scissors, glue sticks, tape, etc.

Handouts
- Be a STAR!, p. 354

Facilitator's Tip
Some facilitators will find it especially hard to learn how to overcome the behavior of people who are disagreeable or argumentative within the group. Generally, these individuals disagree with whatever is said and may be angry or combative. Individuals who display these behaviors may truly be angry or upset by the opinions or comments of others. They may feel they are being ignored or are not able to make comments in a constructive manner. So, what are some possible solutions? You could simply recognize the individual's feelings and continue or you can open their comments to the larger group.

Facilitator's Tip, cont.

Ask if anyone else is feeling the same way in an attempt to solicit input from a peer. Above all, remain calm and don't respond to attacks. If necessary, talk with the individual privately about their comments and how it appears to be impacting the group. If it can't be resolved, you may need to ask the individual to leave the session or the entire group.

Notes

Both of these roadblocks deal with the direction one is going and the tools needed to get to the destination (the goal). While both roadblocks focus mainly on changing goals, it will only briefly be touched upon here (the section on goal setting comes later in this module).

Agenda

10 minutes **Introduction**
1. Begin on time and welcome all participants.
2. Review the agenda for today's session.

20 minutes **Driving in Circles**
1. Read pp. 299-300 (begin at "Driving in Circles" and end at "Thrown Off Track").
2. Lead a discussion using the following questions:
   a. Have you ever felt like you were "driving in circles"?
   c. What do you think are the most important things we can do to overcome this roadblock?

30 minutes **Step-by-Step: *Creating a Road Map for Life***
Getting from one place to another requires us to have a plan or a map of how to get there. This activity will give participants a creative way of designing a clear road map for their lives.
1. Using the concept of a road map, have participants use art supplies to create how they view (or would like to see) their life. Have them include any of the items commonly found on a road map (such as the main highways, roadblocks, bridges, scenic points, exits, hills, lakes, or historical markers, etc.).
2. When they have finished, ask for volunteers who would be willing to share their maps and explain them to the group.

10 minutes **Break**
Remind participants to return at the scheduled time.

30 minutes **Feeling Lost: *Old Habits Die Hard***
The ability to change our habits is key to overcoming these roadblocks. While changing habits is difficult—many estimate it takes six weeks to completely change a habit—this exercise will examine the types of supports we need to make the new behavior "stick."

Cont.   **Feeling Lost: *Old Habits Die Hard*, cont.**
1. Read p. 307 (begin at "Feeling Lost").
2. Ask participants to pair up with the person sitting next to them.
3. Assign one of these common tasks to each team:
    a. Brushing your hair
    b. Putting on a jacket
    c. Tying their tennis shoes
    d. Making a phone call
    e. Frying an egg
    f. Folding a towel or bed sheet
4. One at a time, have the participants practice completing the task, using only one hand while their partner observes.
5. Then have them attempt it with the opposite hand (if they are left handed, they use their right hand, etc.).
6. Finally, have the pairs work together to complete the task.
7. Lead a discussion using the following question:
    a. What did you learn by attempting these tasks? Some suggestions include:
        - We can make simple changes but it is hard work.
        - Getting help from someone else makes it easier.
        - The more you do it, the easier it gets.
        - Letting someone know what we are trying to do makes us more accountable.
        - Trying to do things in a different way can help us find a new way.

10 minutes   **"Be a STAR!"**
1. Hand out the next star.
2. Read the quotation and have participants attach the pieces together with the ribbon.

10 minutes   **Review the Day's Session**
1. Provide the reading assignment for the next session.
2. Remind the group of the next session and thank them for coming.

Personal Notes

_____

_____

_____

_____

Session #9
Thrown Off-Track by Symptoms

Overview
Session #9 examines how the presence of symptoms can be a roadblock to recovery. Participants will also meet in their small groups to continue planning their presentations.

Goals
During this session, participants will:
1. Identify at least two self-care tools they use to reduce or eliminate symptoms.
2. Identify at least two ways to "reframe" relapse.
3. Meet with their small group to work on their presentations.

Readings
Chapter 9, pp. 300-302

Quote
"Love yourself first and everything else falls into line. You really have to love yourself to get anything done in this world." (Lucille Ball, *Pathways to Recovery*, p. 301)

Materials
- *Pathways to Recovery* text
- Flip chart or white board and markers
- Pens/pencils

Handouts
- "Re-frame" Relapse, p. 358
- Be a STAR!, p. 355

Facilitator's Tip
It is quite common to have people in your group who will be experiencing symptoms although it is very possible for them to participate fully in the activities. Occasionally, there may be individuals who are experiencing severe symptoms and may have more difficulty joining in. As the facilitator, encourage that individual's participation at whatever level they may be comfortable (often, just sitting in the group is helpful in reducing symptoms). Having designated peer supporters to join these individuals or spend time alone with them can also be helpful. If you need to speak with the individual, do so privately. If the symptoms do become disruptive, remember that your responsibility is with the *whole* group. You may need to take a short break to talk with the individual or help them seek additional support.

Notes
Examining one's symptoms along with previous periods of relapse provides a good opportunity for participants to listen more to themselves and rely less on others for their well-being. If individuals understand the cycles of their illness and practice healthy self-care, it can indicate that they are not necessarily responsible for a relapse. While relapse is hard, being able to look at it from a different perspective can help one recover from the relapse quicker and feel better about themselves.

Agenda

10 minutes — **Introduction**
1. Begin on time and welcome all participants.
2. Review the agenda for today's session.

20 minutes — **Self-Care of Symptoms**
1. Read pp. 300-301 (end at the exercise).
2. Create a list of the self-care tools group members have used to help manage their psychiatric symptoms.
3. Write the ideas on the flip chart or white board.

20 minutes — **Sharing Our Stories: *Donna***
The concept that Donna talks about is a common one in recovery.
1. Read Donna's story on p. 302.
2. Lead a discussion using the following questions:
   a. What do you think about Donna's comments?
   b. In what ways have you been able to "reframe" relapse?

10 minutes — **Break**
Remind participants to return at the scheduled time.

20 minutes — **"Re-Frame" Relapse**
This exercise is one way for participants to rethink or "reframe" their experiences with relapse. Encourage them to use the frame when they are tempted to view the challenges in life in a negative perspective.
1. Hand out the "Re-Frame Relapse" worksheet.
2. In the space provided, have participants list the ways they have (or can) look at the experience of relapse.
3. Encourage them to use or review these ideas as needed.

20 minutes — **Small Group Project Planning**
1. Provide time for the small groups to work on their project.
2. If they have not already done so, help the groups decide on the topic or activity they will present.

10 minutes   **"Be a STAR!"**
1. Hand out the next star.
2. Read the quotation and have participants attach the pieces together with the ribbon.

10 minutes   **Review the Day's Session**
1. Provide the reading assignment for the next session.
2. Remind the group of the next session and thank them for coming.

Personal Notes

Session #10
Riding the Brake Pedal

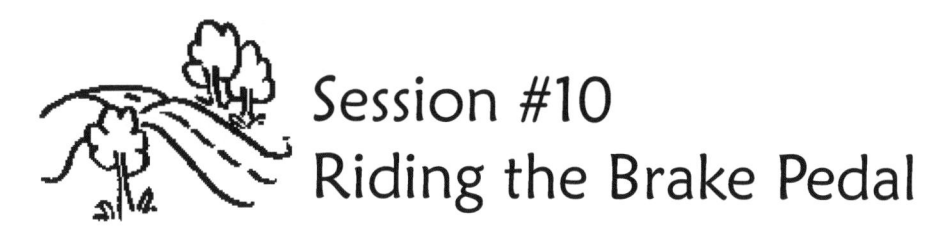

Overview
Session #10 looks at two factors that can substantially limit recovery — fear of failure and fear of success.

Goals
During this session, participants will:
1. Discuss the commonalities between the fear of failure and fear of success.
2. Complete two self-assessments to determine what fears they have.
3. Learn to use a "Daily Success" chart.
4. Create a "fear box" to use for releasing their own personal fears.

Readings
Chapter 9, pp. 302-306

Quote
"You may be disappointed if you fail, but you are doomed if you don't try."
(Beverly Sills, *Pathways to Recovery*, p. 302)

Materials
- *Pathways to Recovery* text
- Flip chart or white board and markers
- Pens/pencils
- A small box for each participant
- Art supplies (paper, old greeting cards or magazines, ribbon, stickers, scissors, glue sticks, tape, etc.)

Handouts
- Be a STAR!, p. 355

Facilitator's Tip
A good facilitator encourages interaction *between* participants, not just between themselves and the group. Help group members to ask questions of and challenge each other.

Notes
The activity for today, the "fear box," is similar to the Guatemalan tradition of "worry dolls." The idea behind the dolls is that if you are worrying about

Notes, cont.

something, you tell the dolls, place them under your pillow at night and the dolls will take your worries away. The same concept is true for the "fear box." Participants can use their "fear box" to place their fears and let them go as needed.

Agenda

10 minutes
Introduction
1. Begin on time and welcome all participants.
2. Review the agenda for today's session.

40 minutes
Fear of Failure vs. Fear of Success
Each of the quotes in this section are helpful reminders as to why it is important to let go of our fears. Encourage participants to use one of these quotes as a positive motivator to begin taking more risks.
1. Read p. 302 (the final paragraph only).
2.. Lead a discussion using the following questions:
    a. How are fear of failure and fear of success the same?
    b. In what ways are they different?
3. Many of us "awful-ize" what can happen to us without ever trying in the first place.
    a. Read the quote by Beverly Sills on p. 302.
    b. In what ways can fear impact our recovery journey?
4. Have participants complete the self-assessment on p. 303.
5. Have participants complete the second self-assessment on p. 304.
6. Continue the discussion using the following questions:
    a. Why does "pulling the covers over our head" not help us take risks?
    b. How can taking risks help us move past our fears (of failure or success)?
    c. What is one risk you can identify which you can take?

10 minutes
Break
Remind participants to return at the scheduled time.

20 minutes
How to Counteract Fears
Babe Ruth, the baseball great, was known for striking out. He once said, "Never let the fear of striking out get in your way." Share this with the group as an introduction to the activity.
1. Read p. 305 (end at "My Daily Successes").
2. Are there things you have done in the past to help you get past your fears? (List the responses on the flip chart or white board.) Some of these might include:
    a. Determining the *cause* of the fear. Often figuring this out can remove the fear.
    b. Talking with others who have overcome fear.

Cont. **How to Counteract Fears, cont.**
- c. Just doing it! Once we get over the fear of something by *doing* it, we are no longer afraid.
- d. As suggested in *Pathways* on p. 305, keep a list of daily successes (the more we "see" our success, the more risks we will be willing to take).

20 minutes **Creating a "Fear Box"**
1. Explain the concept of the "fear box."
2. Using a variety of art materials, have participants decorate their own box.
3. Have pieces of paper in which group members can write their fears.
4. Remind them that when fears arise, they can use the box in a symbolic way to "put away their fears," take a risk and move on. They could also use it as a place to "store" their fears until they are ready to face them.

10 minutes **"Be a STAR!"**
1. Hand out the next star.
2. Read the quotation and have participants attach the pieces together with the ribbon.

10 minutes **Review the Day's Session**
1. Provide the reading assignment for the next session.
2. Remind the group of the next session and thank them for coming.

Personal Notes

_____
_____
_____
_____
_____
_____
_____
_____

Session #11
When the Going Gets Boring

Overview
This session examines what happens when the recovery journey gets boring and what to do that will help participants overcome the boredom. In addition, the group will have an opportunity to evaluate their experience in the group up to this point.

Goals
During this session, participants will:
1. Examine where and when they are bored.
2. Create a "Self-Nurture Calendar" to help alleviate boredom.
3. Share their personal experience about using *Pathways to Recovery*.

Readings
Chapter 9, pp. 306-307

Quote
"Life is either a daring adventure or nothing."(Helen Keller, *Pathways to Recovery*, p. 306)

Materials
- *Pathways to Recovery* text
- Flip chart or white board and markers
- Pens/pencils

Handouts
- Self-Nurture Calendar, p. 359
- Mid-Session Satisfaction Survey, 344
- Facilitator Self-Assessment, p. 345
- Be a STAR!, p. 355

Facilitator's Tip
Feeling a little bored as a facilitator? Try treating each session as a new learning experience for you. There is always something new to try, some new insight to find or a different technique to master. Keep your skills fresh and you will be more effective.

Notes
After examining all the roadblocks, some participants may feel a bit weary. Sometimes when individuals are working on new goals or trying to change how they look at things,

Notes, cont.

they may appear to be disinterested or even disheartened. This is normal (remember "recovery whiplash?"). Encourage the group to continue as new information can take quite a while to "sink in."

Agenda

10 minutes **Introduction**
1. Begin on time and welcome all participants.
2. Review the agenda for today's session.

20 minutes **What Does it Mean to Be Bored?**
1. Read p. 306 (only the first two paragraphs starting at "When the Going").
2. Lead a discussion using the following questions:
   a. What are you like when you are bored?
   b. Are there certain times of the day (or week) when you find yourself bored?
   c. Are there things you have been wanting to do but haven't taken the time for?

10 minutes **Overcoming Boredom**
These can be ideas of things that they have been wanting to do and that are easy to incorporate into their daily routine. There are some examples listed on pp. 306-307 but could also include things like reading the comics, taking a 10 minute walk, calling a friend, writing or drawing, etc.).
1. One way to overcome boredom is to make plans each day to do something special or fun for yourself.
2. Pass out the "Self-Nurture Calendar."
3. For each day of the week, have participants decide on one thing they will do during each day to nurture themselves.
4. Challenge them to use the list during the coming week/s.

10 minutes **Break**
Remind participants to return at the scheduled time.

30 minutes **Mid-Session Evaluation**
Evaluation can be a powerful tool in giving voice to participants. Encourage and respect open and honest comments.
1. Lead a discussion focusing on how the participants view the success of the sessions thus far. Use all or part of these questions:
   a. How has the experience of attending the sessions benefited your recovery?
   b. What is your favorite part of the group? Why?
   c. What is your least favorite part of the group? Why?

Cont. **Mid-Session Evaluation, cont.**
       d. What do I (the facilitator or co-facilitators) do to help you learn?
       e. What suggestions can you offer to make the group better?
       f. What could I (the facilitator or co-facilitators) do to improve the group?
       g. As a group, do you feel we are staying true to the "Partnership Pact"?
       h. Do you feel you are able to uphold the "Recovery Pledge"? Why or why not?
       i. Does anyone have a need for support around his or her recovery efforts?

10 minutes **Written Evaluation**
Be sure to let participants know their comments are anonymous and that their comments will only be used to make positive changes to the group as needed.
1. Pass out "Mid-Session Satisfaction Survey."
2. Ask the group to complete the form and leave with you.

20 minutes **"Be a STAR!"**
1. Hand out the final star for the roadblock and the back cover.
2. Read the quotation and have participants attach the pieces together with the ribbon.
3. Celebrate completing the roadblocks section by announcing everyone is a "STAR!"

10 minutes **Review the Day's Session**
1. Provide the reading assignment for the next session.
2. Remind the group of the next session and thank them for coming.

Personal Notes

_____
_____
_____
_____
_____
_____
_____
_____

Session #12
Meditation & Visualization

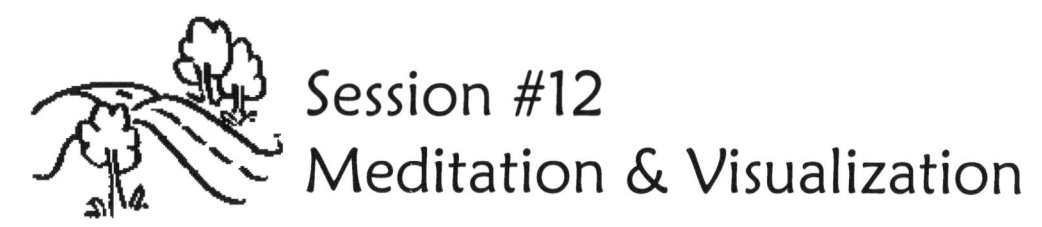

Overview
This session will explain the "supercharging" techniques of meditation and visualization and give participants the opportunity to practice both activities.

Goals
During this session, participants will:
1. Examine meditation and visualization as tools to use for greater focus.
2. Learn one meditation and one visualization exercise they can use outside of the group.

Readings
Chapter 11, pp. 355-357

Quote
"Peace can be reached through meditation on the knowledge which dreams give. Peace can also be reached through concentration upon that which is dearest to the heart."
~ Patanjali (*Pathways to Recovery*, p. 355)

Materials
- *Pathways to Recovery* text
- Flip chart or white board and markers
- Pens/pencils

Facilitator's Tip
Good facilitators make time to practice. There is no better way to feel confident than to spend time preparing and using visualization techniques to imagine how you would like the session to flow. Seek out other facilitators that you admire and ask them how they prepare and what techniques work best for them. They may even be willing to observe you and provide feedback.

Notes
Both these techniques have recently become much more common tools but some facilitators may find themselves uncomfortable with explaining and presenting them to group members. This can be an excellent opportunity to invite an expert from a local hospital, yoga or wellness center to visit (be sure to let group members know ahead of time so they won't be caught off guard by a new person at the group).

Agenda

10 minutes — **Introduction**
1. Begin on time and welcome all participants.
2. Review the agenda for today's session.

20 minutes — **Introduction to Meditation**

Since meditation has evolved from so many different sources, there are several ways it can be done. Encourage the group to learn more about whichever type of meditations may interest them.

1. Introduce the practice of meditation by reading p. 355 (begin at "Supercharging Strategy").
2. Lead a discussion about meditation by asking the following questions:
   a. How familiar are you with meditation?
   b. Have any of you used meditation before? In what form?
   c. If so, how has it helped you?
   d. How do you feel about using meditation as a wellness practice?
   e. Do you think it could be helpful for you?

20 minutes — **Meditation Exercise**

Arrange the room so it is comfortable and quiet. If someone does not want to participate, simply ask them to sit quietly.

1. Read the instruction for the exercise on p. 356.
2. Slowly walk the group through the deep breathing for about 5 minutes so they get a chance to try it.
3. End with a positive note or word (such as "peace" or "thanks").

10 minutes — **Break**

Remind participants to return at the scheduled time.

20 minutes — **Introduction to Visualization**
1. Read "Supercharging Strategy #4" on p. 356.
2. Lead a discussion using the following questions:
   a. How would you describe the process of visualization?
   b. In what ways have you used visualization to help relax you or give you guidance?

30 minutes — **Visualization Exercises**

As with the meditation exercise, arrange the room so it is comfortable and quiet. If someone does not want to participate, simply ask them to sit quietly. The first exercise is a good one to use for times when individuals are anxious or are having a hard time concentrating. The second exercise will help individuals "see" themselves succeeding at a specific goal.

Cont. **Visualization Exercises, cont.**
1. Using the "Creating a Place of Peace" exercise on p. 357, have participants try this visualization activity.
   a. Give participants 3-5 minutes to decide on the "place" they would like to use for this exercise.
   b. Ask for silence and slowly read each section of the exercise, giving time between movements for the group to develop the visualization.
2. Have the group try the second exercise, "Succeeding at a Goal."
   a. Read the exercise.
   b. Give participants 3-5 minutes to decide on a goal they would like to use for the exercise.
   c. Ask for silence and give the group 3-5 minutes to "try" this visualization.
3. Lead a discussion using the following questions:
   a. How did these exercises work for you? Were you able to do them?
   b. Was one easier than the other? Which one? Why?
   c. When do you think it would be helpful to do one of these visualizations?

10 minutes **Review the Day's Session**
1. Provide the reading assignment for the next session.
2. Remind the group of the next session and thank them for coming.

Personal Notes

_____
_____
_____
_____
_____
_____
_____
_____
_____
_____

Session #13
Changing Our Course

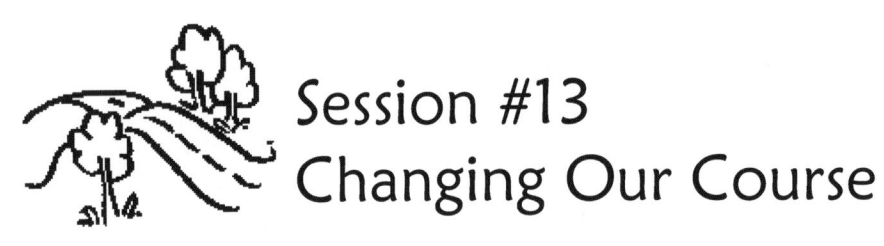

Overview
This session is the beginning step to help participants identify the personal strengths they possess.

Goals
During this session, participants will:
1. List a minimum of 2-3 personal strengths.
2. Discuss how their personal experiences have led to a "negative mental roadmap."
3. Discover why it is important to focus on personal strengths instead of deficits.

Readings
Chapter 4, p. 73-77

Quote
"If you constantly think of illness, you eventually become ill; if you believe yourself to be beautiful you become so." (Shakti Gawain, *Pathways to Recovery*, p. 75)

Materials
- *Pathways to Recovery* text
- Flip chart or white board and markers
- Pens/pencils

Facilitator's Tip
Confucius said, "What I hear, I forget. What I see, I remember. What I do, I understand." So, one of the best ways for facilitator's to help participants learn is to plan for them to 'do' things. By actively participating, group members will be more likely to take the information learned and start to use it or in some way change their behavior.

Notes
Identifying strengths can be another difficult exercise for some. Over the years, many individuals become much more comfortable with their deficits and will find listing their strengths quite challenging. As always, remind participants they are starting "where they are." Explain that the group will be spending several sessions on strengths so everyone will have an opportunity to become more comfortable with the process.

Agenda

10 minutes **Introduction**
1. Begin on time and welcome all participants.
2. Review the agenda for today's session.

15 minutes **Exploring Our Strengths**
Review the strengths list that was developed by group members during Module One, Session #4.
1. Read p. 73 (end at "My Initial Strengths List").
2. Have group members complete the questions on pp. 73-74.
3. Lead a discussion using the questions that participants just completed.

15 minutes **Sharing Our Stories:** *Linda*
Group members will likely be able to identify with this writer AND with the quote on the bottom of p. 74.
1. Read Linda's story on p. 74.
2. Lead a short discussion with the group using these questions:
   a. How does Linda's story relate to what we have been talking about?
   b. How was Linda able to use her strengths to "take back" pieces of herself?

20 minutes **Negative Roadmaps**
There are a variety of ways we are taught to have a "negative roadmap." This is common for many individuals; again, identifying these barriers will make it easier to make a positive change.
1. Read pp. 74-75 (begin at "Charting Our Course").
2. Lead a discussion using the following questions:
   a. What kind of things can you identify that cause you to have negative thinking?
   b. In what ways will continuing a negative perspective make the recovery journey more difficult?

10 minutes **Break**
Remind participants to return at the scheduled time.

10 minutes **Changing Our Orientation**
1. Read p. 76 (end at "Moving from a Problem").
2. Explain that changing our orientation will take time and effort but it does make the recovery journey easier.
3. Lead a short discussion using the following question:
   a. As a group, how do you think we can better focus on the positive?

15 minutes   **Small Group Activity:** *Moving to a Strengths Orientation*
Even though changing one's orientation from a deficit to a strengths-based one will take time and effort, it can make the recovery journey much easier.
1. Divide participants into small groups of 3-4 people and ask them to choose one person to record their ideas.
2. Ask the small groups to do the following:
   a. Read the last paragraph on p. 76 as well as the chart on p. 77.
   b. List 2-3 things they can do to help change their current orientation.

15 minutes   **Group Discussion**
1. Ask each reporter to share highlights from their discussion; list these on the flip chart or white board.
2. Lead a discussion using the following questions:
   a. Do you see any common themes within this list?
   b. What reactions did you have to the chart?
   c. Are there alternative ways of identifying our deficits versus our strengths?

10 minutes   **Review the Day's Session**
1. Provide the reading assignment for the next session.
2. Remind the group of the next session and thank them for coming.

Personal Notes

_____
_____
_____
_____
_____
_____
_____
_____
_____
_____

Session #14
Getting Going

Overview
Session #14 starts the process of identifying the various sources of our strengths, including those derived from our unique knowledge as well as our talents and skills. Participants will also meet in their small groups to continue planning their presentations.

Goals
During this session, participants will:
1. Examine the various sources of strengths.
2. List at least three strengths that come from things they have learned in life.
3. Decide on at least two things they would like to learn more about.
4. List at least two personal talents or skills.
5. Identify at least one talent or skill to develop.
6. Meet with their small groups to continue planning their presentation.

Readings
Chapter 4, pp. 78-82

Quote
"If you do not ask yourself what it is you know, you will go on listening to others and change will not come because you will not hear your own truth." (St. Bartholomew, *Pathways to Recovery*, p. 78)

Materials
- *Pathways to Recovery* text
- Flip chart or white board and markers
- Pens/pencil
- Index cards for the "Strengths Encounters" exercise

Handouts
- Strengths Encounters, p. 360

Facilitator's Tip
Find out early in the group what the participants consider their strengths and interests. Once you can identify these, you will be able to design activities and share examples that are relevant to the group members.

Notes
Remember that it can be quite difficult for participants to identify their strengths. Always encourage group members to help each other.

You will want to prepare the "Strengths Encounters" cards prior to the session. Also, get an update on the progress of the small group projects. If barriers or problems are present, schedule a brainstorming time to help them.

Agenda

10 minutes — **Introduction**
1. Begin on time and welcome all participants.
2. Review the agenda for today's session.

10 minutes — **Identifying the Sources of Our Strengths**
1. Read p. 78 (end at "Strengths that Come"), having the group think about the questions listed.
2. Explain the different types of strengths that will be covered during the next three sessions. These include strengths from:
   a. Our unique knowledge
   b. Our skills & talents
   c. Our cultural identity & resources
   d. The community
   e. Our personal qualities
   f. The things we are proud of
   g. The perception of others

15 minutes — **Group Activity: *Strengths Encounters***
This activity will give group members the opportunity to share their own strengths as well as learn about the strengths of others in the group.
1. Give each member of the group one of the "Strengths Encounters" cards.
2. Pair the participants up and have them ask and answer the questions on the card. Give them 1-2 minutes.
3. Have participants swap questions and repeat the process with different pairs until each has asked a question of someone else.

15 minutes — **Group Discussion**
1. Lead a discussion using the following questions:
   a. How difficult was it to think of a strength you have?
   b. Did you remember a strength you have that you had forgotten about?
   c. Did you hear about a skill from someone else that you would like to learn more about?
2. Encourage the group to continue discussing this exercise during the break.

10 minutes	**Break**
	Remind participants to return at the scheduled time.

15 minutes	**Strengths from My Unique Knowledge**

1. Read pp. 78-79 (begin at "Strengths that Come").
2. Pose the questions on p. 79 to the group. Have them discuss their answers and complete the questions in the workbook.
3. Have participants complete the self-reflection on p. 80. Encourage them to list as many answers as possible.

15 minutes	**Strengths from My Strengths & Talents:** *Phillip's Story*

1. Read p. 81, including Phillip's story.
2. Like Phillip, can participants identify at least one talent that they can use (or are using) to support their recovery?
3. Have participants complete the exercise on p. 82. Encourage them to list as many answers as possible.

20 minutes	**Small Group Project Planning**

1. Provide time for groups to work on their project.
2. Assist them with planning as needed.

10 minutes	**Review the Day's Session**

1. Provide the reading assignment for the next session.
2. Remind the group of the next session and thank them for coming.

Personal Notes

_____
_____
_____
_____
_____
_____
_____
_____
_____

Session #15
Getting Going, cont.

Overview
Session #15 continues the process of identifying personal strengths, including those found as part of one's cultural identity and from resources within the community. Group members will also identify personal qualities as well as things in which they can be proud.

Goals
During this session, participants will:
1. List at least three strengths that come from their cultural identity.
2. Name at least three strengths that come from community resources.
3. Identify at least three personal qualities.
4. Describe three strengths in which to be proud.

Readings
Chapter 4, pp. 83-94

Quote
"A weakness is a strength not yet developed." (Benjamin Franklin, *Pathways*, p. 89)

Materials
- *Pathways to Recovery* text
- Flip chart or white board and markers
- Pens/pencils

Handouts
- Strengths You See in Me (2-3 copies per group member), pp. 361-363

Facilitator's Tip
Avoid the "isms." This includes racism, sexism, ageism, mentalism, etc. Individuals can be very sensitive to even the slightest hint of stigma or prejudice. Be careful to treat each person equally and without offense.

Notes
Remember that strengths are often the thoughts or feelings that sustain individuals and give them the ability to hold on to hope and courage. Strengths come from many different areas; the important thing to remember is that strengths come from a person's thoughts, not from what others may have said.

Notes, cont.

The homework assignment for today can be a very helpful resource for participants. However, encourage them NOT to go to individuals who have a negative attitude or who would not be supportive of them; there is no need to affirm any negative thoughts. You might want to have group members complete the homework handout as a group as participants will have known each other longer and could give more specific answers. It could also help boost morale before group members do the activity with others.

Agenda

10 minutes   **Introduction**
1. Begin on time and welcome all participants.
2. Review the agenda for today's session.
3. Review the strengths definition on p. 78. Have the group members list what kinds of things make up strengths. This will include:
    a. Things routinely done.
    b. Things excelled at in the past or mastered.
    c. Unrealized potential (things you THINK you can do but may not have tried).
    d. Abilities and interests to develop.

20 minutes   **Strengths from My Cultural Identity**
Strengths that come from our cultural identify are often overlooked. This section is a good one for the entire group to complete together.
1. Read p. 83 (the first paragraph only).
2. As a group, have participants identify their own cultural strengths. Write all the responses on the flip chart or white board.
3. Have participants add their own strengths to the exercise on p. 84. Encourage them to list as many answers as possible.

20 minutes   **Strengths from My Community Resources**
Being part of and participating in the community is a key element of the recovery journey. Our communities are rich in resources, both formal (like the YMCA/YWCA, hospital, pharmacy, etc.) and informal (such as a neighborhood reading group or where to find a good sandwich).
1. Read pp. 85-86 (end at the exercise).
2. Divide the group into pairs and have them discuss their ideas about community strengths.
3. Participants should then complete the exercise on p. 86.

10 minutes   **Break**
Remind participants to return at the scheduled time.

20 minutes	**Personal Qualities that are My Strengths**
	1. Read p. 87 (including the stories).
	2. Remind the group that their stories are probably similar to those of Kathy and Sandy.
	3. Have participants complete the exercise on p. 88.
20 minutes	**Strengths that are Things I Have to Be Proud Of**
	Being proud can have many meanings. Some may find listing things they are proud of as boastful or egotistic. Others may simply feel they have nothing in which to be proud. Encourage the group to think of the things that give them satisfaction or provide a positive sense of self-esteem or self-respect.
	1. Read p. 89 (including the story).
	2. Have the group identify the strengths that are listed in Linda's story.
	3. Finish by having participants complete the exercise on p. 90.
10 minutes	**Homework Assignment: *Strengths Others See in Me***
	Others are often able to see strengths in us that we are unable to see in ourselves. While this assignment can be difficult for some, it can be very helpful in identifying other strengths we possess. Group members should choose people with whom they feel comfortable and safe. This could include family or friends, neighbors, a minister or mentor, mental health providers or even someone else in the group. Also, remind participants that homework such as this exercise can enhance the work they are already doing during the group.
	1. Give each participant 2-3 copies of "Strengths You See in Me."
	2. Review the questions on the handout and answer any questions the group may have.
	3. Encourage them to talk to at least one person before the next session to ask for their help in completing the questionnaire.
10 minutes	**Review the Day's Session**
	1. Provide the reading assignment for the next session.
	2. Remind the group of the next session and thank them for coming.

Personal Notes

_____

_____

_____

_____

_____

Session #16
Making the Most of Our Strengths

Overview
Session #16 gives participants the opportunity to combine all they have learned about their strengths in the past sessions. They will begin to map out and test drive how to enhance one strength.

Goals
During this session, participants will:
1. Discuss the process of having a supporter share their perceptions of their strengths.
2. Identify at least two people, places or things that encourage and support them.
3. Identify one strength to "test drive."

Readings
Chapter 4, pp. 97-100

Quote
"One of the most important results you can bring into the world is the you that you really want to be." (Robert Fritz, *Pathways to Recovery*, p. 97)

Materials
- *Pathways to Recovery* text
- Flip chart or white board and markers
- Pens/pencils

Facilitator's Tip
A good facilitator is enthusiastic about the topic. If you are excited about the day's material, participants will be more motivated to learn. If you appear bored or apathetic, your group members will likely be so too.

Notes
Depending on the comfort level of the group, you may want to consider using small groups for the strengths self-reflection activity. The "test driving" exercise could also be assigned as homework if needed.

Agenda

10 minutes — **Introduction**
1. Begin on time and welcome all participants.
2. Review the agenda for today's session.

20 minutes — **Discussion of the Homework Assignment**
1. Lead a discussion using the following questions:
    a. How was the experience of asking others to tell you about your strengths?
    b. Who did you ask to do the exercise?
    c. How did you do the exercise? (Did you meet the person, give them the handout, talk on the phone?, etc.)
    d. Did anything you found out surprise you? Did anything disappoint you?
    e. Did you get any answers that you would disagree with?
    f. How do you think doing this exercise has been helpful to you? Why or why not?

20 minutes — **Mapping Your Strengths Terrain**
This final exercise in identifying strengths looks at the people, places and things that help support and encourage. As the group completes this, remind them of the strengths they have identified so far and what might support them best.
1. Introduce the exercise on p. 95.
2. Have the participants individually complete the questions.
3. Once everyone has had a chance to answer the questions, provide time for the group to share their answers.

10 minutes — **Break**
Remind participants to return at the scheduled time.

30 minutes — **Strengths Self-Reflection**
By this time, participants have developed a rather long list of strengths. The following discussion will provide an opportunity for group members to reflect on the experience and share perspectives.
1. Lead a discussion using the questions on pp. 96-97.
2. Since identifying personal strengths makes up much of the remaining work in *Pathways*, it's important for the group to share how this experience has felt to them. Encourage and welcome each person's participation in this discussion.
3. To finish, read the quote by Huston Smith on p. 96.

5 minutes — **Sharing Our Stories: *Cindy***
1. Read Cindy's story on p. 97.
2. Most people will strongly relate to Cindy's comments; remind the group to think of these words when they feel like "giving in."

15 minutes **Test Driving One Strength**
While identifying strengths is the first step, group members now have a chance to "test drive" one of their strengths.
1. Read through the exercise on pp. 98-99.
2. Using the questions at the beginning, help each person choose one strength on which they would like to focus.
3. Have the participants complete the exercise on their own. If they are unable to complete it during group time, encourage them to do it as homework.
4. Also encourage them to celebrate the progress they have made on identifying and using their strengths. Some suggestions are listed on p. 100.

10 minutes **Review the Day's Session**
1. Provide the reading assignment for the next session.
2. Remind the group of the next session and thank them for coming.

Personal Notes

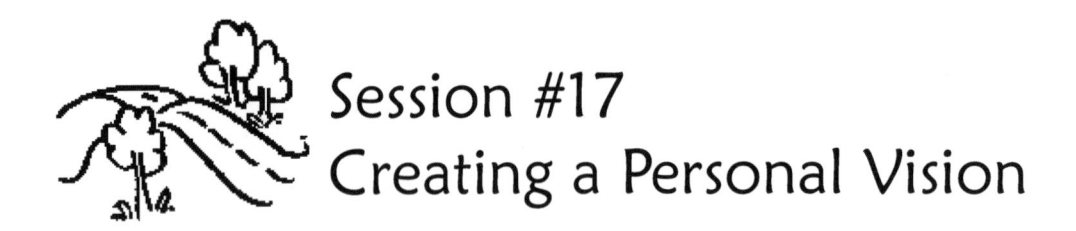

Session #17
Creating a Personal Vision

Overview
Session #17 will explore how to create a personal vision that will allow participants to move from the past and develop their own preferred future. Participants will also meet in their small groups to continue planning their presentations.

Goals
During this session, participants will:
1. Review their progress on "test driving" one of their strengths.
2. Examine the seven guideposts for creating a personal vision.
3. Learn how to identify their preferred future.
4. Meet with their small groups to finalize their presentation.

Readings
Chapter 4, pp. 97-100

Quote
"I want to recover so I can be there for people who have never seen someone who has been there and back." (Marcia Lovejoy, *Pathways to Recovery*, p. 112)

Materials
- *Pathways to Recovery* text
- Flip chart or white board and markers
- Pens/pencils

Facilitator's Tip
You've probably heard the old expression, "You've got to talk the talk, and walk the walk." That's important to facilitators. If you don't believe in and live by what you are sharing, group members *will* see that and be less likely to integrate the concepts and ideas into their own lives.

Notes
Creating a vision of what is wanted in life needs to be realistic and based on what the individual wants. For some, this is a hard concept to understand, especially if they don't feel in control of their own life. These persons may need to look at a simple, basic vision until a larger vision of the future can be identified.

Agenda

10 minutes — **Introduction**
1. Begin on time and welcome all participants.
2. Review the agenda for today's session.

10 minutes — **Review of Test Driving One Strength**
Hopefully, participants have been able to at least begin the process of "test driving" one of their strengths. This discussion will give them an opportunity to further explore their progress and get support from the group for their efforts.
1. Lead a discussion using the following questions:
   a. Have you been able to work on the test driving exercise?
   b. How is it going? Do you need help?

30 minutes — **Vision Guidepost**
This exercise begins the process of creating a personal vision for the future. In order for one to have the future they want, they must begin to "see" it. For some, being able to visualize their future is very difficult. Continue to remind them to draw from their list of strengths as needed.
1. Read p. 105 (end at "Vision Guideposts").
2. Review the visioning exercise conducted during Session #12 and reinforce the importance of being able to visualize our future. Both the quotes and Chris's story about chili are also good ways to show how visioning is something we can all do rather easily.
3. Read each guidepost (pp. 105-108) individually, giving group members time to answer the questions in their workbook. Ask for ideas and suggestions from the group as needed.

10 minutes — **Break**
Remind participants to return at the scheduled time.

10 minutes — **Identifying Your Preferred Future: *Desired Accomplishments***
1. Read the instructions to the exercise on p. 108.
2. Have group members list the things they would like to accomplish and why. Encourage them to add as many things as possible.

20 minutes — **Identifying Your Preferred Future: *Building My Vision***
Before having group members complete the exercise individually, you may want to "test drive" a response with the entire group so they have a better understanding of the task.
1. Read the directions for the exercise on p. 109.
2. Using the list developed on p. 108, have the group answer the questions in their workbook.

Cont. **Identifying Your Preferred Future:** *Building My Vision*, **cont.**
3. One way to make a vision feel more "real" is to create something that will not only remind us of our vision but encourage us to continue striving for our goal and our preferred future. Encourage participants to read and try the "special projects" described on pp. 110-112 (this would also be a good activity to do during Session #20).

20 minutes **Small Group Project Planning**
1. Provide time for the small groups to finalize their project.
2. Assist them with planning as needed.

10 minutes **Review the Day's Session**
1. Provide the reading assignment for the next session.
2. Remind the group of the next session and thank them for coming.

Personal Notes

___
___
___
___
___
___
___
___
___
___
___
___
___
___
___
___

Session #18
Setting a Course to Succeed

Overview
Today's session examines how to set long and short-term goals, the practical tools participants will need to better plan for the future.

Goals
During this session, participants will:
1. Define the difference between a long and short-term goal.
2. Develop a "travel plan" to outline at least one long-term goal.
3. Identify at least one method they will use to remember their long-term goal.
4. Examine the five key elements in writing a successful goal.
5. Practice writing short-term goals.

Readings
Chapter 5, pp. 112-121

Quote
"I believe the longest road to recovery is approximately 1.5 feet. When a person realizes that healing is as far from the top of our head to the bottom of your heart, you've found the longest road." (Marc Kelso, *Pathways to Recovery*, p. 114)

Materials
- *Pathways to Recovery* text
- Flip chart or white board and markers
- Pens/pencils

Facilitator's Tip
Giving participants a choice is an important element of each group. For example, while you may have planned for a general discussion, participants may feel more comfortable by sharing with one or two others. Still others may prefer to work alone. By giving group members a choice, you give them an opportunity to more fully express themselves.

Notes
For some, this might be the first time they have tried to write a goal; others may have little experience at it. Using something visual is a good way to explain the process of setting goals. While you can find lots of resources to do this, one way would be to use a travel theme, having participants draw a map of how they will reach their goal. Others like using a "goal ladder" where each short-term goal is placed on one rung. As goals are achieved, you take a step up until you reach your

Notes, cont.
long-term goal. However you feel comfortable explaining goals, make sure that each person has a good understanding of the process as they will be writing and using their goals in Module Three.

Agenda

10 minutes
Introduction
1. Begin on time and welcome all participants.
2. Review the agenda for today's session.

10 minutes
Forming Long-Term Goals
1. Read pp. 112-113 (begin at "Setting a Course").
2. Review the specifics of setting long-term goals. These include:
   a. Translating one's vision into statements of where they intend to be.
   b. Specifying the action to be taken.
   c. Accomplishable within a 3-6 month period.

20 minutes
Exercise: *Develop a Long-Range Travel Plan*
1. Read the example of setting goals on p. 114.
2. Ask for other examples from the group of long-term goals.
3. Have participants complete the exercise questions on p. 115.
4. Either individually or as a group, ask for participants to share what they have developed. Provide suggestions as needed.

10 minutes
You Have a Compass to Point the Way
1. Read p. 116.
2. Have the group share ways they will remember their long-term goals. Write responses on the flip chart or white board.

10 minutes
Break
Remind participants to return at the scheduled time.

15 minutes
Small Group Activity: *Elements of a Short-Term Goal*
1. Divide the participants into five groups.
2. Assign each group one element of a short-term goal (pp. 117-120).
3. Explain the following:
   a. Each small group will read and briefly discuss their topic.
   b. After the discussion, each group will have no more than 5 minutes to present their topic to the large group.

25 minutes	**Small Group Presentations** 1. In order, have each group present their topic. 2. Ask for and answer any questions there may be about why and how to write a short-term goal.
10 minutes	**Exercise: *Assessing Your Goals*** 1. As a group, complete the exercise on p. 121.
10 minutes	**Review the Day's Session** 1. Provide the reading assignment for the next session. 2. Remind the group of the next session and thank them for coming.

Personal Notes

_____

_____

_____

_____

_____

_____

_____

_____

_____

_____

_____

_____

_____

_____

Session #19
Bringing it All Together

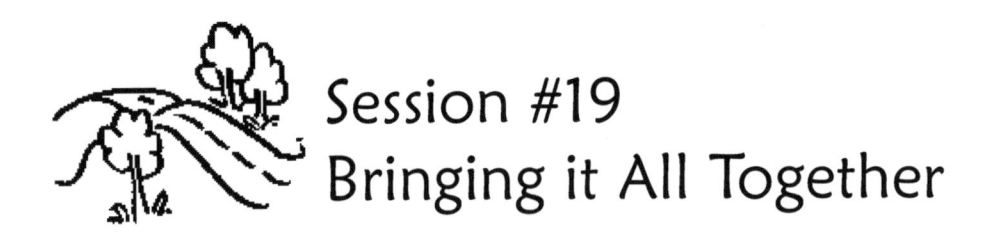

Overview
Session #19 provides participants the opportunity to develop and use the skills learned from Chapter 5 to develop a plan to achieve one long-term goal. Participants will also meet in their small groups to finalize their presentations.

Goals
During this session, participants will:
1. Write one long-term goal.
2. Write at least 2-3 short-term goals.
3. Develop a creative group project to highlight Module Two learning.
3. Meet with their small groups to continue planning their presentation.

Readings
Chapter 5, pp. 121-123

Quote
"May you live all the day's of your life." (Jonathan Swift, *Pathways to Recovery*, p. 123)

Materials
- *Pathways to Recovery* text
- Flip chart or white board and markers
- Pens/pencils
- One large piece of poster board, cut like a jigsaw puzzle (there should be as many pieces of the puzzle as there are participants in the group)
- Art supplies (paper, old greeting cards or magazines, ribbon, stickers, scissors, glue sticks, tape, etc.)

Facilitator's Tip
Use stories, give examples and paint verbal pictures in order to illustrate specific points. Remember that adults learn best when they can translate theory or concepts into real-life situations.

Notes
This is a good time to begin discussing the importance of setting dates to each goal. If there is no completion date, there is a tendency to procrastinate and goals are never really accomplished. Also, if the date is set with too little time, it can be frustrating and individuals can feel as though they have failed for not getting things done.

Agenda

10 minutes — **Introduction**
1. Begin on time and welcome all participants.
2. Review the agenda for today's session.

15 minutes — **Review of Long and Short-Term Goals**
Creating long and short-term goals will be important as the group examines the "Personal Recovery Plan" during Module Three. It is very important to make sure participants understand both the importance of setting goals as well as how to write them.
1. Lead a discussion using the following questions:
   a. Does anyone have any questions about "why" it is important to set goals?
   b. Does anyone have any questions about "how" to set long or short-term goals?
2. Explain that setting both types of goals will be further explored during Module Three.

25 minutes — **Exercise:** *Bringing It All Together*
1. Have participants turn to p. 122 in the text.
2. Read the instructions and help participants complete the exercise (the long-term goal can be transferred from the work completed on p. 115). Make sure the participant's short-term goals meet the five elements of a successful goal (from Session #18).
3. If time permits, ask for volunteers to share the goals they have written.

10 minutes — **Break**
Remind participants to return at the scheduled time.

30 minutes — **Your Piece of the Puzzle**
While starting out with a blank puzzle may seem odd, this activity will help participants not only review what they have learned but see their role as part of the larger group. Don't be surprised by the completed puzzle—it will be beautiful!
1. Give each participant one blank puzzle piece.
2. Using the art supplies of their choice, have each person decorate their piece to represent what they have learned during this module (review the sessions as needed).
3. Once everyone has finished, have them briefly explain their work and add their piece to the larger puzzle.
4. Lead a discussion using the following questions:
   a. What makes this completed puzzle special? (Each person's contribution leads to a greater work, all the pieces are needed to complete the whole, etc.)

Module Two

20 minutes **Small Group Project Planning**
This will be the last scheduled time for groups to meet.
1. Provide time for the small groups to finalize their project.
2. Assist them with planning as needed.

10 minutes **Review the Day's Session**
1. Provide the reading assignment for the next session.
2. Remind the group of the next session and thank them for coming.

Personal Notes

_____
_____
_____
_____
_____
_____
_____
_____
_____
_____
_____
_____
_____
_____
_____
_____
_____
_____
_____
_____

Session #20
Facilitator's Choice

Overview
This session allows the group to further explore subjects of interest or to examine sections of the *Pathways to Recovery* text not covered during Module Two.

Goals
During this session, participants will (*to be determined by the group &/or the subject chosen*). List your goals below:

1.

2.

3.

Readings
To be determined by the group &/or the subject chosen

Quote
"All acts performed in the world begin in the imagination." (Barbara Grizzuti Harrison, *Pathways to Recovery*, p. 113)

Materials
- *Pathways to Recovery* text
- Flip chart or white board and markers
- Pens/pencils

Handouts
To be determined by the group &/or the subject chosen

Facilitator's Tip
Patience is another skill that will be useful to you as a facilitator. This can be difficult when there are disruptive individuals or persons with slower learning styles. An impatient facilitator can negatively impact a group and cause participants to lose trust in you &/or the group process.

Notes
There are a variety of options for this session, including:

1. Covering previous topics in which the group needed more time.
2. The group may choose a topic in which they would like more information. However remember that, as the facilitator, you may need to spend time preparing materials.
3. Arrange for a special speaker to share with the group. This might include a peer role model or a panel of individuals who can talk about their recovery.
4. You may have local sites or museums that the group would like to visit.

At the end of the session, talk with the group about the upcoming end of Module Two. Discuss how they would like to celebrate the completion of the sessions. Each group is different and they will come up with unique ideas that will fit the members of the group. Here are some of the ways other *Pathways to Recovery* groups have celebrated:

- Have a pizza party or potluck dinner
- Coordinate a craft or activity day
- Get a movie and a pizza
- Have lunch or dinner at a restaurant
- Spend the day at the park (with a picnic, nature walk or other park activities)
- Attend a free concert
- Take a special hike
- Volunteer in the community together

You will also want to make some decisions on activities to recognize the progress and outcomes of this group. Recognition and validation is extremely important! Be creative and have fun!

Agenda

10 minutes — **Introduction**
1. Begin on time and welcome all participants.
2. Review the agenda for today's session.

40 minutes — **Group Activity**
To be determined by the group &/or the subject chosen.

10 minutes — **Break**
Remind participants to return at the scheduled time.

30 minutes — **Group Activity**
To be determined by the group &/or the subject chosen.

20 minutes　　**Celebration Planning**
1. Talk with the group about the celebration during Session #24.
2. Provide a list of possible activities (see "Notes" section).
3. Decide what activity most represents the group.
4. If possible, ask the group members to share in the planning and preparation of the celebration.

10 minutes　　**Review the Day's Session**
1. Provide the reading assignment for the next session.
2. Remind the group of the next session and thank them for coming.

Personal Notes

_____
_____
_____
_____
_____
_____
_____
_____
_____
_____
_____
_____
_____
_____
_____
_____

Session #21
Small Group Project Presentations

Overview
Session #21 allows participants—within a small group format—to share more in-depth information on a topic of recovery.

Goals
During this session, participants will:
1. Present recovery-oriented information to the other group members.
2. Identify at least four aspects of recovery from the small group assignment presentations.

Readings
Small group participants will provide their own readings if needed

Quote
"One starts an action because one must do something." (T.S. Eliot, *Pathways*, p. 61)

Materials
Small group participants will provide their own materials as needed

Handouts
Small group participants will provide their own handouts if needed

Facilitator's Tip
While some competition among group members can be good, too much can make participants feel anxious and out of place. Continually remind the group that they travel their recovery journey at their own pace and in their own style.

Notes
Remember, your role as facilitator is to keep the presentations moving and on time. Don't allow one group to take more time than allotted. Keeping the groups on time shows respect for the other groups who have spent time planning and preparing for their presentation.

Take time to review the presentations with the group. Be sure to celebrate and recognize the accomplishments of each group. Encourage members to talk with their peers if they are interested in learning more about a specific topic.

Agenda

10 minutes — **Introduction**
1. Begin on time and welcome all participants.
2. Review the agenda for today's session.

40 minutes — **Small Group Presentations**
1. Allow a few extra minutes if a group needs to do any set up for their presentation.
2. Introduce each small group, their members and their project.
3. Validate each group's efforts in presenting information to the larger group.

10 minutes — **Break**
Remind participants to return at the scheduled time.

40 minutes — **Small Group Presentations, cont.**
1. Continue the presentations.

10 minutes — **Discussion and Thanks**
1. Briefly discuss what group members have learned from their peers in today's session.
2. Thank each group and acknowledge them for their efforts and courage in presenting to their peers.

10 minutes — **Review the Day's Session**
1. Provide the reading assignment for the next session.
2. Remind the group of the next session and thank them for coming.

Personal Notes

_____
_____
_____
_____
_____
_____
_____

Session #22
Small Group Project Presentations

Overview
Session #22 continues the small group presentations, allowing participants—within a small group format—to share more in-depth information on a topic of recovery.

Goals
During this session, participants will:
1. Present recovery-oriented information to the other group members.
2. Identify at least four aspects of recovery from the small group presentations.

Readings
Small group participants will provide their own readings if needed

Quote
"Determine that the thing can and shall be done, and then...find the way." (Abraham Lincoln, *Pathways to Recovery*, p. 265)

Materials
Small group participants will provide their own materials as needed

Handouts
Small group participants will provide their own handouts if needed

Facilitator's Tip
Remember group members will not all see the world in the same way, nor will they always want to take the same approach to reach a conclusion. The value of participating in a group is in the variety of opinions, experiences and ideas that come together. Encourage creativity and difference.

Notes
Remember, your role as facilitator is to keep the presentations moving and on time. Don't allow one group to take more time than allotted. Keeping the groups on time shows respect for the other groups who have spent time planning and preparing for their presentation.

Take time to review the presentations with the group. Be sure to celebrate and recognize the accomplishments of each group. Encourage members to talk with their peers if they are interested in learning more about a specific topic.

Agenda

10 minutes — **Introduction**
1. Begin on time and welcome all participants.
2. Review the agenda for today's session.

40 minutes — **Small Group Presentations**
1. Allow a few extra minutes if a group needs to do any set up for their presentation.
2. Introduce each small group, their members and their project.
3. Validate each group's efforts in presenting information to the larger group.

10 minutes — **Break**
Remind participants to return at the scheduled time.

40 minutes — **Small Group Presentations, cont.**
1. Continue the presentations.

10 minutes — **Discussion and Thanks**
1. Briefly discuss what group members have learned from their peers in today's session.
2. Thank each group and acknowledge them for their efforts and courage in presenting to their peers.

10 minutes — **Review the Day's Session**
1. Provide the reading assignment for the next session.
2. Remind the group of the next session and thank them for coming.

Personal Notes

Session #23
Module Evaluation & Looking

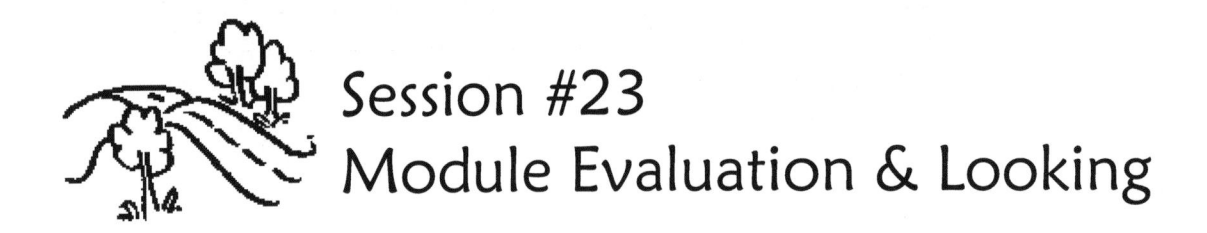

Overview
Session #23 will allow participants to reflect on the past sessions and share any ideas or comments about what they have learned. It will also allow group members to formally evaluate their experience and begin planning for future sessions.

Goals
During this session, participants will:
1. State at least three learning experiences from participating in Module Two.
2. State what they liked and disliked about the sessions.
3. Identify their personal readiness to continue with the *Pathways to Recovery* series.

Readings
None

Quote
"Nothing happens unless first a dream." (Carl Sandburg, *Pathways to Recovery*, p. 114)

Materials
- *Pathways to Recovery* text
- Flip chart or white board and marker
- Pens/pencils

Handouts
- Final Session Satisfaction Survey, p. 350
- Facilitator Self-Assessment, p. 345

Facilitator's Tip
Provide opportunities for group members to give each other feedback, either by working in pairs or small groups. This gives them the chance to share ideas and hear feedback in a less threatening manner.

Notes
Remember, evaluation is vital to becoming a better facilitator. Be prepared for compliments and criticisms. This is an opportunity for you to make changes to provide a greater learning experience for all group members. You may also want to invite someone to take notes or record participant's answers on the flip chart or white board. If you are

Notes, cont.

uncomfortable or you would like to give the group an opportunity to be completely honest, consider asking someone who is not part of the group to conduct the evaluation. Finally, be sure to complete your own self-assessment.

Agenda

10 minutes **Introduction**
1. Begin on time and welcome all participants.
2. Review the agenda for today's session.

15 minutes **Small Group Activity:** *Review of Module Two*
1. Divide participants into small groups of 3-4 people and ask them to choose one person to record their ideas.
2. Ask the small groups to make a list of the things they have learned in the group.

25 minutes **Group Discussion**
1. Ask each reporter to share highlights from their discussion.
2. On the flip chart or white board, list the ideas given in categories for the different topics discussed (for example, recovery, identifying strengths, things needed for the journey, etc.)
3. If possible, record the responses and make copies for everyone.

10 minutes **Break**
Remind participants to return at the scheduled time.

30 minutes **Final Session Evaluation**
While some may feel sad the sessions are ending, remind them of all the things they have learned from the earlier discussion. Encourage participants to share and support each other in this stage of change. Allow ample time to share their feelings about the group.
1. Explain the importance of evaluating the participant's experiences during Module Two.
2. Lead a discussion using the following questions:
    a. What did you like about this module? Not like?
    b. What was your favorite session?
    c. What was your least favorite session?
    d. What would you change about the group?
    e. Have any of you had problems or experienced anything negative around your recovery so far? If so, how have you dealt with it or how do you plan to make changes?
    f. Does anyone need help with anything related to recovery or with what we have discussed during the sessions?

10 minutes — **Written Satisfaction Survey**
Let participants know that the written forms are anonymous and will be used only to improve the next sessions. Share your appreciation for their honesty.
1. Hand out the "Final Session Satisfaction Survey."
2. Have participants complete the evaluation.

10 minutes — **Celebration Planning**
1. Take this time to finalize plans for the celebration activities during Session #24.
2. If needed, remind participants of any details for the celebration (for example, change of location, time, things to bring, etc.).

10 minutes — **Review the Day's Session**
1. Provide the reading assignment for the next session.
2. Remind the group of the next session and thank them for coming.

Personal Notes

_____
_____
_____
_____
_____
_____
_____
_____
_____
_____
_____
_____
_____
_____
_____

Session #24
Celebration!

Overview
Session #24 reviews Module Two, with participants reflecting on their experience and learning. It also provides all group members the opportunity to celebrate individual and group accomplishments.

Goals
During this session, participants will:
1. Identify accomplishments, individually and for each member.
2. Celebrate the completion of Module Two.

Readings
To be decided by the facilitator or the group

Quote
"The question isn't who is going to let me; it's who is going to stop me." (Ayn Rand, *Pathways to Recovery*, p. 368).

Materials
Supplies for today's session will depend on what the group decides to do

Handouts
- Certificate of Achievement (or similar recognition), p. 364

Facilitator's Tip
Always have a back up plan! While most activities will take longer than planned, you never know when something will take less time or if participants will not be interested (or they may already know the information). A good facilitator always has a few extra discussion questions or activities that can be done when time runs short.

Notes
The activities for this final session should be predetermined by the participants. Let them know there will be much more to learn in the upcoming modules and encourage them to continue in the group. Also let them know that if they have any doubts or are simply not ready for this journey, you and the group members will understand.

Notes, cont.

The main goal for today is to celebrate the accomplishments of coming together as a group to work on the journey of recovery. Getting to know one another better in a social setting will reinforce the peer support needed for work that will be done in future modules.

You should also recognize individual accomplishments made during the sessions. Some suggestions include:

- Certificates of attendance or accomplishment
- Small gifts individualized for each person
- The same gift for each person
- A card or note with your personal thanks

Above all, make sure that *each* person is recognized and celebrated.

Agenda

10 minutes — **Introduction**
1. Begin on time and welcome all participants.
2. Review the agenda for today's session.

10 minutes — **Highlights of Module Two**
1. Start by having the group recite the "Recovery Pledge" (p. 20).
2. Using the flip chart or white board, make a list of the highlights and outcomes for Module Two.

90 minutes — **Celebration!**
1. Conduct the celebration activities.
2. Be sure to recognize each individual and their accomplishments during the session.

10 minutes — **Review the Day's Session**
1. Invite participants to join in attending Module Three.
2. Thank each group member for participating.

Personal Notes

_____
_____
_____
_____
_____

Module Three

"I've learned that people will forget what you said, people will forget what you did, but people will never forget how you made them feel."

~ Maya Angelou

Introduction to Module Three

"Fill your life with as many moments and experiences of joy and passion as you humanly can. Start with one experience and build on it."
~ Marcia Wieder

Module Three continues the exploration of *Pathways to Recovery* and provides twenty-four, 2-hour sessions. This section includes the following chapters:

- Chapter 6: Moving Forward on the Journey: Mapping Our Goals Across Major Life Domains

- Chapter 7: Travel Companions & Social Support for the Journey (pp. 217-224)

- Chapter 8: Developing Your Personal Recovery Plan

In addition, two supercharging strategies from Chapter 12 — exercise and humor — will also be explored.

This module is really the heart and soul of the *Pathways to Recovery* text. Although it covers over 100 pages of the text, participants will get the opportunity to explore each of the life domains in greater depth. However, because there *is* a lot of information, you will want to encourage the group participants to read and/or complete some of the exercises and questions on their own. Better yet, they could discuss them in an informal social setting or share them with one of their supporters.

While the domains cover the common ones (like housing, health, education and career), they also include sections on sexuality and intimacy as well as spirituality. Admittedly, these can be difficult subjects for some facilitators and/or group members to discuss. But we would encourage you NOT to shy away from these sessions. Both topics are very important in the human spectrum and are often two of the subjects rated most important in a recovery journey.

REMEMBER...

If you have not already done so, it is important for you to read the introduction to this guide. In it you will find key elements and guidelines for facilitating a successful, recovery-focused and positive experience for all.

Don't hesitate to add your own ideas, activities, resources and energy. Your ability to be creative will enhance the positive nature of the group and help to build a safe, supportive and fun environment for all participants. Examine your own creative style as you prepare for each session. The important point is to include the activities and exercises that will best help group members understand and apply the concepts learned.

Session #1
Welcome & Introductions

Overview
Session #1 allows participants to get to know each other better while reviewing the structure and function of the group.

Goals
During this session, participants will:
1. Introduce/reintroduce themselves to each member of the group and continue the process of building group unity.
2. Discuss how the *Pathways to Recovery* group will be conducted.
3. Discuss the basic group process, commitment and expectations.

Readings
Pathways to Recovery, Preface, pp. iii-viii (begin at "How to Use This Workbook")

Quote
"A journey of a thousand miles must begin with a single step." (Chinese Proverb, *Pathways to Recovery*, p. iv)

Materials
- An individual copy of *Pathways to Recovery* text for each person in the group
- A binder or folder for each participant (for handouts and other materials)
- Flip chart or white board and markers
- Pens/pencils

Handouts
- Reasons to Participate in the *Pathways to Recovery* Group, 335
- Questions to Ask Yourself About Participating in the *Pathways to Recovery* Group, p. 336
- Handy Reminder for Group Members, 337
- The Partnership Pact, p. 338
- My Favorite Things, p. 365

Facilitator's Tip
Always welcome group participants to the sessions. Greet them by name. A relaxed smile and informal conversation will go a long way in reducing any anxieties that may be present. It will also help to get participants focused on the session and begin on time.

Notes
Remember that new participants will change the complexion of the group. It is important for you to do your best to help them feel supported. Watch for levels of discomfort and address them with the group. Find ways for each person to participate. Remind the group that while you are working on common goals together, you do want them to enjoy each other and the activities. As in previous modules, establishing group guidelines early on helps you better incorporate new members who will feel supported and willing to participate.

Agenda

20 minutes **Introduction & Icebreaker Activity:** *My Favorite Things*
1. Begin on time and welcome all participants.
2. Review the agenda for today's session.
3. Conduct the icebreaker activity.
    a. Have participants find a partner.
    b. Hand out "My Favorite Things."
    c. Have the pairs answer the questions. If time permits, have them share their answers with the larger group.

20 minutes **Why participate in the *Pathways to Recovery* group?**
1. Hand out "Questions to Ask Yourself about Participating in the *Pathways to Recovery* Group."
2. Have participants complete the form and discuss their ideas as a group.
3. Hand out "Reasons to Participate in the *Pathways to Recovery* Group."
4. Review each guideline and ask for questions.

20 minutes **Group Guidelines, Process & Commitment**
If you are just starting the Modules with this session, hand out personal copies of Pathways to Recovery to each participant; give them a few minutes to look over the workbook.
1. Go over each item found on pp. 32-35 of the facilitator's guide (start at "Beginning the Session" and end at "Group Support") and explain or remind the group how the sessions will be conducted.
2. Discuss the benefits of making a commitment to the group.
    a. Remind participants that group dynamics takes hard work and commitment from each member.
    b. Encourage a supportive and recovery-focused environment.
    c. The group can be successful if everyone is consistent with their attendance and participates actively.
    d. Remind group members that sharing is more likely to occur when a positive connection is developed.

10 minutes	**Break** *Remind participants to return at the scheduled time.*
20 minutes	**Group Expectations** 1. Hand out "*Pathways to Recovery* Handy Reminder for Group Members." 2. Discuss these items as they will serve as the group expectations.

20 minutes	**The "Partnership Pact"**
	The pact is the agreement made between group members to insure a safe, supportive and strengths-focused group based on the individual's unique values and needs.
	1. Review the concept of the "Partnership Pact."
	2. Develop or review a list of items to include in the pact (see suggestions on p. 42 of Module One) that will serve as ground rules and expectations. These include:
	   a. Everyone in the group should agree with the items.
	   b. Write all the remarks on the flip chart or white board.
	   c. Participants can add remarks at any time.
	   d. Development of the pact will continue during the next session and everyone will receive a copy of it.

10 minutes	**Review the Day's Session** 1. Review the day's session and ask participants if they have any final questions about the group. 2. Provide the reading assignment for the next session. 3. Remind the group of the next session and thank them for coming.

Personal Notes

_____
_____
_____
_____
_____

Session #2
Moving Forward on the Journey

Overview
Session #2 provides an introduction to the major life domains and begins the process of helping participants explore the direction they want to head in the future.

Goals
During this session, participants will:
1. Continue the process of group building.
2. Finalize the "Partnership Pact."
3. Review the key components of the "Recovery Pledge."
4. Examine the importance of reclaiming our lives for ourselves.
5. Describe the factors involved in moving forward.

Readings
Chapter 6, pp. 127-130

Quote
"There is one thing which gives radiance to everything. It is the idea of something around the corner." (G.K. Chesterton, *Pathways to Recovery*, p. 127)

Materials
- *Pathways to Recovery* text
- *Pathways to Recovery* text for new participants
- Flip chart or white board and markers
- Pens/pencils

Facilitator's Tip
During difficult tasks or activities, you may want to give participants an "escape route" in case the activity is too difficult. If individuals are uncomfortable, provide alternatives, such as working with a partner or in a small group.

Notes
You may find some members who can only concentrate on one or two of the life domains. For various reasons, they may not be able to focus on the others. This would be a good time to mention the importance of balance in life and how that will help to develop individuality and a sense of this being *their* life.

Agenda

10 minutes — **Introduction**
1. Begin on time and welcome all participants.
2. Review the agenda for today's session.

15 minutes — **The "Partnership Pact"**
1. Building on the work done in Session #1, add any new ideas to the list (especially from individuals new to the group.)
2. Remind participants they will finalize the pact during Session #3.

15 minutes — **The "Recovery Pledge"**
1. Read or review the "Recovery Pledge" (*Pathways* text, p. 20).
2. Lead a discussion using the following questions (for groups only doing Module Three, use the discussion questions on p. 46):
   a. Is this pledge still important to you?
   b. Does it mean anything different to you now?
   c. Do you believe the group is upholding the pledge?
   d. How can we work together to make the pledge real and be more effective?

20 minutes — **Introduction to the Life Domains**
1. Read pp. 127-129 (do not include the stories).
2. Lead a discussion using the following questions:
   a. In what ways has your psychiatric disability been your "full-time job?" What has helped you move on to find more meaning and purpose?
   b. What roles have you had to claim in your recovery? What roles have you had to reclaim?
   c. In what other ways have you reclaimed your life "through the process of recovery?"
   d. As we begin looking at the different areas of our life, what stands out as most important to you?

10 minutes — **Break**
Remind participants to return at the scheduled time.

15 minutes — **Small Group Activity: *Our Stories***
1. Divide participants into small groups of 3-4 people and ask them to choose one person to record their ideas.
2. Assign one of the stories on pp. 127-129 to each group.
3. Ask the small groups to discuss the stories by using the following questions:
   a. What is the main point the writer is making?
   b. Do you agree or disagree with their comments? Why or why not?

15 minutes   **Group Discussion**
  1. Ask each reporter to share highlights from their discussion.
  2. What common themes do you see in each story?

10 minutes   **Introduction to Module Three Information**
  1. Read p. 130.
  2. Ask if there are any questions about Module Three.

10 minutes   **Review the Day's Session**
  1. Provide the reading assignment for the next session.
  2. Remind the group of the next session and thank them for coming.

Personal Notes

_____
_____
_____
_____
_____
_____
_____
_____
_____
_____
_____
_____
_____
_____

Session #3
Heading Toward Home

Overview
Session #3 begins the examination of the life domains by looking at the importance of home.

Goals
During this session, participants will:
1. Finalize the "Partnership Pact."
2. Discuss the six factors that make "home" important to positive mental health.
3. Complete a self-assessment of their current living situation.
4. Identify at least two of their current housing strengths and two past strengths.
5. Write at least one housing goal.

Readings
Chapter 6, pp. 131-135

Quote
"Tell me the landscape in which you live and I will tell you who you are." (Jose Ortega y Gassett, *Pathways to Recovery*, p. 132)

Materials
- *Pathways to Recovery* text
- Flip chart or white board and markers
- Pens/pencils
- One copy of the "Partnership Pact" for everyone to sign

Facilitator's Tip
Be aware of environmental factors that can influence both comfort and learning. Try to have comfortable chairs, tables to write on and a quiet space with few distractions. The room should fit the size of your group (not too large *or* too small), be easily accessible and maintain a comfortable temperature. Also, be sure that participants feel comfortable in letting you know when there are things in the learning environment which are not helpful.

Notes
Since this is the first session to cover how you will use your strengths to reach your goals, you may want to have the group provide an example and work through the session together. Participants can then complete or add to their responses as homework.

Notes, cont.

For individuals in your group who are experiencing homelessness or whose living situations are difficult or unsafe, this could be a challenging session. Help participants focus on the future but with realistic expectations and an understanding of where they are and why. Even small changes to their living situation can make a big difference.

Finally, in order to end in a positive manner, each domain session will conclude with "Do It Today," an activity to give participants the chance to begin making simple changes.

Agenda

10 minutes **Introduction**
1. Begin on time and welcome all participants.
2. Review the agenda for today's session.

15 minutes **The "Partnership Pact"**
Remind the group members they are making a commitment to conduct themselves according to the agreed upon items.
1. Review the "Partnership Pact."
   a. Ask for and add any new items.
   b. Pass out one copy and have participants sign the form.
   c. If possible, at break, make individual copies for everyone; if not, have copies ready for the next session.

15 minutes **Small Group Activity: *Why is Home Important?***
1. Read the first paragraph on p. 131.
2. Divide participants into small groups of 3-4 people and ask them to choose one person to record their ideas.
3. Assign 1-2 of the topics listed on p. 131 to each group.
4. Ask the small groups to answer the following:
   a. Are there other reasons why this idea is important?
   b. What are 3-4 specific ways members of the group carry out these ideas? (For example, to express individuality, the group might list hanging personal art work, setting up a space to do crafts, framing pictures of family, etc.)

20 minutes **Group Discussion**
1. Ask each reporter to share highlights from their discussion; list these on the flip chart or white board.
2. After each group has reported back, ask for further suggestions from all the group members and add these to the list.

10 minutes **Self-Assessment**
1. Have group members complete the self-assessment on p. 132, followed by the exercise on p. 133.

10 minutes	**Break** *Remind participants to return at the scheduled time.*
30 minutes	**Using Your Strengths to Reach Your Housing Goals** 1. Have participants turn to p. 134-135 in their workbooks. 2. Using a sample goal listed on p. 133 (or have the group decide on one), walk through the exercise on p. 134-135. 3. Have participants decide on one goal and add to the list on p. 266. Let them know you will be adding goals to this sheet in coming sessions.

10 minutes	**Do It Today:** *Enhancing Your Current Home*
	1. Have the group brainstorm 2-3 ways that, beginning today, they could increase the comfort of their living situation. Encourage them to be simple yet creative with their ideas. Some sample ideas include:
	    a. Create a space or shelf to hold meaningful items.
	    b. Have a home blessing with family and friends.
	    c. Spend a day cleaning & organizing your home (or just one room).
	    d. Rearrange the furniture in one room.
	    e. For those experiencing homelessness, include something special in a backpack (or even a pocket) to help envision a future living space.

10 minutes	**Review the Day's Session** 1. Provide the reading assignment for the next session. 2. Remind the group of the next session and thank them for coming.

Personal Notes

_____

_____

_____

_____

_____

_____

_____

Session #4
Learning as We Go

Overview
Session #4 examines the domain of education and learning.

Goals
During this session, participants will:
1. Define education.
2. Identify why education is important to the recovery journey.
3. Identify at least three current learning strengths.
4. Write at least one educational goal.

Reading
Chapter 6, pp. 136-140

Quote
"Learning is a treasure that will follow its owner everywhere." (Chinese Proverb, *Pathways to Recovery*, p. 137)

Materials
- *Pathways to Recovery* text
- Flip chart or white board and markers
- Pens/pencils
- Index cards

Facilitator's Tip
Good facilitators are not born with the necessary skills; rather, they are constantly learning and growing. You can enhance your skills by reading books, practicing or co-facilitating with more experienced individuals and paying attention to feedback from the group. Actively search for new tools and ideas to continue your own growth.

Notes
Throughout this session, remind participants that "learning" covers *all* areas of life; education doesn't just happen in a school-type setting. Expand on what group members already know, such as their "street smarts," the understanding they have of their illness or knowing what's available in the community. Encourage them to share these with others.

Agenda

10 minutes — **Introduction**
1. Begin on time and welcome all participants.
2. Review the agenda for today's session.

20 minutes — **Learning As We Go**
1. Read pp. 136-137 (do not include the stories at this time).
2. Lead a discussion using the following questions:
    a. During the past year, what are some of the learning experiences you have had?
    b. In what ways have your educational activities helped you grow?

20 minutes — **Sharing Our Stories:** *JoAnn & Others*
1. Read the stories by JoAnn and the other individual on p. 137.
2. Lead a discussion using the following questions:
    a. In what ways can you identify with these writers?
    b. In what ways have the writers used their learning experiences to enhance their recovery?

10 minutes — **Exploring Educational Strengths**
1. Have participants complete p. 138.
2. Next, have them identify one strength from Module Two that could be used to write an educational goal. Provide ideas and suggestions as needed.

10 minutes — **Break**
Remind participants to return at the scheduled time.

30 minutes — **Using Your Strengths to Reach Your Educational Goals**
This activity offers a good opportunity for group members to help each other. Take your time and provide ideas and support as needed.
1. As a group, read through each question on pp. 138-140 and have them write their answers in the workbook.
2. Have participants decide on one goal and add it to the education section on p. 266.

10 minutes — **Do It Today:** *Enhancing Your Learning*
1. Have the group brainstorm 2-3 ways that, beginning today, they could use to write an educational goal. Encourage them to be simple yet creative with their ideas. Sample ideas include:
    a. Check out library books on a topic of interest.
    b. Call the local community college and request a catalog of classes.

Cont. **Do It Today:** *Enhancing Your Learning*
   c. Call a friend to see if they would like to join you for a free community workshop.
2. Here's an alternate activity that will allow group members to learn from each other:
   a. Give each participant an index card.
   b. Have them write down one thing they would like to learn.
   c. Collect the cards; read each idea, asking if anyone in the group has knowledge or experience in that area.
   d. Encourage the participants to talk and schedule time to learn from each other.

10 minutes **Review the Day's Session**
1. Provide the reading assignment for the next session.
2. Remind the group of the next session and thank them for coming.

Personal Notes

_____

_____

_____

_____

_____

_____

_____

_____

_____

_____

_____

_____

_____

_____

_____

_____

Session #5
Ticket to Ride

Overview
Session #5 is the first of two sessions to look at the domain of assets. In addition, the small group project will be introduced.

Goals
During this session, participants will:
1. Define "assets."
2. Identify why assets are important to the recovery journey.
3. List at least three current asset strengths.
4. Create a "balance sheet" comparing their assets and liabilities (bills or loans).
3. Develop groups for the small group project.

Readings
Chapter 6, pp. 141-144, 148-150

Quote
"It's good to have money and the things that money can buy, but it's good too, to check up once in a while and make sure you haven't lost the things that money can't buy." (George Lucas Lorimer, *Pathways to Recovery*, p. 141)

Materials
- *Pathways to Recovery* text
- Flip chart or white board and markers
- Pens/pencils

Handouts
- Small Group Project Presentation: *Instruction Sheet,* p. 366

Facilitator's Tip
Remember that content and resources change. Participants will expect the information you are sharing is the most current and up-to-date available. While that *may* be true, there are new ideas and concepts being developed all the time. Stay abreast of new trends and recent developments. If you find yourself uncomfortable with a topic, consider inviting someone who is more knowledgeable in that particular area.

Notes
It is important to note while discussing assets that, while it is true many individuals with psychiatric disabilities do have limited incomes and resources, not everyone is in this situation. What *is* true is that we can all learn ways of increasing both our monetary and outside resources. Help each person according to their situation and lifestyle; don't assume that everyone is alike!

Also during this session, participants will be introduced to the small group project. As part of this assignment, group members will design their own project and are free to be creative in developing a 10-15 minute presentation on a topic of interest from Module Three. Some examples for this module might include:

- Presenting a humorous skit
- Exploring any one of the domains further
- Developing a handbook of local community resources
- Further exploring any aspect of one of the domains (for example, job accommodations, volunteer options in the community, alternative health practices, etc.)
- Leading the group in an interesting exercise activity

Encourage participants to be creative in developing their group project. Brainstorm with the groups if they have a hard time beginning.

Agenda

10 minutes — **Introduction**
1. Begin on time and welcome all participants.
2. Review the agenda for today's session.

20 minutes — **Small Group Project Presentations**
Having small groups develop and present on a topic of interest provides a wonderful experience for learning. Groups will create their own project and develop a 10-15 minute presentation to be given during Sessions #21 & 22.
1. Hand out the "Small Group Project Presentation: *Instruction Sheet*" for this module.
2. Review the project instructions, helping participants brainstorm ideas for a topic.
3. Divide the class into groups of 3-5 people.
4. Give the groups time to meet and brainstorm potential topics.
5. Since the presentations will be done during two separate sessions, have them decide the order in which they will present.

30 minutes — **Defining Assets**
1. Read pp. 141.
2. Ask the group how they would define "asset." List the answers on the flip chart or white board.

Cont. **Defining Assets, cont.**
    3. Lead a discussion using the following questions:
       a. Why is it important to think about our assets?
       b. Why is it important to think about our assets as more than just money?
       c. What does Pat Deegan mean when she says "We are often encouraged to adjust to the unnatural state of extreme poverty" (*Pathways* text, p. 141, paragraph 4)?
       d. What information would it be helpful for you to have so you could increase your assets?

10 minutes **Break**
Remind participants to return at the scheduled time.

30 minutes **The "Balance Sheet"**
Completing this entire exercise, especially p. 144, may be uncomfortable for some, either because they are not sure how to answer the questions or because they need more privacy. Be sensitive to this and encourage the group to complete the exercise at home as needed.
1. Read the instructions to the exercise on p. 142.
2. Using the table on p. 143, have group members check off which assets they already have.
3. Next, check which assets they feel they need to get.
4. Finally, brainstorm with the group what ideas they have or what they may need to do to get more assets or resources.

10 minutes **Strengths About Assets**
1. Have participants complete p. 148.
2. Next, have them identify one strength from Module Two that could be used to write a goal to enhance their assets. Provide ideas and suggestions as needed.

10 minutes **Review the Day's Session**
1. Provide the reading assignment for the next session.
2. Remind the group of the next session and thank them for coming.

Personal Notes

_____

_____

_____

Session #6
Ticket to Ride, cont.

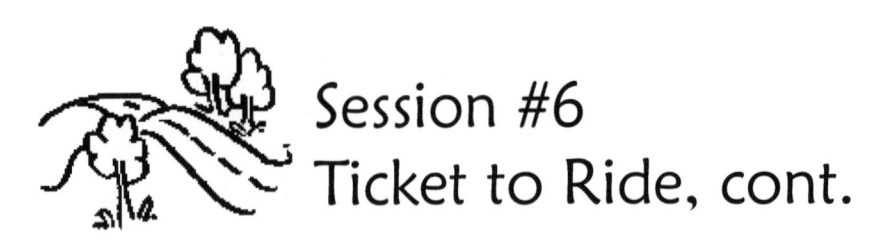

Overview
Session #6 continues the examination of assets. Participants will identify their strengths and goals and learn tips that will help them build their assets.

Goals
During this session, participants will:
1. Write at least one goal to increase assets.
2. Identify at least two of their current asset strengths.
2. List at least two ways they can begin to build their assets.

Readings
Chapter 6, pp. 145-150

Quote
"Don't be run so much by what you lack as by what you have already achieved." (Marcus Arelius, *Pathways to Recovery*, p. 142)

Materials
- *Pathways to Recovery* text
- Flip chart or white board and markers
- Pens/pencils

Facilitator's Tip
Always wear comfortable clothes and shoes. Unless otherwise required, try to dress in a similar manner as participants. This will help them feel more comfortable and recognize that you are there as the facilitator, not as an authority figure.

Notes
For those who have a hard time believing in a future or who have very low self-esteem, understanding they have assets or can achieve additional assets, defies their current beliefs. They may make jokes or suggest new assets that are unrealistic to avoid thinking about the topic. They might also be embarrassed over what they feel they don't have. Help them identify at least one realistic asset and how to expand upon or improve it.

Agenda

10 minutes — **Introduction**
1. Begin on time and welcome all participants.
2. Review the agenda for today's session.

20 minutes — **Using Your Strengths to Reach Your Asset Goals**
This exercise offers a good opportunity for group members to help each other. Take your time and provide ideas and support as needed.
1. As a group, read through each question on pp. 149-150 and have them write their answers in the workbook.
2. Have participants decide on one goal and add it to the asset section on p. 266.

30 minutes — **Small Group Activity: *Tips & Ideas for Building Assets***
1. Divide participants into three groups and ask them to choose one person to record their ideas.
2. Assign each group one page from the text (pp. 145-147).
3. Have the small groups to do the following:
    a. Read the tips on their assigned page.
    b. Discuss, then summarize each tip.
    c. For each tip, list one or two specific ideas about "why" this tip would or would not work for you.

10 minutes — **Break**
Remind participants to return at the scheduled time.

30 minutes — **Group Discussion**
1. Ask each reporter to share highlights from their discussion.
2. Lead a discussion using the following questions:
    a. Of everything we've discussed about assets, what do you think is the most important to you?
    b. How will you use this information to enhance your assets?
    c. Is there one tip you think will be especially helpful to you? Why? What will you do to incorporate it into your life?

10 minutes — **Do It Today: *Increasing Your Assets***
1. Have the group brainstorm 2-3 ways that, beginning today, they could do to increase their assets. Encourage them to be simple yet creative with their ideas. Some sample ideas include:
    a. Start a "piggy bank" of loose change.
    b. Organize an area in your home to do bills.
    c. Create a visual representation of your assets or where you would like to be if you had more assets.

10 minutes **Review the Day's Session**
1. Provide the reading assignment for the next session.
2. Remind the group of the next session and thank them for coming.

Personal Notes

_____
_____
_____
_____
_____
_____
_____
_____
_____
_____
_____
_____
_____
_____
_____

Session #7
Building a Career Path

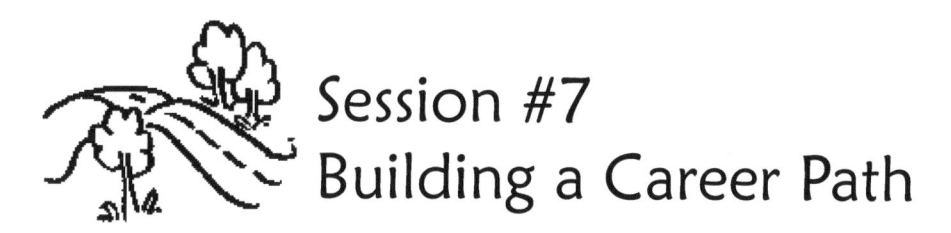

Overview
Session #7 begins the look at work and how to be successful at it. Participants will specifically examine the benefits of working as well as the basics of the world of work.

Goals
During this session, participants will:
1. List at least three benefits of working.
2. Complete a motivation self-assessment.
3. Identify at least two interests that could be used within a work setting.
4. List at least two characteristics of a workplace that are personally important.
5. Identify the resources available to help find or keep a job.
6. Discuss the value of "shifting gears."

Readings
Chapter 6, pp. 151-160

Quote
"Vocation...would include finding out the place where the need of the world coincides with your own gifts, where that which you can give is joyfully received." (James Carroll, *Pathways to Recovery*, p. 151)

Materials
- *Pathways to Recovery* text
- Flip chart or white board and markers
- Pens/pencils

Facilitator's Tip
One mistake some facilitators make is to present themselves as the "authority." It's much more effective, however, to let the group know that you also have questions or do not know something. Remember to use the collective experience of the group because together, the group knows more than you individually do.

Notes
Most people who have experienced psychiatric symptoms have had difficulty working at some point in their life (hasn't everyone?). Some may have even lost jobs because of their symptoms or been "forced" to take jobs that didn't match their interests or activities.

Notes, cont.

While work can be very stressful, so is unemployment. Remind the group that going back to work does not necessarily mean *returning* to a former job or career; it *is* possible to find a new kind of work that will be enjoyable and one in which they will find a good "fit." Also remember one also doesn't have to be symptom-free to work.

During this session, be mindful that some group members may already have a job while others may not feel they are ready to work. Use the diversity in the group to help group members learn from each other. There is also a large amount of information about work and career in the *Pathways* text. Encourage participants to use this material with a vocational counselor or other person who may be helping them examine work options.

Agenda

10 minutes — **Introduction**
1. Begin on time and welcome all participants.
2. Review the agenda for today's session.

10 minutes — **The Benefits of Working**
1. Read p. 151 (end at "Exploring the World").
2. Using the flip chart or white board, have the group add their ideas about the benefits of working.

20 minutes — **Exploring the World of Work: *Motivation***
Motivation is an important factor in determining one's ability to be successful at working. If motivation is high, the chances of being employed are also high.
1. Have participants complete the motivation assessment on p. 152.
2. Lead a discussion using the following questions:
   a. Are you motivated to work?
   b. Can you name some of the things that would/do motivate you to work? List the responses on the flip chart or white board.
3. Read the list of motivational ideas on p. 153.

10 minutes — **Exploring the World of Work: *Interests & Aptitudes***
Encourage participants to more fully complete this on their own and/or share it with those who may be helping them look for work.
1. Read p. 153 (start at "Honor Your Interests").
2. Lead a discussion using Griff's question at the top of p. 155 (What makes you feel awake and alive?).

10 minutes — **Sharing Our Stories: *Crystal***
1. Read the story on p. 155.
2. Lead a short discussion using the following question:
   a. What can you do (like Crystal) to help make your interests and passions part of your work?

10 minutes   **Break**
Remind participants to return at the scheduled time.

10 minutes   **Exploring the World of Work: *What is Important***
1. Read p. 155 (begin at "Identify What is Important").
2. Have participants complete the question at the top of p. 156.

10 minutes   **Exploring the World of Work: *Resources for Working***
1. Briefly review the resources that are available. These include:
    a. Community Resources
    b. Employee Rights
    c. Reasonable Accommodations
2. Have participants suggest ways to learn more about these resources; encourage them to follow up with one or more of these ideas.

20 minutes   **Sharing Our Stories: *Suzette***
1. Read the story on p. 155.
2. Lead a discussion using the following questions:
    a. Can you relate to the experiences Suzette describes?
    b. What do you see as the most important thing to do that will enable you to "shift gears"?
3. Encourage participants to read pp. 159-160 (end at "Volunteerism") before the next session.

10 minutes   **Review the Day's Session**
1. Provide the reading assignment for the next session.
2. Remind the group of the next session and thank them for coming.

Personal Notes

_____

_____

_____

_____

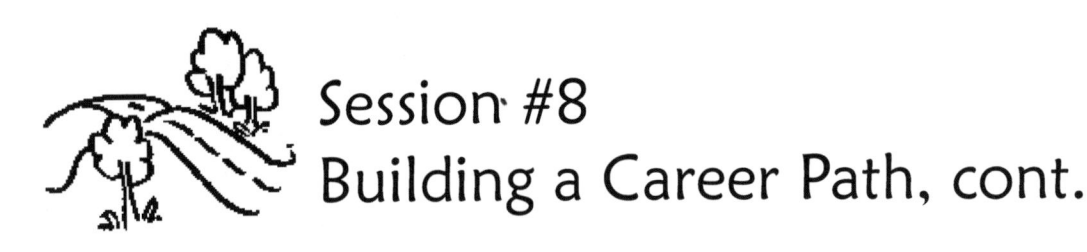

Session #8
Building a Career Path, cont.

Overview
Session #8 continues the exploration of the career path by examining volunteerism. Participants will also identify their current vocational strengths and set goals for working.

Goals
During this session, participants will:
1. Review the material from Session #7.
2. Explore the benefits of volunteering.
3. Identify at least three current vocational strengths.
4. Write at least one vocational goal.

Readings
Chapter 6, pp. 160-165

Quote
"There is a wonderful mythical law of nature that the three things we crave most in life—happiness, freedom and peace of mind—are always attained by giving them to someone else." (Peyton Conway March, *Pathways to Recovery*, p. 161)

Materials
- *Pathways to Recovery* text
- Flip chart or white board and markers
- Pens/pencils

Facilitator's Tip
Using technology in your group can be one more method to enhance learning for participants. Whether that includes interactive Internet activities or simply an overhead projector, be sure that you either know how to use the technology (or make sure someone is available to help you) or that you learn prior to the group. Just remember that, while we are all becoming more comfortable with the technological advances that have occurred in recent years, it certainly doesn't replace the value of personal connection with others.

Notes
Volunteering can be a great way to give back and help others. It can also be a good first step for individuals wanting to explore interests and learn skills. Most communities offer a wide range of volunteer opportunities. If you have a local volunteer center, you could invite them to speak to the group.

Agenda

10 minutes — **Introduction**
1. Begin on time and welcome all participants.
2. Review the agenda for today's session.

20 minutes — **Review**
1. Lead a discussion using the following questions:
    a. Do you have any questions about the material we covered in the last session?
    b. What do you like/dislike about the idea of working?
    c. Why would you consider working at this time?

20 minutes — **Why Volunteer?**
1. Read pp. 160-161 (begin at "Volunteerism" and end before the questions on p. 161).
2. Lead a discussion using the following questions:
    a. Do any of you currently volunteer? What do you do?
    b. What do you think about volunteering?
    c. How has volunteering helped you in the past?
    d. How are working and volunteering similar? How are they different?
    e. What would be your main reasons for volunteering?

10 minutes — **Break**
Remind participants to return at the scheduled time.

10 minutes — **Exploring Vocational Strengths**
1. Have participants complete p. 163.
2. Next, have them identify one strength from Module Two that could be used to write a work or vocational goal. Provide ideas and suggestions as needed..

10 minutes — **Role Models**
1. Ask participants to think of a person they know who is successfully working.
2. Next, have them list at least 2-3 characteristics of why they think this person is successful (for example, they are motivated, they are making a difference, they are happier, etc.).
3. As a group, list all the characteristics on the flip chart or white board.

20 minutes — **Using Your Strengths to Reach Your Vocational Goals**
This activity offers a good opportunity for group members to help each other. Take your time and provide ideas and support as needed.

Cont. **Using Your Strengths to Reach Your Vocational Goals, cont.**
1. As a group, read through each question on pp. 164-165 and have them write their answers in the workbook.
2. Have participants decide on one goal and add it to the vocation section on p. 266.

10 minutes **Do It Today:** *Enhancing Your Ability to Work*
1. Have the group brainstorm 2-3 ways that, beginning today, they could start looking at the possibility of working or volunteering. Encourage them to be simple yet creative with their ideas. Some sample ideas include:
    a. Putting together a work history or resume.
    b. Further examining what factors are important in a job.
    c. Ask for ideas from someone who is already working.
    d. Looking at current want ads to see what types of jobs might be available.
    e. Calling a local volunteer center or organization and ask about volunteer opportunities.

10 minutes **Review the Day's Session**
1. Provide the reading assignment for the next session.
2. Remind the group of the next session and thank them for coming.

Personal Notes

_____
_____
_____
_____
_____
_____
_____
_____
_____
_____
_____

Session #9
Recharging Our Batteries

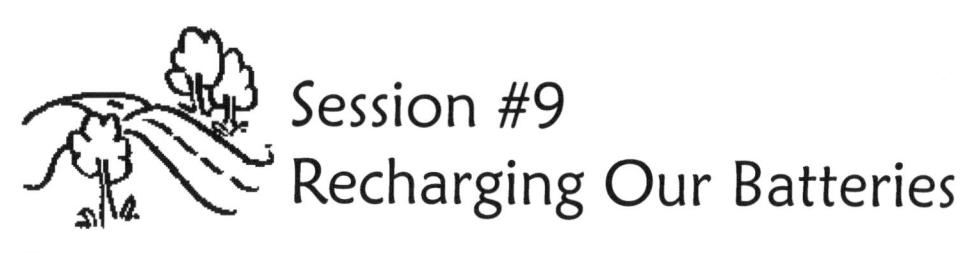

Overview
Session #9 explores leisure and recreation interests. Participants will also meet in their small groups to continue planning their presentations.

Goals
During this session, participants will:
1. Identify at least three current leisure or recreational strengths.
2. Write at least one leisure goal.
3. Meet with their small groups to continue planning their presentation.

Readings
Chapter 6, pp. 166-171

Quote
"Life is about enjoying yourself and having a good time." (Cher, *Pathways to Recovery*, p. 166).

Materials
- *Pathways to Recovery* text
- Flip chart or white board and markers
- Pens/pencils

Facilitator's Tip
Feed their minds, feed their bodies! Most group participants will appreciate some sort of drink or refreshment. Fresh, healthy food (such as fruits and vegetables) will help keep people awake and alert. If you are unable to provide this, you could encourage group members to bring their own snack or perhaps rotate bringing snacks among the participants.

Notes
Remind participants that leisure and recreational activities can be done alone or with others—a friend, family member, neighbor, pet, etc. If it's difficult to set aside part of a day for fun activity, suggest making a commitment to ask one person to meet for a "play time" (see Module One, Session #6 for ideas).

Agenda

10 minutes — **Introduction**
1. Begin on time and welcome all participants.
2. Review the agenda for today's session.

15 minutes — **Do You Need a Tune-Up?**
The work of recovery can sometimes feel hard and not much fun. But it's important to include activities that help "recharge" us.
1. Read p. 166 (end at the Catherine's story).
2. Lead a discussion using the questions on p. 168.

10 minutes — **Exploring Leisure & Recreational Strengths**
1. Have participants complete p. 169.
2. Next, have them identify one strength from Module Two that could be used to write a leisure or recreational goal. Provide ideas and suggestions as needed.

15 minutes — **Using Your Strengths to Reach Your Leisure Goals**
This exercise offers a good opportunity for group members to help each other. Take your time and provide ideas and support as needed.
1. As a group, read through each question on pp. 170-171 and have them write their answers in the workbook.
2. Have participants decide on one goal and add to the leisure section on p. 266.

10 minutes — **Break**
Remind participants to return at the scheduled time.

20 minutes — **Sharing Our Stories: *Catherine***
1. Read Catherine's story on pp. 166-167.
2. Lead a discussion using the following questions:
   a. What things led to Catherine learning about what she enjoyed?
   b. How does Catherine's story relate to what we've been talking about?

20 minutes — **Small Group Project Planning**
1. Provide time for the small groups to work on their project.
2. If they have not already done so, help the groups decide on the topic or activity they will present.

10 minutes — **Do It Today: *Enhancing Your Leisure & Recreation***
1. Have the group brainstorm 2-3 ways that, beginning today, they could increase their leisure or recreational activities. Encourage

Cont. **Do It Today: *Enhancing Your Leisure & Recreation*, cont.**
them to be simple yet creative with their ideas. Some sample ideas include:
   a. Calling the local community center to find out what team sports are available.
   b. Asking a friend to show you how to do a specific craft.
   c. Inviting a friend over to play board games or cards.

10 minutes **Review the Day's Session**
1. Provide the reading assignment for the next session.
2. Remind the group of the next session and thank them for coming.

Personal Notes

Session #10
Feeling Good Along the Way

Overview
This session gives participants an opportunity to look at how to live or enhance a healthy lifestyle. In addition, the group will discuss how to use the supercharging strategy of exercise to improve their health and wellness.

Goals
During this session, participants will:
1. Examine the definition of wellness.
2. List at least one complementary or alternative health practice they could use.
3. Complete a lifestyle self-assessment.
4. Identify at least three current health or wellness strengths.
5. Write at least one health goal.
6. Examine the types of exercise available and its potential health benefits.
7. Identify at least two types of exercise they might like to try.

Readings
Chapter 6, pp. 172-179, Chapter 11, p. 358

Quote
"We live in our minds so much of the time that we have almost forgotten our bodies." (Ray Kybartas, *Pathways to Recovery*, p. 172)

Materials
- *Pathways to Recovery* text
- Flip chart or white board and markers
- Pens/pencils

Handouts
- The Benefits of Exercise, p. 367

Facilitator's Tip
Don't underestimate the importance of getting people moving, especially if participants are joining the group after a meal. One minute of leg lifts or walking around the room is often enough to get people energized and ready to work.

Notes
Our health and the activities we choose to promote our wellness are highly individualized. Be sure to share the note on p. 174 of the *Pathways* text, reminding the group that, while there are many choices and options for alternative health care practices and exercise, it is important to talk with their medical provider and to research ideas they may have.

If the group would prefer, this is a good session to actually practice the topic! The group could take a walk, play volleyball or go to the park. It could also be a good time to invite a local expert on wellness to talk about how to create a healthier lifestyle.

Agenda

10 minutes **Introduction**
1. Begin on time and welcome all participants.
2. Review the agenda for today's session.

15 minutes **Definition of Wellness**
1. Read pp. 172-173 (end at "Integrative Health Practices).
2. Lead a discussion using the following questions:
    a. Does the definition by Travis & Ryan include everything you consider when thinking about wellness? Is there anything you would like to add?
    b. How you do you think wellness plays a role in a recovery journey?

15 minutes **Healthy Lifestyle Self-Assessment**
1. Provide instructions for completing the self-assessment on pp. 175-176.
2. Either as a group or individually, have participants complete the form.

10 minutes **Exploring Health & Wellness Strengths**
1. Have participants complete p. 177.
2. Next, have them identify one strength from Module Two that could be used for writing their health and wellness goal. Provide ideas and suggestions as needed.

10 minutes **Break**
Remind participants to return at the scheduled time.

15 minutes **Using Your Strengths to Reach Your Health Goals**
This activity offers a good opportunity for group members to help each other. Take your time and provide ideas and support as needed. The self-assessment completed earlier can be very helpful for participants in setting this goal.

Cont. **Using Your Strengths to Reach Your Health Goals, cont.**
1. As a group, read through each question on pp. 178-179 and have group members write their answers in the workbook.
2. Have them decide on one goal and add to the leisure section on p. 266.

25 minutes **Supercharging Strategy: Exercise — *Use It or Lose It!***
We all know that exercise can be a benefit to our life. While it can be difficult at times, it can also be fun!
1. Read supercharging strategy #5 on p. 358.
2. Lead a discussion using the following questions:
    a. Do you exercise? What do you do and how often?
    b. What benefits do you get from exercising?
3. On the flip chart or white board, have the group list as many benefits to exercise as possible.
4. Next, make a list of different types of exercise.
5. Pass out "The Benefits of Exercise."
6. Have participants complete the handout and discuss.

10 minutes **Do It Today:** *Enhancing Your Health & Wellness*
1. Read pp. 173-174 (begin at "Integrative Health Practices").
2. Using these ideas and those generated during the session, have the group brainstorm 2-3 ways that, beginning today, they could increase their level of health and wellness. Encourage them to be simple yet creative with their ideas. Some sample ideas include:
    a. Rereading the section in Module Two about meditation and visualization; try using it once before the next session.
    b. Picking one of the complimentary practices listed and look for more information on the topic.
    c. Talking with a friend who uses one of these practices.

10 minutes **Review the Day's Session**
1. Provide the reading assignment for the next session.
2. Remind the group of the next session and thank them for coming.

Personal Notes
___
___
___
___

Session #11
Private Pleasures

Overview
Session #11 explores the seldom discussed but important topic of intimacy and sexuality.

Goals
During this session, participants will:
1. Discuss why intimacy and sexuality are important aspects or recovery.
2. Examine how trauma impacts sexuality.
3. Explore the impact of psychiatric medication on sexual expression.
4. Define personal intimacy.
5. Identify at least two ways to enhance a sexual partnership.

Readings
Chapter 6, pp. 180-187

Quote
"Be mindful of the power...that intimacy creates." (Daphne Rose Kingma, *Pathways to Recovery*, p. 185)

Materials
- *Pathways to Recovery* text
- Flip chart or white board and markers
- Pens/pencils

Facilitator's Tip
A good facilitator needs to be able to balance the process of the group versus the results desired. This can be hard when you feel you need to cover a certain amount of material or only have a limited amount of time left in the session. Trust your instincts and remember that often the best learning experiences come from unplanned discussions or activities.

Notes
As *Pathways to Recovery* states, "intimacy and sexuality are important, but seldom discussed, areas of recovery" (p. 180). Some individuals find this topic extremely significant to their lives; others find sexuality and intimacy less important. For some facilitators, it will be tempting NOT to include this session for group discussion. Just remember these feelings are common to almost everyone. Sexuality and intimacy **are** important in our lives and positive relationships have been strongly proven to help our personal health and well-being.

Notes, cont.

We strongly encourage you **NOT** to shy away from this session. Please read through it (and Session #12) so you are familiar with the material included. Most groups are very willing to talk about sexuality if done in an open, frank and honest manner. Ask the group for their ideas and examine their comfort levels. If individuals are extremely uncomfortable, assure them this is common and don't force the topic. Do encourage them to explore the material on their own or with a safe person. Finally, if necessary, consider inviting someone to lead the session who is trained and can provide the information in an informative and helpful manner (remember to let the group know if this will happen). Often there are individuals from local health departments or HIV/AIDS organizations who would be glad to present the information.

Many individuals who experience psychiatric symptoms have also been impacted by trauma. While it is important to recognize that the experiences of trauma, abuse and a history of bad relationships certainly impact our sexual lives, we would discourage you from having an in-depth discussion on the topic. If individuals in the group who have been impacted by trauma have not already done so, encourage them to seek further help from their health care providers or a professional counselor.

Above all, try to be comfortable and relaxed when you are facilitating these sessions. The agenda has been designed to allow a healthy discussion without censoring the material. Do recognize that some topics are very personal and private (such as the self-pleasure section—you may want to assign this section to read on one's own). Do your best to be respectful of the intense feelings and reactions that may occur. As more discussions of sexuality and intimacy are encouraged to happen, your willingness to include the topic will help in overcoming the barriers and stigma that many individuals (like the writer who shares their story on p. 182) have encountered.

Agenda

10 minutes **Introduction**
1. Begin on time and welcome all participants.
2. Review the agenda for today's session.

15 minutes **Sshhh...Don't Talk About It!**
1. Read pp. 180-181 (end at "The Impact of Trauma"). Either individually or as a group, have participants complete the question at the top of p. 181.
2. Lead a discussion using the following questions:
    a. Why do you think it is so difficult for most people to discuss this topic (not just those who experience psychiatric symptoms)?
    b. Reread Pat Deegan's quote on p. 180. Why are Pat's words so important?
    c. Other than the ones listed, are there other ideas you have on how to get over negative feelings about sexuality?

15 minutes	**The Impact of Trauma on Sexuality**
	1. Read pp. 181-182 (begin at "The Impact" and end at "Sexual Expression").
	2. Lead a discussion using the following questions:
	   a. How can the impact of trauma effect individuals?
	   b. What has helped you (or someone you know) to overcome the effects of trauma?

15 minutes	**Sexual Expression and Psychiatric Medication**
	1. Read pp. 182-183 (begin at "Sexual Expression" and end at "Self-Pleasuring").
	2. Lead a discussion using the following questions:
	   a. Would you agree or disagree that common side-effects should be labeled on medications? Why or why not?
	   b. The person in Pat Deegan's discussion talks about not wanting to accept the side effects of their medication. What do you think about this person's comments?

10 minutes	**Break** *Remind participants to return at the scheduled time.*

15 minutes	**Defining Intimacy**
	1. Read pp. 184-186 (begin at "Intimacy" and end at the story).
	2. Lead a discussion using the following questions:
	   a. How do you define intimacy?
	   b. From your perspective, are intimacy and sexuality the same thing? Why or why not?
	   c. Why are sexuality and intimacy important to one's recovery journey?

10 minutes	**Sharing Our Stories:** *Anonymous*
	1. Read the story on p. 186.
	2. Lead a short discussion using the following questions:
	   a. What do you think of this writer's comments?
	   b. What solution do you see to the attitudes described here?

10 minutes	**Enhancing Sexual Partnerships** *Encouraging safe sex practices and partnerships is important to overall sexual health and well-being. Stress the importance of gathering information and examining personal thoughts, values and feelings about sexuality and intimacy.* 1. Read or discuss pp. 186-187 (begin at "Enhancing Sexual Partnerships" and end at the questions). 2. Lead a short discussion using the following question: a. What do you think is the main idea of this passage? Why would you consider this important?

10 minutes   **Review the Day's Session**
1. Provide the reading assignment for the next session.
2. Remind the group of the next session and thank them for coming.

Personal Notes

Session #12
Private Pleasures, cont.

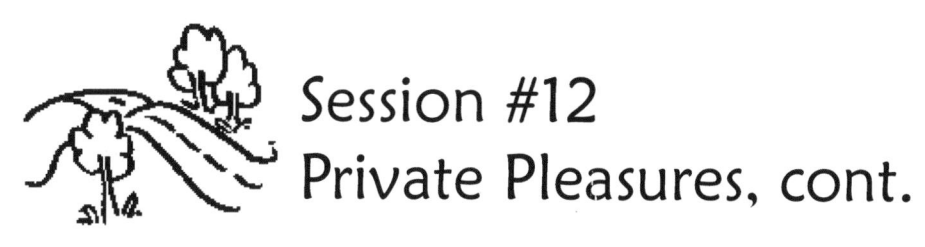

Overview
Session #12 continues the discussion of sexuality and intimacy. In addition, participants will have an opportunity to evaluate their experience in the group up to this point.

Goals
During this session, participants will:
1. Identify at least three intimacy &/or sexuality strengths.
2. Write at least one goal to address their intimacy &/or sexuality goals.
3. Share their personal experience about using *Pathways to Recovery*.

Readings
Chapter 6, pp. 188-190

Quote
"Butterflies mean 'a lot' in life. Remember how they live in a cocoon before they thrive as beautiful creatures. But never forget how they feel in your stomach." (Millie Crossland, *Pathways to Recovery*, p. 184)

Materials
- *Pathways to Recovery* text
- Flip chart or white board and markers
- Pens/pencils

Handouts
- Mid-Session Satisfaction Survey, p. 344
- Facilitator Self-Assessment, 345

Facilitator's Tip
Good facilitators must maintain their own personal integrity. This includes being honest and open with the group, maintaining confidentiality and honoring and respecting each individual for who they are and what they bring to the process.

Notes
Today's session continues to build upon the discussion of sexuality and intimacy and gives individuals an opportunity to determine their strengths and set goals in this area. Remember that, just as ANY of the domains discussed in the group, some individuals will find this topic significant while others view it as less important. The more comfortable and relaxed you are, the more group members will feel safe to share their thoughts and ideas.

Notes, cont.
As the group takes time to evaluate the sessions so far, remember to be prepared for compliments and criticisms. This is an opportunity for you to make changes to provide for a greater learning experience for all group members. Also remember that you should ask someone to take notes or record participant's answers on the flip chart or white board. If you are uncomfortable or you would like to give the group an opportunity to be completely honest, you might consider asking someone who is not part of the group to conduct the evaluation. Finally, be sure to complete your own self-assessment.

Agenda

10 minutes — **Introduction**
1. Begin on time and welcome all participants.
2. Review the agenda for today's session.

10 minutes — **Questions & Review**
Some facilitators may find it important to check in with participants after the last session. If so, give the group an opportunity to share their ideas and comments.
1. Lead a short discussion using the following question:
   a. Did you find the last session helpful to you? Do you have any questions or comments for the group?

10 minutes — **Exercise: *Exploring Intimacy and Sexuality Strengths***
1. Have participants complete p. 188.
2. Next, have them identify one strength from Module Two that could be used for a goal in this area. Provide ideas and suggestions as needed.

20 minutes — **Using Strengths to Reach Your Intimacy & Sexuality Goals**
This activity offers a good opportunity for group members to help each other. Take your time and provide ideas and support as needed.
1. As a group, read through each question on pp. 189-190 and have group members write their answers in the workbook.
2. Have them decide on one goal and add to the sexuality section on p. 266.

10 minutes — **Do It Today: *Enhancing Your Personal Intimacy***
1. Have the group brainstorm 2-3 ways that, beginning today, they could enhance their sense of personal intimacy. Encourage them to be simple yet creative with their ideas. Some sample ideas include:

Cont. **Do It Today: *Enhancing Your Personal Intimacy*, cont.**
        a. Get information from the local health clinic on safe sex practices
        b. Discuss what has been learned in the sessions with a partner
        c. Make plans to talk with a medical provider about the sexual side-effects of medications

10 minutes **Break**
Remind participants to return at the scheduled time.

30 minutes **Mid-Session Evaluation**
Evaluation can be a powerful tool in giving voice to participants. Encourage and respect open and honest comments.
1. Lead a discussion focusing on how the participants view the success of the sessions thus far. Use all or part of these questions:
    a. How has the experience of attending the sessions benefitted your recovery?
    b. What is your favorite part of the group? Why?
    c. What is your least favorite part of the group? Why?
    d. What do I (the facilitator or co-facilitators) do to help you learn?
    e. What suggestions can you offer to make the group better?
    f. What could I (the facilitator or co-facilitators) do to improve the group?
    g. As a group, do you feel we are staying true to the "Partnership Pact?"
    h. Do you feel you are able to uphold the "Recovery Pledge?" Why or why not?
    i. Does anyone have a need for support around his or her recovery efforts?

10 minutes **Written Evaluation Survey**
Be sure to let participants know their comments are anonymous and that their comments will only be used to make positive changes to the group as needed.
1. Pass out the "Mid-Session Satisfaction Survey."
2. Ask the group to complete the form and leave it with you. Be sure to let them know their comments are anonymous and will only be used to make changes in the group as needed.

10 minutes **Review the Day's Session**
1. Provide the reading assignment for the next session.
2. Remind the group of the next session and thank them for coming.

Personal Notes

Session #13
Forging a Higher Path

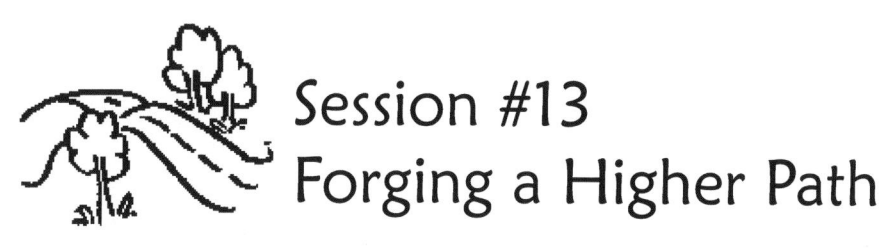

Overview
Session #13 begins the overview of spirituality as part of the recovery journey.

Goals
During this session, participants will:
1. Define spirituality.
2. Identify at least three reasons why spirituality is important to the recovery journey.
3. List at least three characteristics of their personal spirituality.

Readings
Chapter 6, pp. 191-204

Quote
"The first peace, which is the most important, is that which comes within the souls of people when they realize their relationship, their oneness with the universe and all it's powers, and when they realize at the center of the universe dwells the Great Spirit, and that this center is really everywhere, it is within each of us." (Black Elk, *Pathways* text , p. 194)

Materials
- *Pathways to Recovery* text
- Flip chart or white board and markers
- Pens/pencils

Facilitator's Tip
In order for participants to begin to use the concepts and ideas presented during each session, they will need to be able to retain or remember the information. As facilitator, you have an opportunity to make the connections between the group learning and how participants will apply it in their everyday lives. The amount of information retained can be enhanced by reviewing material, using a variety of hands-on activities and encouraging the use of new tools outside the group structure.

Notes
Sessions #13 & 14 cover a vast amount of information. There is no way to cover all the material in these sessions. This may be a topic that the group would like to further explore during Session #20 (Facilitator's Choice) or you can suggest they complete the workbook at home or with a trusted friend or spiritual mentor.

Notes, cont.
The topic of spirituality is a *very* personal one. While some participants may be eager for discussion, others may be hesitant. Remind the group that the discussions are about *spirituality* and not religion. Be particularly respectful of feelings and beliefs; don't let the discussion turn into a time for some members to monopolize the session or attempt to push their values and beliefs on other participants.

Agenda

10 minutes — **Introduction**
1. Begin on time and welcome all participants.
2. Review the agenda for today's session.

10 minutes — **The Definition of Spirituality**
1. Read pp. 191-192 (end at the questions).
2. Lead a discussion using the following questions:
    a. Do you agree with the definition given? Why or why not?
    b. Do you have your own definition of spirituality? How is it different?
    c. Are there levels of spirituality that you have explored? How did you do this and what did you learn?

20 minutes — **The Benefits of Spirituality**
1. Read the three benefits stated on pp. 194-196. These include:
    a. Spirituality is a source of important beliefs and values.
    b. It is a source of positive relationships and builds a sense of community.
    c. Spiritual practices are a source of comfort and healing.
2. Lead a discussion using the following questions:
    a. Are these benefits ones you have experienced?
    b. Are there other benefits that spirituality gives you?
    c. Can you give an example of how spirituality has benefitted your recovery journey?

20 minutes — **Telling Our Stories: *Carrie***
1. Read Carrie's story on p. 195.
2. Lead a discussion using the following questions:
    a. Do you agree that there is a difference between spirituality and religion? How do you see them as similar? How do you see them as different?

10 minutes — **Break**
Remind participants to return at the scheduled time.

25 minutes **Small Group Exercise:** *Expanding the Definitions*
This exercise will help participants creatively expand their meaning of spirituality.
1. Draw 2-3 flowers on the flip chart or white board (use a circle in the middle with multiple petals).
2. Place words associated with spirituality (such as love, peace, faith, etc.) in the center circle.
3. For each flower, ask participants to add any word they believe are core characteristics of the topic (for example, for "faith," they may include word petals like sustaining, comfort, values, etc.).
4. Divide the participants into small groups of 3-4 people and assign one flower to each group (you could also have the group choose only one flower for everyone to examine). Ask the groups to do the following:
    a. Select a group reporter.
    b. Discuss their "flower" using the following questions:
        1. Do you agree or disagree that these words represent this topic?
        2. Why are the "petals" important to the topic?

15 minutes **Group Discussion**
1. Ask each reporter to share highlights from their discussion.
2. Lead a discussion using the following questions:
    a. Do you feel you have a greater understanding of the topic? Why or why not?
    b. Of all the characteristics listed, which ones are most important to you? Why?

10 minutes **Review the Day's Session**
1. Provide the reading assignment for the next session.
2. Remind the group of the next session and thank them for coming.

Personal Notes

_____
_____
_____
_____
_____
_____

Session #14
Forging a Higher Path, cont.

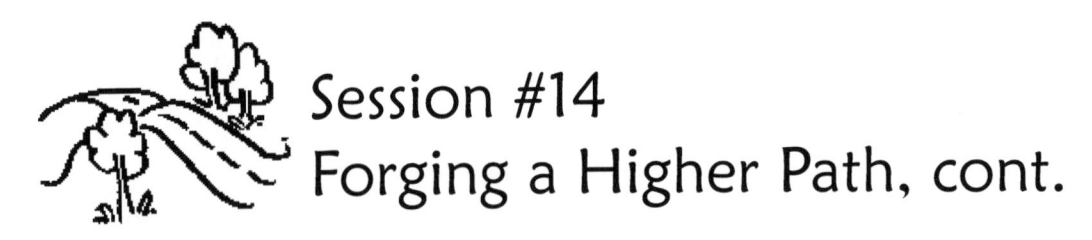

Overview
Session #14 continues the discussion of spirituality, specifically exploring the impact of spirituality and mental illness. Participants will also meet in their small groups to continue planning their presentations.

Goals
During this session, participants will:
1. Explore how spirituality can influence the recovery journey.
2. Complete a spirituality self-assessment.
3. Identify at least three current spirituality strengths.
4. Write at least one goal about spirituality.
5. Meet with their small groups to continue planning their presentation.

Readings
Chapter 6, pp. 200-204

Quote
"Stand by the roads and look, and ask for the ancient paths, where the good way is; and walk in it, and find rest for your souls." (Jeremiah 6:16, *Pathways to Recovery*, p. 199)

Materials
- *Pathways to Recovery* text
- Flip chart or white board and markers
- Pens/pencils

Facilitator's Tip
Maintaining their objectivity can be hard for some facilitators. You will need to be able to set aside any strong personal opinions and avoid negative responses to group comments. Always do your best to remain neutral and impartial.

Notes
Remember and remind the group that the topic of spirituality is a *very* personal one and the discussion for this session is about *spirituality* and not religion. Be particularly respectful of feelings and beliefs; don't let the discussion turn into a time for some members to monopolize the session or attempt to push their values and beliefs on other participants.

It's also time to get an update on the progress of the small group project presentations. If barriers or problems are present, schedule a brainstorming time to help them.

Agenda

10 minutes — **Introduction**
1. Begin on time and welcome all participants.
2. Review the agenda for today's session.

30 minutes — **The Spiritual Rewards of Psychiatric Disability**
1. Read p. 200 (start at "The Spiritual Rewards" and end at the question).
2. Lead a discussion using the following questions:
   a. How has your illness impacted your spirituality?
   b. How have you used your spirituality to make your recovery journey easier or different?
   c. In what way does your spirituality influence your thoughts and behaviors?
   d. What do you do to celebrate your spiritual self?

10 minutes — **Exercise: *Exploring Spiritual Strengths***
1. Have participants complete p. 202.
2. Next, have them identify one strength from Module Two that could be used to write a spirituality goal. Provide ideas and suggestions as needed.

10 minutes — **Break**
Remind participants to return at the scheduled time.

20 minutes — **Using Your Strengths to Reach Your Spirituality Goals**
This exercise offers a good opportunity for group members to help each other. Take your time and provide ideas and support as needed.
1. As a group, read through each question on pp. 203-204 and have them write their answers in the workbook.
2. Have participants decide on one goal and add it to the spirituality section on p. 266.

20 minutes — **Small Group Project Planning**
1. Provide time for the small groups to work on their project.
2. Assist them with planning as needed.

10 minutes — **Do It Today: *Enhancing Your Spirituality***
1. Have participants complete the self-assessment on p. 201 (remind them that if they don't feel such effects as these, that is okay).
2. Have the group brainstorm 2-3 ways that, beginning today, they could increase their spirituality. Encourage them to be simple yet creative with their ideas. Some sample ideas include:

Cont.

Do It Today: *Enhancing Your Spirituality*, cont.

    a. Make a commitment to read a short passage from a favorite book or religious material.
    b. Light a candle daily and take a moment to contemplate.
    c. Talk with a friend or family member about being a spiritual mentor.

10 minutes

Review the Day's Session

1. Provide the reading assignment for the next session.
2. Remind the group of the next session and thank them for coming.

Personal Notes

Session #15
Travel Companions & Social

Overview
Session #15 examines the importance of social support, including its definition, benefits and personal importance in the journey of recovery.

Goals
During this session, participants will:
1. Define social support.
2. Examine the benefits of having social support.
3. Identify at least three current social support strengths.
4. Write at least one social support goal.

Readings
Chapter 7, pp. 217-220, pp. 251-253

Quote
"Call it a clan, call it a network, call it a tribe, call it a family. Whatever you call it, whoever you are, you need one." (Jane Howard, *Pathways to Recovery*, p. 219)

Materials
- *Pathways to Recovery* text
- Flip chart or white board and markers
- Pens/pencils

Facilitator's Tip
Facilitation is not just showing up; it involves hard work and thought as well as preparation. You will be called on to make decisions, carry out tasks and then, live with the consequences. Accepting responsibility and having the discipline to carry out the work for the group can be daunting. But the positive reward of seeing group members grow and change is also exciting and, for most facilitators, well worth the effort put forth.

Notes
In order to include their social support goals in their recovery plan, participants will only begin the process of exploring social supports during this session. The remainder of Chapter 7 will be covered in greater depth during Module Four.

It will also important to point out the difference between social supports and professional supports. If individual group members are identifying their therapist,

Notes, cont.
case manager, doctor or other provider as their social support, you may need to help them get a view of the larger picture.

Agenda

10 minutes — **Introduction**
1. Begin on time and welcome all participants.
2. Review the agenda for today's session.

20 minutes — **The Definition of Social Support**
1. Read pp. 218-219 (begin at "What is Social Support" and end at "What are the Benefits").
2. Lead a discussion using the following questions:
   a. In addition to the definition included in the workbook, is there anything you would like to add?
   b. What has been the most important piece of social support for you in your life?

30 minutes — **The Benefits of Social Support**
While examining the benefits of social support are important, also remind the group that Module Four will include ways for increasing and enhancing their relationships with others.
1. Read pp. 219-220.
2. Lead a discussion using the following questions:
   a. How has social support been helpful to your recovery?
   b. Of the benefits listed on p. 220, which do you find you have the most of in your life? Are any lacking?

10 minutes — **Break**
Remind participants to return at the scheduled time.

10 minutes — **Exercise: *Exploring Social Support Strengths***
1. Have participants complete p. 251.
2. Next, have them identify one strength from Module Two that could be used to write a social support goal. Provide ideas and suggestions as needed.

20 minutes — **Using Your Strengths to Reach Your Social Support Goals**
This exercise offers a good opportunity for group members to help each other. Take your time and provide ideas and support as needed.
1. As a group, read through each question on pp. 252-253 and have them write their answers in the workbook.
2. Have participants decide on one goal and add it to the social supports section on p. 266.

10 minutes   **Do It Today:** *Enhancing Your Social Support*
1. Have the group brainstorm 2-3 ways that, beginning today, they could enhance or increase their social support. Encourage them to be simple yet creative with their ideas. Some sample ideas include:
   a. Call a friend to have lunch.
   b. Do a simple kindness for another person.
   c. Send a special card to a family member.

10 minutes   **Review the Day's Session**
1. Provide the reading assignment for the next session.
2. Remind the group of the next session and thank them for coming.

Personal Notes

Session #16
Writing the Personal Recovery Plan

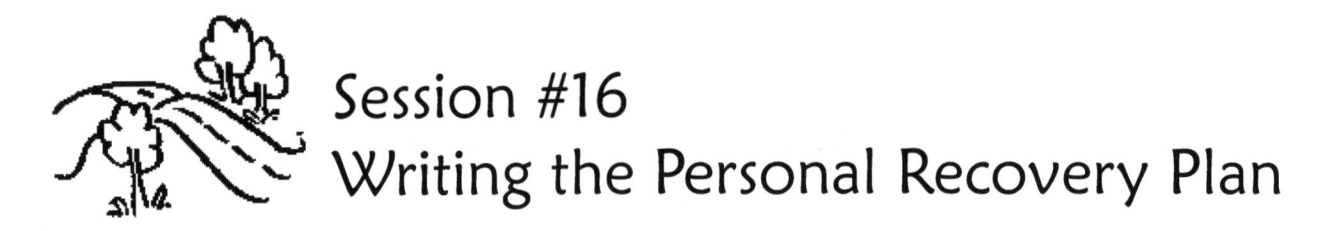

Overview
Session #17 begins the development of the "Personal Recovery Plan," including the elements of a successful plan.

Goals
During this session, participants will:
1. Examine the "Personal Recovery Plan."
2. Discuss the six elements of a successful plan.
3. Begin to combine all the lists of strengths they have created.

Readings
Chapter 8, pp. 259-265

Quote
"Determine that the thing can and shall be done, and then...find the way." (Abraham Lincoln, *Pathways to Recovery*, p. 265)

Materials
- *Pathways to Recovery* text
- Flip chart or white board and markers
- Pens/pencils
- Bottles of "White Out" for each participant (see "Vicki's Story")

Facilitator's Tip
Sometimes facilitators never personally use the tools they are sharing with the group. Doesn't it make sense that if we believe what we are sharing will help the participants, that it would do the same for us? In addition, completing the same materials as the group will give you a better idea of how to explain the activity as well as being able to identify where others may have difficulty.

Notes
Taking a look at all the strengths the participants have developed since Module Two, it can be helpful to start thinking about other questions they could ask themselves in order to further develop and use their strengths (for example, "I am motivated to do what? In which life domains? By when? By whom?" or "How many ways does this strength fit into my plan?").

Agenda

10 minutes — **Introduction**
1. Begin on time and welcome all participants.
2. Review the agenda for today's session.

10 minutes — **The Roadmap for Movement**
Although the group will not actually begin writing the plan until the next session, looking at the plan at this time will help them know what to expect and reduce fears about completing the form.
1. Read the first two paragraphs on p. 259.
2. Have the participants turn to p. 274 in *Pathways to Recovery* and look at a blank copy of the recovery plan.
3. Ask for and answer any questions the group may have about the plan at this time.

30 minutes — **Sharing Our Stories: *Vicki***
In this story, Vicki outlines many good tips that she used to incorporate her strengths into a plan of action.
1. Read Vicki's story on pp. 261-262.
2. Lead a discussion using the following questions:
    a. What was your first impression of Vicki's story?
    b. What is the main idea she is sharing?
    c. Thinking back on all we have discussed and accomplished so far, how does this story help you put all the pieces together?
    d. How does Vicki's story motivate you?
3. End by giving each participant their own bottle of "White Out." (If you can't or don't want to give the "White Out," have the group take Vicki's story and turn it into *their* story (using *their* ideas, goals, strengths, etc. instead of Vicki's)

10 minutes — **Break**
Remind participants to return at the scheduled time.

20 minutes — **Making the Plan a Success**
There are six suggestions listed for making the "Personal Recovery Plan" successful. If participants are uncomfortable writing, have them pair up to complete this task.
1. Briefly go over each of the six suggestions on pp. 259-265.
2. Write each suggestion on a large piece of paper and hang around the room; give each participant a colored marker.
3. Ask participants to move around the room and add any comments they have to the suggestions.
    a. Their comments could include specific ideas, tips they have learned, questions they have or resources available.

Module Three

Cont. **Making the Plan a Success, cont.**
　　　　b.　Remind them to recall the materials they have discussed in this and previous modules.
　　　　c.　Encourage them to add something to each suggestion if possible.

30 minutes **Group Discussion**
1. Read the comments from each suggestion.
2. Lead a short discussion using the following questions:
　　a.　Do you have any questions about the ideas that were shared?
　　b.　Can you identify at least one comment from this suggestion that you can use in your life?
3. Finish by thanking participants for their ideas and comments.

10 minutes **Review the Day's Session**
1. Provide the reading assignment for the next session.
2. Remind the group of the next session and thank them for coming.

Personal Notes

_____
_____
_____
_____
_____
_____
_____
_____
_____
_____
_____
_____
_____
_____

Cont.

Session #17
Bringing It All Together

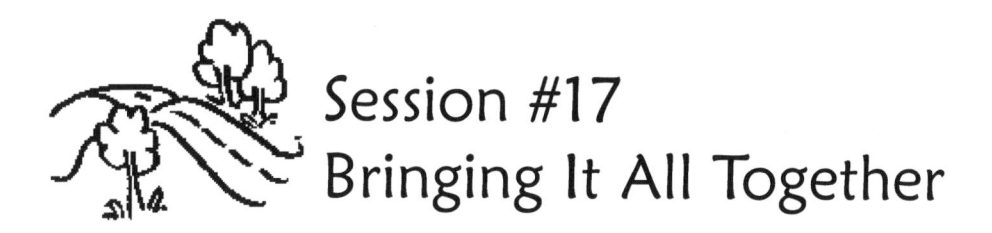

Overview
Session #17 continues the process of developing the "Personal Recovery Plan" in a step-by-step manner.

Goals
During this session, participants will:
1. Review the goals that have been developed throughout Module Three.
2. Select one goal to begin working on first.
3. Develop a list of long-term and short-term goals.
4. Identify at least two resources and two supports to include in the plan.

Readings
Chapter 8, pp. 266-268

Quote
"The tragedy of life doesn't lie in not reaching your goal. The tragedy lies in having no goal to reach." (Benjamin Mays, *Pathways to Recovery*, p. 267)

Materials
- *Pathways to Recovery* text
- Flip chart or white board and markers
- Pens/pencils

Facilitator's Tip
Good facilitators recognize the importance of language. As participants learn new concepts, they will also learn new terms, new words and new definitions. You can make these new words "real" by incorporating them in your examples and questions. The more comfortable individuals are with the language, the more they will use it.

Notes
The group will be taking the information created in previous sessions and incorporating it into their overall plan. Make sure each participant understands the process fully before moving on to the next section of the plan.

Agenda

10 minutes — **Introduction**
1. Begin on time and welcome all participants.
2. Review the agenda for today's session.

10 minutes — **Group Discussion: *Wandering & Wondering***
1. Read the quote on p. 266.
2. Lead a discussion using the following questions:
    a. What is the main point of this quote?
    b. How are you feeling about beginning this process of exploring your goals?

15 minutes — **Steps #1 & 2: *Reviewing & Identifying Your Goals***
1. Review the nine areas in which the participants have developed goals during the previous sessions.
2. Have participants complete the following:
    a. Reread the goals they have previously listed on p. 266.
    b. Add &/or adapt any goals that they would like to change prior to beginning the personal plan.

15 minutes — **Step #3: *Selecting a Priority Goal***
While participants have hopefully identified several goals, encourage them to choose the one they would most like to achieve. Help them prioritize if needed.
1. Read step #3.
2. Have participants choose their "top priority" goal and write it in the space given.

10 minutes — **Break**
Remind participants to return at the scheduled time.

20 minutes — **Step #4: *Setting Long and Short Term Goals***
1. Read step #4 and review how to write long and short-term goals (see Module Two, Session #18 if needed).
2. Have the participants list their goals in the space provided.

20 minutes — **Step #5: *Identifying Resources***
1. Read step #5. Remind the group of the strengths and resources they have already identified in earlier sessions. Encourage them to review their own notes and comments in their workbook.
2. Have participants list the resources and supports they anticipate needing to accomplish their goal.
3. Finally, let the group know they will be looking at two sample plans during the next session and will have an opportunity to begin writing their own.

10 minutes **Small Group Project Planning**
This will be the last scheduled time for groups to meet.
1. Provide time for the small groups to finalize their project.
2. Assist them with planning as needed.

10 minutes **Review the Day's Session**
1. Provide the reading assignment for the next session.
2. Remind the group of the next session and thank them for coming.

Personal Notes

_____
_____
_____
_____
_____
_____
_____
_____
_____
_____
_____
_____
_____
_____
_____
_____

Session #18
Bringing It All Together, cont.

Overview
During Session #18, the group will examine two sample recovery plans and begin the process of creating their own. Participants will also meet in their small groups to finalize their presentations.

Goals
During this session, participants will:
1. Examine one sample recovery plan designed to make a stated goal a reality.
2. Examine one sample recovery plan that is used to explore a potential goal.
3. List six functions of a "Personal Recovery Plan."
4. Practice creating their own recovery plan.
5. Meet with their small groups to finalize details for their upcoming presentation.

Readings
Chapter 8, pp. 268-276

Quote
"Even if you are on the right track, you will get run over if you just sit there." (Will Rogers, *Pathways to Recovery*, p. 271)

Materials
- *Pathways to Recovery* text
- Flip chart or white board and markers
- Pens/pencils

Facilitator's Tip
How about writing your own personal plan? By developing your own plan, you can continue to develop as a facilitator or take a look at other options for your life. Perhaps you have gained enough confidence as a facilitator that you would like to find a job where you can use those skills. Maybe you'd like to explore a new creative outlet or go back to school. Whatever your goals or ideas, try adapting the plan to fit your own needs.

Notes
As an alternative, you may want to have the group decide on a goal and create another sample plan so they can see how the process develops. While some individuals in the group may be able to create the plan they will use, this session is planned for group members to learn "how" to complete the plan, not necessarily to complete one today.

Agenda

10 minutes — **Introduction**
1. Begin on time and welcome all participants.
2. Review the agenda for today's session.

15 minutes — **Jim's Plan**
Jim has designed his plan based on a firm decision already made. He uses his plan to focus on his vision of becoming an artist.
1. Read pp. 268-269 (begin at "Design a Plan").
2. As a group, review Jim's plan on p. 269.

10 minutes — **The Functions of a Personal Recovery Plan**
The functions listed here use Jim's plan as an example.
1. Read p. 271-272 (end at "Setting a Personal").
2. Ask for and answer any questions.

15 minutes — **Pam's Plan**
Pam has designed her plan based on her desire to explore her vision of having companionship. By comparing her plan with Jim's, the group will now have options for how they can use the plan to reach their own goals.
1. Read p. 272.
2. As a group, review Pam's plan on p. 273.

10 minutes — **Group Discussion**
1. Lead a discussion using the following questions:
    a. Are you able to see the different approaches Jim and Pam took to develop their plan?
    b. Before you begin to write your own plan, do you have any questions?

10 minutes — **Break**
Remind participants to return at the scheduled time.

30 minutes — **Creating Your Own Personal Recovery Plan**
The participants now have the opportunity to test their skills at creating their own plan. They will be using the information they created in Session #17 to "fill in the blanks" and practice developing a plan.
1. Have participants turn to p. 274 in the workbook.
2. Using the information they listed on pp. 266-268, help the group create their vision, long-term goal and at least 2-3 short-term goals.
3. If anyone in the group appears to be struggling, they could work together with a partner or you could engage the entire group to help.

10 minutes · **Get the Rubber on the Road**
1. Read p. 276, reminding the group that the important part of the recovery journey is to "keep moving."
2. Read p. 277 and encourage the participants to develop at least one thing they will do to celebrate their progress.

10 minutes · **Review the Day's Session**
1. Provide the reading assignment for the next session.
2. Remind the group of the next session and thank them for coming.

Personal Notes

Session #19
Supercharging Strategy: Humor

Overview
Session #19 gives participants an opportunity to not only learn more about humor, but to practice it and develop ways to bring more humor to life.

Goals
During this session, participants will:
1. Discuss the benefits of including humor in their lives.
2. Take time to "use" humor by telling funny stories or jokes.
3. Develop a list of "101 Things to Do to Create Humor."

Readings
Chapter 12, pp. 365-366

Quote
"A good time for laughing is when you can." (Jessamyn West, *Pathways to Recovery*, p. 365)

Materials
- *Pathways to Recovery* text
- Flip chart or white board and markers
- Pens/pencils

Handouts
- 101 Things to Do to Create Humor, p. 368

Facilitator's Tip
Don't forget to maintain a sense of humor! This doesn't mean that you need to use jokes or tell funny stories—although some find that a good technique. Keeping your ability to laugh is essential and will help you get through most situations. Being able to laugh at yourself and the situation will provide an environment that is comfortable and relaxed.

Notes
The benefits of humor are well known to improve both our physical and mental health. It can reduce stress, lower blood pressure and provide instant relief from tension, anxiety and anger. Humor helps us be more creative, connects us to others and can even boost our immune system. Being able to laugh not only makes us feel good but often helps us put things in perspective.

Notes, cont.

Today is a day to laugh and have fun! We all need to take time out to find humor in our lives. Give the group plenty of time to share stories, jokes and funny moments. Be ready with your own stories, jokes, etc. in case the group has trouble coming up with their own.

Agenda

10 minutes

Introduction
1. Begin on time and welcome all participants.
2. Review the agenda for today's session.

20 minutes

The Benefits of Humor
1. Read p. 365 (end at the story).
2. Lead a discussion using the following questions:
   a. What type of humor (fun, light, dry, dark, silly, absurd, etc.) do you enjoy most? Why?
   b. What benefits do you receive from finding humor and laughing? Write the responses on the flip chart or white board.
   c. What do you think is the best thing about humor? Why?

20 minutes

Sharing Our Stories: *Amy & JoAnn*
1. Read the stories on pp. 365-366.
2. Lead a discussion using the following questions:
   a. How can laughter help us heal (as Amy describes)?
   b. How important is laughter to our recovery journey?

10 minutes

Break
Remind participants to return at the scheduled time.

20 minutes

Group Activity: *Let's Laugh!*
Most likely, group members will be ready to share their own humorous stories. Use this time to laugh and have a good time, just make sure that the humor is not directed "against" anyone or of a genre not comfortable to those in the group.

1. Ask the participants to share their funny stories.
2. If needed, you may need to use a *prompt* to encourage the stories. These might include:
   a. Any item in the room (for example, a chair, a poster, a piece of chalk, etc.). There are stories about everything!
   b. Categories of stories (for example, things that were funny in school, ways we may have laughed at ourselves, etc.).
   c. Read stories or jokes that you have collected or found in books or magazines.

20 minutes   **Group Activity: "101 Things to Do to Create Humor"**
This is a great exercise that allows participants to have fun and be creative.
1. Explain to the group that you are going to create a list of "101 Things to Do to Create Humor."
2. Pass out the form.
3. Using the flip chart or white board, write down all the ideas that are offered. Have the group add the suggestions to their own sheet. Make sure the ideas are specific (for example, instead of listing "read something funny," you would add "read the comics in the daily paper," "read a favorite joke book," etc.)
4. If the group is unable to come up with 101 items, encourage them to add to the list as they think of more ideas.

10 minutes   **Do It Today:** *Nurturing a Sense of Humor*
1. Have the group brainstorm 2-3 ways that, beginning today, they could nourish their sense of humor. Encourage them to be simple yet creative with their ideas. Some sample ideas include:
    a. Watch a funny movie or television program.
    b. Check out a joke book from the library.
    c. Keep track of funny moments that happen; reread them when you need a laugh.
    d. Read the comics in the daily newspaper.

10 minutes   **Review the Day's Session**
1. Provide the reading assignment for the next session.
2. Remind the group of the next session and thank them for coming.

Personal Notes

_____
_____
_____
_____
_____
_____
_____
_____

Session #20
Facilitator's Choice

Overview
This session allows the group to further explore subjects of interest or to examine sections of the *Pathways to Recovery* text not covered during Module Three.

Goals
During this session, participants will (*to be determined by the group &/or the subject chosen*). List your goals below:

1.

2.

3.

Readings
To be determined by the group &/or the subject chosen

Quote
"We are not permitted to choose the frame of our destiny. But what we put into it is ours." (Dag Hammerskjold, *Pathways to Recovery*, p. 352)

Materials
- *Pathways to Recovery* text
- Flip chart or white board and markers
- Pens/pencils

Handouts
To be determined by the group &/or the subject chosen

Facilitator's Tip
Keep in mind that, as adults, participants want to be able to actually *use* the information they are gathering in the group. Encourage group members to make connections between what they already know and what they are learning.

Notes

There are a variety of options for this session, including:

1. Covering previous topics in which the group needed more time.
2. The group may choose a topic in which they would like more information. However remember that, as the facilitator, you may need to spend time preparing materials.
3. Arrange for a special speaker to share with the group. This might include a peer role model or a panel of individuals who can talk about their recovery.
4. You may have local sites or museums that the group would like to visit.

At the end of the session, talk with the group about the upcoming end of Module Three. Discuss how they would like to celebrate the completion of the sessions. Each group is different and they will come up with unique ideas that will fit the members of the group. Here are some of the ways other *Pathways to Recovery* groups have celebrated:

- Have a pizza party or potluck dinner
- Coordinate a craft or activity day
- Get a movie and a pizza
- Have lunch or dinner at a restaurant
- Spend the day at the park (with a picnic, nature walk or other park activities)
- Attend a free concert
- Take a special hike
- Volunteer in the community together

You will also want to make some decisions on activities to recognize the progress and outcomes of this group. Recognition and validation is extremely important! Be creative and have fun!

Agenda

10 minutes	**Introduction**	

1. Begin on time and welcome all participants.
2. Review the agenda for today's session.

40 minutes	**Group Activity**

To be determined by the group &/or the subject chosen.

10 minutes	**Break**

Remind participants to return at the scheduled time.

30 minutes	**Group Activity**

To be determined by the group &/or the subject chosen.

20 minutes   **Celebration Planning**
   1. Talk with the group about the celebration during Session #24.
   2. Provide a list of possible activities (see "Notes" section).
   3. Decide what activity most represents the group.
   4. If possible, ask the group members to share in the planning and preparation of the celebration.

10 minutes   **Review the Day's Session**
   1. Provide the reading assignment for the next session.
   2. Remind the group of the next session and thank them for coming.

Personal Notes

Session #21
Small Group Project Presentations

Overview
Session #21 allows participants—within a small group format—to share more in-depth information on a topic of recovery.

Goals
During this session, participants will:
1. Present recovery-oriented information to the other group members.
2. Identify at least four aspects of recovery from the small group assignment presentations.

Readings
Small group participants will provide their own readings if needed

Quote
"Let the insight that the journey brought you pervade your day to day experience." (Anonymous, *Pathways to Recovery*, p. 166)

Materials
Small group participants will provide their own materials as needed

Handouts
Small group participants will provide their own handouts if needed

Facilitator's Tip
Encourage clarity from participants. If you do not understand someone's comment, ask them to further explain or give an example. Your ability to ask for clarity will give others permission to do the same.

Notes
Remember, your role as facilitator is to keep the presentations moving and on time. Don't allow one group to take more time than allotted. Keeping the groups on time shows respect for the other groups who have spent time planning and preparing for their presentation.

Take time to review the presentations with the group. Be sure to celebrate and recognize the accomplishments of each group. Encourage members to talk with their peers if they are interested in learning more about a specific topic.

Agenda

10 minutes — **Introduction**
1. Begin on time and welcome all participants.
2. Review the agenda for today's session.

40 minutes — **Small Group Presentations**
1. Allow a few extra minutes if a group needs to do any set up for their presentation.
2. Introduce each small group, their members and their project.
3. Validate each group's efforts in presenting information to the larger group.

10 minutes — **Break**
Remind participants to return at the scheduled time.

40 minutes — **Small Group Presentations, cont.**
1. Continue the presentations.

10 minutes — **Discussion and Thanks**
1. Briefly discuss what group members have learned from their peers in today's session.
2. Thank each group and acknowledge them for their efforts and courage in presenting to their peers.

10 minutes — **Review the Day's Session**
1. Provide the reading assignment for the next session.
2. Remind the group of the next session and thank them for coming.

Personal Notes

_____
_____
_____
_____
_____
_____
_____

Session #22
Small Group Project Presentations

Overview
Session #22 continues the small group presentations, allowing participants—within a small group format—to share more in-depth information on a topic of recovery.

Goals
During this session, participants will:
1. Present recovery-oriented information to the other group members.
2. Identify at least four aspects of recovery from the small group assignment presentations.

Readings
Small group participants will provide their own readings if needed

Quote
"The longest journey is the journey inward." (Dag Hammerskjold, *Pathways to Recovery*, p. 198)

Materials
Small group participants will provide their own materials as needed

Handouts
Small group participants will provide their own handouts if needed

Facilitator's Tip
Building trust within a group is vital to its success. Participants must be free to ask questions, share their personal experiences and participate in discussions as they choose. That means no criticism or preferential treatment; each person's voice and contribution is important.

Notes
Remember, your role as facilitator is to keep the presentations moving and on time. Don't allow one group to take more time than allotted. Keeping the groups on time shows respect for the other groups who have spent time planning and preparing for their presentation.

Take time to review the presentations with the group. Be sure to celebrate and recognize the accomplishments of each group. Encourage members to talk with their peers if they are interested in learning more about a specific topic.

Agenda

10 minutes — **Introduction**
1. Begin on time and welcome all participants.
2. Review the agenda for today's session.

40 minutes — **Small Group Presentations**
1. Allow a few extra minutes if a group needs to do any set up for their presentation.
2. Introduce each small group, their members and their project.
3. Validate each group's efforts in presenting information to the larger group.

10 minutes — **Break**
Remind participants to return at the scheduled time.

40 minutes — **Small Group Presentations, cont.**
1. Continue the presentations.

10 minutes — **Discussion and Thanks**
1. Briefly discuss what group members have learned from their peers in   today's session.
2. Thank each group and acknowledge them for their efforts and courage in presenting to their peers.

10 minutes — **Review the Day's Session**
1. Provide the reading assignment for the next session.
2. Remind the group of the next session and thank them for coming.

Personal Notes

_____
_____
_____
_____
_____
_____
_____

Session #23
Module Evaluation & Looking

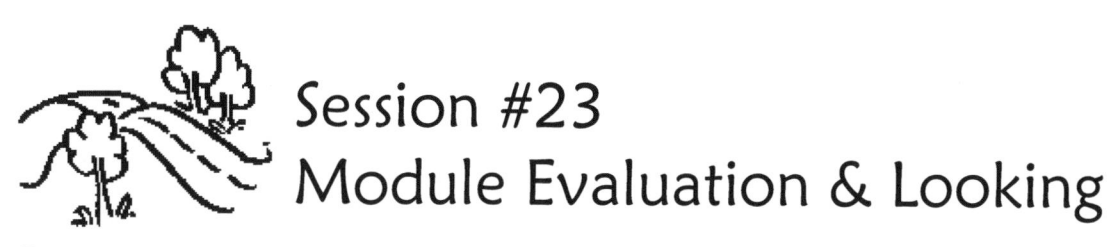

Overview
Session #23 will allow participants to reflect on the past sessions and share any ideas or comments about what they have learned. It will also allow group members to formally evaluate their experience and begin planning for future sessions.

Goals
During this session, participants will:
1. State at least three learning experiences from participating in Module Three.
2. State what they liked and disliked about the sessions.
3. Identify their personal readiness to continue with the *Pathways to Recovery* series.

Readings
None

Quote
"There is one thing which gives radiance to everything. It is the idea of something around the corner." (G.K. Chesterton, *Pathways to Recovery*, p. 127)

Materials
- *Pathways to Recovery* text
- Flip chart or white board and marker
- Pens/pencils

Handouts
- Final Session Satisfaction Survey, p. 350
- Facilitator Self-Assessment, p. 345

Facilitator's Tip
Even though you may have specific times scheduled to allow participants to provide their feedback, consider checking with them on occasion to see how they feel they are learning and incorporating the material. You may find you need to return to an earlier session for review or that participants would like to be moving at a faster pace.

Notes
Remember, evaluation is vital to becoming a better facilitator. Be prepared for compliments and criticisms. This is an opportunity for you to make changes to provide a greater learning experience for all group members. You may also

Notes, cont.

want to invite someone to take notes or record participant's answers on the flip chart or white board. If you are uncomfortable or you would like to give the group an opportunity to be completely honest, consider asking someone who is not part of the group to conduct the evaluation. Finally, be sure to complete your own self-assessment.

Agenda

10 minutes — **Introduction**
1. Begin on time and welcome all participants.
2. Review the agenda for today's session.

15 minutes — **Small Group Activity: *Review of Module Three***
1. Divide participants into small groups of 3-4 people and ask them to choose one person to record their ideas.
2. Ask the small groups to make a list of the things they have learned in the group.

25 minutes — **Group Discussion**
1. Ask each reporter to share highlights from their discussion.
2. On the flip chart or white board, list the ideas given in categories for the different topics discussed (for example, recovery, identifying strengths, things needed for the journey, etc.).
3. If possible, record the responses and make copies for everyone.

10 minutes — **Break**
Remind participants to return at the scheduled time.

30 minutes — **Group Discussion: Final Session Evaluation**
While some may feel sad the sessions are ending, remind them of all the things they have learned from the earlier discussion. Encourage participants to share and support each other in this stage of change. Allow ample time to share their feelings about the group.
1. Explain the importance of evaluating the participant's experiences during Module Three.
2. Lead a discussion using the following questions:
    a. What did you like about this module? Not like?
    b. What was your favorite session?
    c. What was your least favorite session?
    d. What would you change about the group?
    e. Have any of you had problems or experienced anything negative around your recovery so far? If so, how have you dealt with it or how do you plan to make changes?
    f. Does anyone need help with anything related to recovery or with what we have discussed during the sessions?
    g. Are you ready to start Module Four? Why or why not?

10 minutes **Written Satisfaction Survey**
Let participants know that the written forms are anonymous and will be used only to improve the next sessions. Share your appreciation for their honesty.
1. Hand out the "Final Session Satisfaction Survey."
2. Have participants complete the evaluation.

10 minutes **Celebration Planning**
1. Take this time to finalize plans for the celebration activities during Session #24.
2. If needed, remind participants of any details for the celebration (for example, change of location, time, things to bring, etc.).

10 minutes **Review the Day's Session**
1. Provide the reading assignment for the next session.
2. Remind the group of the next session and thank them for coming.

Personal Notes

Session #24
Celebration!

Overview
Session #24 reviews Module Three, with participants reflecting on their experience and learning. It also provides all group members the opportunity to celebrate individual and group accomplishments.

Goals
During this session, participants will:
1. Identify accomplishments, individually and for each member.
2. Celebrate the completion of Module Three.

Readings
To be decided by the facilitator or the group

Quote
"Be ye merry: You have cause. So have we all of joy." (William Shakespeare, *Pathways to Recovery*, p. 205)

Materials
Supplies for today's session will depend on what the group decides to do

Handouts
- Certificates of Achievement (or similar recognition), p. 369

Facilitator's Tip
If you do decide to ask a guest speaker to join the group, be sure to discuss with them what you'd like them to cover—in detail (include the topic, length of presentation, time to arrive, the location of the group, etc.). Don't be afraid to add comments or ask questions of the presenter. You may even need to help them refocus if they get off topic. Try to also allow time for a question and answer period to give the group members a chance to learn more from the presenter. Be sure to send a personal thank you to the presenter after the session.

Notes
The activities for this final session of Module Three should be predetermined by the participants. Let them know there will be much more to learn in the final module and encourage them to continue in the group. Also let them know that if they have any doubts or are simply not ready for this journey, you and the group members will understand.

Notes, cont.
The main goal for today is to celebrate the accomplishments of coming together as a group to work on the journey of recovery. Getting to know one another better in a social setting will reinforce the peer support needed for work that will be done in future modules.

You should also recognize individual accomplishments made during the sessions. Some suggestions include:

- Certificates of attendance or accomplishment
- Small gifts individualized for each person
- The same gift for each person
- A card or note with your personal thanks

Above all, make sure that *each* person is recognized and celebrated.

Agenda

10 minutes **Introduction**
1. Begin on time and welcome all participants.
2. Review the agenda for today's session.

10 minutes **Highlights of Module Three**
1. Start by having the group recite the "Recovery Pledge" (p. 20).
2. Using the flip chart or white board, make a list of the highlights and outcomes for Module Three.

90 minutes **Celebration!**
1. Conduct the celebration activities.
2. Be sure to recognize each individual and their accomplishments during the session.

10 minutes **Review the Day's Session**
1. Provide the reading assignment for the next session.
2. Remind the group of the next session and thank them for coming.

Personal Notes

_____
_____
_____
_____
_____

Module Four

"The past is behind, learn from it.
The future is ahead, prepare for it.
The present is here, live it.
~ Thomas S. Monson

Introduction to Module Four

"Today a new sun rises for me; everything lives, everything is animated, everything seems to speak to me of my passion, everything invites me to cherish it."
~ Ninon de Lenclos

Module Four continues the exploration of *Pathways to Recovery* and provides twenty-four, 2-hour sessions. This section includes the following chapters:

- Chapter 7: Travel Companions and Social Support for the Journey (pp. 224-256)
- Chapter 10: Rest Stops and Travel Tips
- Chapter 12: Transformations: Sharing Our Stories of Recovery

In addition, two supercharging strategies from Chapter 12—affirmations and gratitude—will also be explored.

During this module, participants will continue the discussion of social support. They will have the opportunity to assess their current level of support and learn how to both expand and enhance the supportive relationships in their lives.

The journey of recovery can be a long and winding road. While the group has spent much time planning and preparing for the future, Chapter 10 provides numerous tips on how to take breaks and rest stops when needed. Participants will learn simple and inexpensive ways to "tune up" their lives and make the journey more fun and relaxing.

Sharing one's personal story can be a deep and transformational experience. Every person has an important and healing story to tell. Chapter 12 begins by focusing on the importance of sharing one's recovery story and will lead participants step-by-step in creating their own unique story.

While this module completes the exploration of the material in *Pathways to Recovery*, it really is only the beginning. Participants will continue to find new dreams and develop the goals and resources to achieve those. Much has been learned and incorporated into the daily lives of the group members and it is important to evaluate and recognize the effort that has gone into making the workbook real. It has been a long trip but with the tips and tools provided, group members now have a wonderful new way of living the journey!

REMEMBER...

If you have not already done so, it is important for you to read the introduction to this guide. In it you will find key elements and guidelines for facilitating a successful, recovery-focused and positive experience for all.

Don't hesitate to add your own ideas, activities, resources and energy. Your ability to be creative will enhance the positive nature of the group and help to build a safe, supportive and fun environment for all participants. Examine your own creative style as you prepare for each session. The important point is to include the activities and exercises that will best help group members understand and apply the concepts learned.

Session #1
Welcome & Introductions

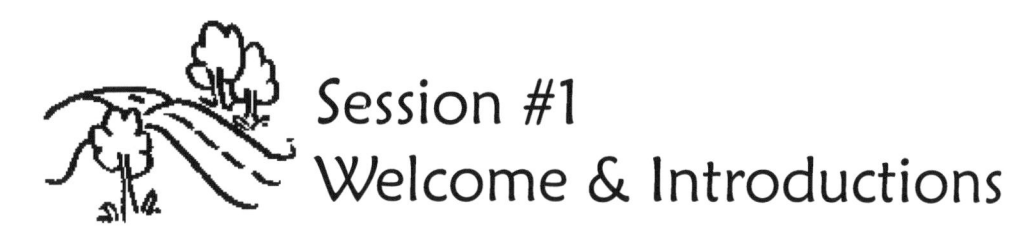

Overview
Session #1 will allow participants to get to know each other better while reviewing the structure and functioning of the group.

Goals
During this session, participants will:
1. Introduce/reintroduce themselves to each member of the group and continue the process of building group unity.
2. Discuss how the *Pathways to Recovery* group will be conducted.
3. Discuss the basic group process, commitment and expectations.

Readings
Pathways to Recovery, Preface, pp. iii-viii (begin at "How to Use This Workbook")

Quote
"The most difficult thing in life is to know yourself." (Thales, *Pathways to Recovery*, p. 81)

Materials
- An individual copy of *Pathways to Recovery* text for each person in the group
- A binder or folder for each participant (for handouts and other materials)
- Flip chart or white board and markers
- Pens/pencils

Handouts
- Reasons to Participate in the *Pathways to Recovery* Group, p. 335
- Questions to Ask Yourself About Participating in the *Pathways to Recovery* Group, p. 336
- Handy Reminder for Group Members, 337
- The Partnership Pact, p. 338
- This or That: *Which Will You Choose?*, p. 370

Facilitator's Tip
As facilitator, you hold the collective remembrance of what has occurred within the group. A good facilitator is able to hold the group memory, going back as needed to remind participants of previous discussions, agreements, ideas or activities. This helps keep the group focused and make progress on individual and group goals.

Notes
Remember that new participants will change the complexion of the group. It is important for you to do your best to help them feel supported. Watch for levels of discomfort and address them with the group. Find ways for each person to participate. Remind the group that, while you are working on common goals together, you do want them to enjoy each other and the activities. As in previous modules, establishing group guidelines early on helps you better incorporate new members who will feel safe and willing to participate.

Agenda

20 minutes

Introduction & Icebreaker Activity: *This or That?*
1. Begin on time and welcome all participants.
2. Review the agenda for today's session.
3. Using the handout, pose the questions to the group, asking participants to choose which word they identify with more than the other. Group members can answer by raising their hands, standing up or moving from one side of the room to the other.

20 minutes

Why participate in the *Pathways to Recovery* group?
1. Hand out "Questions to Ask Yourself about Participating in the *Pathways to Recovery* Group."
2. Have participants complete the form and discuss their ideas as a group.
3. Hand out "Reasons to Participate in the *Pathways to Recovery* Group."
4. Review each guideline and ask for questions.

20 minutes

Group Guidelines, Process & Commitment
If you are just starting the Modules with this session, hand out personal copies of Pathways to Recovery to each participant; give them a few minutes to look over the workbook.
1. Go over each item found on pp. 32-35 of the facilitator's guide (start at "Beginning the Session" and end at "Group Support") and explain or remind the group how the sessions will be conducted.
2. Discuss the benefits of making a commitment to the group.
    a. Remind participants that group dynamics takes hard work and commitment from each member.
    b. Encourage a supportive and recovery-focused environment.
    c. The group can be successful if everyone is consistent with their attendance and participates actively.
    d. Remind group members that sharing is more likely to occur when a positive connection is developed.

10 minutes	**Break** *Remind participants to return at the scheduled time.*
20 minutes	**Group Expectations** 1. Hand out *"Pathways to Recovery* Handy Reminder for Group Members." 2. Discuss these items as they will serve as the group expectations.

20 minutes	**The "Partnership Pact"**
	The pact is the agreement made between group members to insure a safe, supportive and strengths-focused group based on the individual's unique values and needs.
	1. Review the concept of the "Partnership Pact."
	2. Develop or review a list of items to include in the pact (see suggestions on p. 42 of Module One) that will serve as ground rules and expectations. These include:
	   a. Everyone in the group should agree with the items.
	   b. Write all the remarks on the flip chart or white board.
	   c. Participants can add remarks at any time.
	   d. Development of the pact will continue during the next session and everyone will receive a copy of it.

10 minutes	**Review the Day's Session** 1. Review the day's session and ask participants if they have any final questions about the group. 2. Provide the reading assignment for the next session. 3. Remind the group of the next session and thank them for coming.

Personal Notes

_____

_____

_____

_____

_____

_____

_____

Session #2
Assessing Your Circle of Support

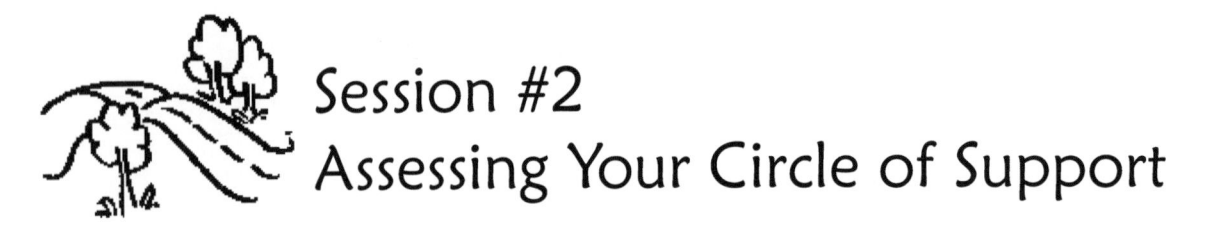

Overview
Session #2 continues the discussion of social support, specifically by completing a self-assessment and examining ideas to help reach personal social support goals.

Goals
During this session, participants will:
1. Finalize the "Partnership Pact."
2. Complete a self-assessment of their current social supports.
3. Identify at least three reasons why social support is personally important.

Readings
Chapter 7, pp. 221-224

Quote
"Nobody, but nobody can make it out here alone." (Maya Angelou, *Pathways* text, p. 224)

Materials
- *Pathways to Recovery* text
- *Pathways to Recovery* text for new participants
- Flip chart or white board and markers
- Pens/pencils

Facilitator's Tip
Be yourself! There is no room for phoniness and a lack of genuine regard will only serve to defeat the group process. Your strength as a facilitator is in your ability to share who you are and what you've learned in a manner that helps the group learn and apply new skills. The presence of an insincere facilitator will only suppress potential learning opportunities.

Notes
As was discussed in Module Three, it's important for social supports to include people and places that are NOT professional in nature. Many times individuals need to talk to or be with someone during the hours that professional offices are closed. If you find group members who are unable to develop peer supports, encourage them to develop a long-term goal with specific short-term steps to help them do this.

Agenda

10 minutes — **Introduction**
1. Begin on time and welcome all participants.
2. Review the agenda for today's session.

10 minutes — **The "Partnership Pact"**
1. Building on the work done in Session #1, add any new ideas to the list (especially from individuals new to the group.)
2. Remind participants they will finalize the pact during Session #3.

20 minutes — **Small Group Activity: *The Contributions of Social Support***
1. Divide participants into two equal groups; have them choose one person to record their ideas.
2. Have the groups discuss the following:
    a. Group #1 will discuss, "What do people do for you that you find supportive?"
    b. Group #2 will discuss, "In what ways are you supportive of others?"

20 minutes — **Group Discussion**
1. Ask each reporter to share the highlights from their group. List the ideas from each group on the flip chart or white board.
2. Lead a discussion using the following questions:
    a. Did your group find this discussion easy or hard? Why or why not?
    b. What common themes do you see in the two lists?
    c. In what ways are the lists similar? How are they different?
    d. For you, what is the most important benefit you get from social support?
    e. If you could create a perfect circle of support, who would it include?

10 minutes — **Break**
Remind participants to return at the scheduled time.

20 minutes — **Group Exercise: *Assessing Your Circle of Support***
In order to understand how to expand the circle of support, this exercise helps participants evaluate where they currently stand and will give them a better idea of how to set goals to increase support.
1. Read the instructions for the exercise on p. 221.
2. Using the form on p. 223, give participants time to complete the support circle. Provide help and ideas as needed.

Module Four

265

20 minutes   **Group Discussion**
1. Read through each of the listed questions on p. 224, giving participants time to individually think about their answers.
2. Lead a discussion using the following questions:
    a. Are you satisfied with your current level of support?
    b. Do you see any specific patterns that have developed (for example, supporters are mostly mental health providers, there are supports missing in one or

more

    areas, there are too few supporters, etc.)?
    c. In what areas would you like to see your supporters increase? Why is this important to you at this time?

10 minutes   **Review the Day's Session**
1. Provide the reading assignment for the next session.
2. Remind the group of the next session and thank them for coming.

Personal Notes

Session #3
Roadblocks to Communication

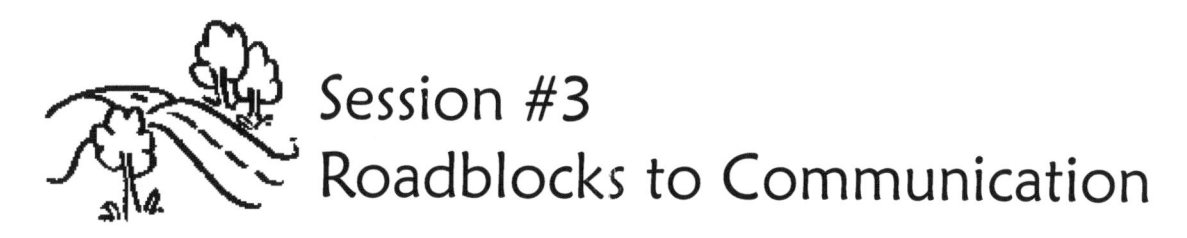

Overview
Session #3 takes a look at the common roadblocks to communication. Participants will examine each roadblock and develop possible solutions for overcoming them.

Goals
During this session, participants will:
1. Finalize the "Partnership Pact."
2. Discuss the five common roadblocks to communication.
3. Identify one personal roadblock and write an action plan for how to overcome it.

Readings
Chapter 7, pp. 224-227

Quote
"To attract good fortune, spend a new penny on an old friend, share an old pleasure with a new friend, and lift up the heart of a true friend by writing his name on the wings of a dragon." (Chinese Proverb, *Pathways to Recovery*, p. 225)

Materials
- *Pathways to Recovery* text
- Flip chart or white board and markers
- Pens/pencils
- One copy of the "Partnership Pact" for everyone to sign

Facilitator's Tip
Conflict *can* work to your advantage as a facilitator. Disagreements among group members are common and usually provides for the inclusion of different points of view or alternative approaches to a problem. While everyone in the group has a right to their opinion, it is up to you as the facilitator to maintain an objective perspective and to insist on consideration and respect for all participants.

Notes
Communication impacts every aspect of our lives. While there is much information on how to build and enhance these skills in the *Pathways to Recovery* text, encourage participants to seek out other resources as needed. This could also be a good project for small groups to consider for their presentations.

Agenda

10 minutes — **Introduction**
1. Begin on time and welcome all participants.
2. Review the agenda for today's session.

10 minutes — **The "Partnership Pact"**
Remind the group members they are making a commitment to conduct themselves according to the agreed upon items.
1. Review the "Partnership Pact."
    a. Ask for and add any new items.
    b. Pass out one copy and have participants sign the form.
    c. If possible, at break, make individual copies for everyone; if not, have copies ready for the next session.

40 minutes — **Overcoming the Roadblocks to Communication**
This activity will take the majority of today's session. Each roadblock will take approximately 10-15 minutes to complete.
1. Briefly review the five roadblocks listed on pp. 225-226.
2. For each roadblock, have the group make a list of the specific impact this roadblock has or could have on a relationship.
3. For each roadblock, lead a discussion using the following questions:
    a. What advice would you give someone who wanted to overcome this barrier?
    b. If this roadblock creates a negative impact on a relationship, in what way would the opposite behavior or action improve a relationship?

10 minutes — **Break**
Remind participants to return at the scheduled time.

30 minutes — **Overcoming the Roadblocks to Communication, cont.**
1. Continue the group activity from before the break.

10 minutes — **Overcoming the Roadblocks: *What Steps will You Take?***
1. Have the participants complete the two questions on p. 227.

10 minutes — **Review the Day's Session**
1. Provide the reading assignment for the next session.
2. Remind the group of the next session and thank them for coming.

Personal Notes

Session #4
Expanding Our Circle of Support

Overview
Session #4 begins a more in-depth discussion of social support. The group will discuss mutual support and learn tools to help them further develop their ability to expand their circle of support. In addition, the small group project will be introduced.

Goals
During this session, participants will:
1. Examine the three ways mutual social support happens.
2. Learn three ways to get the support they need.
3. Discuss the concept of "plum blossom courage" and how to incorporate its meaning into their personal lives.
4. Develop groups for the small group project.

Readings
Chapter 7, pp. 227-231

Quote
"It takes only a minute to get a crush on someone, an hour to like someone, and a day to love someone, but it takes a lifetime to forget someone." (Unknown, *Pathways to Recovery*, p. 230)

Materials
- *Pathways to Recovery* text
- Flip chart or white board and markers
- Pens/pencils

Handouts
- Small Group Project Presentation: *Instruction Sheet*, p. 371

Facilitator's Tip
In order to convey a positive and well-thought out message, do your best to communicate clearly with everyone in the group. Be open and honest in your choice of words, your body language and facial expressions. Clear communication can enhance discussions, reduce negative conflict and promote learning.

Notes
Also during this session, participants will be introduced to the small group project. As part of this assignment, group members will design their own project and are free to be creative in developing a 10-15 minute presentation on a topic of interest from Module Four. Some examples for this module might include:

- Developing a list of "101 Ways to Reduce Stress."
- Further exploring the concept of gratitude (why it's helpful, why it works, etc.).
- Creating a short skit on how to meet someone new.
- Preparing a resource list of places to submit recovery stories for publication (for example, specific websites, addresses of publishers, etc.).
- Designing all or part of the final celebration activity.

Encourage participants to be creative in developing their group project. Brainstorm with the groups if they have a hard time beginning.

Agenda

10 minutes — **Introduction**
1. Begin on time and welcome all participants.
2. Review the agenda for today's session.

10 minutes — **Building Mutual Support**
1. Read p. 228 (end at "Basically there are three ways...").
2. Lead a short discussion using the following question:
    a. Can you name one or two ways you have experienced mutual support?

15 minutes — **Small Group Activity: *Getting the Support We Need***
1. Briefly go over each of the three ways to get needed support.
2. Divide participants into three equal groups and ask them to choose one person to record their ideas.
3. Assign each small group one of the topics and have them read the material.
4. Ask the groups to summarize what they have read and prepare a 5-minute presentation for the entire group. Encourage them to be creative.

25 minutes — **Group Discussion**
1. Ask each group to share their presentation.
2. Following each group, lead a discussion using the following questions:
    a. What was the most important point in the presentation?
    b. What idea from this group can you use in your daily life?

10 minutes	**Break**
	Remind participants to return at the scheduled time.

20 minutes	**Homework Assignment: *Exploring New Relationships***

Exploring potential relationships is important to enhancing the social support needed for a successful recovery journey. Even though the exercise asks for individuals to identify a person a day, giving them an option of choosing one or two people provides a good introduction to the activity.

1. Read the exercise on p. 231.
2. Have the group members identify at least two people who they would like to get to know better and complete the questions.
3. Brainstorm with the group about possible people, roles and/or ways to go about contacting these individuals.
4. Encourage the group to try the exercise prior to the next session.

20 minutes	**Small Group Project Presentations**

Having small groups develop and present on a topic of interest provides a wonderful experience for learning. Groups will create their own project and develop a 10-15 minute presentation to be given during Sessions #21 & 22.

1. Hand out the "Small Group Project Presentations: *Instruction Sheet*" for this module.
2. Review the project instructions, helping participants brainstorm ideas for a topic.
3. Divide the class into groups of 3-5 people.
4. Give the groups time to meet and brainstorm potential topics.
5. Since the presentations will be done during two separate sessions, have them decide the order in which they will present.

10 minutes	**Review the Day's Session**

1. Provide the reading assignment for the next session.
2. Remind the group of the next session and thank them for coming.

Personal Notes

___
___
___
___
___
___
___

Session #5
Exploring Our Relationships

Overview
Session #5 is the first of three sessions that will explore the different types of available relationships.

Goals
During this session, participants will:
1. List one to two peers they would like to know better.
2. Identify at least four qualities found in a role model or mentor.
3. Discuss the qualities necessary in a good friend.
4. Examine their current level of family support.

Readings
Chapter 7, pp. 232-236

Quote
"Here is someone at once so like you that you have come home, and yet so different he opens a thousand windows of the universe." (Michael Drury, *Pathways to Recovery*, p. 234)

Materials
- *Pathways to Recovery* text
- Flip chart or white board and markers
- Pens/pencils

Facilitator's Tip
One of the best skills for a facilitator to learn is that of becoming comfortable with silence. Many individuals need time to think about a response to a question or to decide how they feel about a specific topic. While it is relatively common to fear silence, it can be a very valuable tool for a facilitator.

Notes
As the text describes, for some, certain relationships are extremely important and provide a genuine source of help and healing. For others, some of these relationships have been or are hurtful and problematic. Use these discussions as a way for participants to focus on which relationships they find useful and ones in which they would like to build upon and nurture.

Agenda

10 minutes   **Introduction**
1. Begin on time and welcome all participants.
2. Review the agenda for today's session.

15 minutes   **Discussion of the Homework Assignment**
1. Lead a discussion of the homework assignment on p. 231 using the following questions:
   a. If you were able to try the assignment, what kind of response did you receive?
   c. Were there things that worked well? Things that didn't?
   d. Will this can be a beneficial tool for you to use?

10 minutes   **Deciding What Kind of Relationships to Build**
1. Introduce the types of relationships that will be covered in the next three sessions (pp. 232-242).
2. Lead a short discussion using the following question:
   a. Which of these relationships have you found most important in your life? Are there others?

15 minutes   **Peers & Advisors**
1. Read pp. 232-233 (end at "Friends"). Have the group answer the questions in the text.
2. Lead a discussion using the following questions:
   a. What is the difference between the peer relationship and that of advisor or mentor?
   b. What qualities do you think are important in each of these roles? (List the answers on the flip chart or white board.)
   c. If/when you identify a person you would like to be an advisor or mentor, what questions would you ask them? Why?

10 minutes   **Break**
Remind participants to return at the scheduled time.

20 minutes   **Friends**
1. Read pp. 233-235 (end at "Family").
2. Lead a discussion using the questions in the text.

20 minutes   **Family**
1. Read pp. 235-236 (start at "Family" and end at "Parenting").
2. Lead a discussion using the questions in the text.

10 minutes	***Just Because Someone...***
1. Read the Truman Capote quote on p. 235.
2. Lead a short discussion using the following questions:
   a. Do you agree or disagree with Capote's words? Why?
   b. What personal message do you find in the quote?

10 minutes	**Review the Day's Session**
1. Provide the reading assignment for the next session.
2. Remind the group of the next session and thank them for coming.

Personal Notes

Session #6
Exploring Our Relationships, cont.

Overview
Session #6 continues the exploration of building new relationships. Participants will discuss the roles of parenting, intimate partners, casual relationships, spiritual supporters, pets and the universe.

Goals
During this session, participants will:
1. Compare and contrast the roles of parent, intimate partner and casual relationships.
2. Discuss how community participation can be a source of personal support.
3. Identify at least two qualities they find important in a spiritual supporter.
4. List at least three positive supports that can be provided by pets.
5. List at least two ways they view the universe as a source of support.

Readings
Chapter 7, pp. 236-241

Quote
"Some things have to be believed to be seen." (Ralph Hodgson, *Pathways* text, p. 40)

Materials
- *Pathways to Recovery* text
- Flip chart or white board and markers
- Pens/pencils

Facilitator's Tip
Using icebreakers or simple activities is a great way for facilitators to help people relax and get to know one another better. A good icebreaker is positive, illustrates the topic and helps group members expand their thinking. It can also be a fun and energizing activity! Icebreakers help set the tone for the session or conclude the group in a meaningful and memorable way. Be sure the activity you choose is appropriate to the group and is both physically and psychologically safe.

Notes
By now, participants should be seeing the variety of relationships that are available to them. While some group members may not find certain relationships as important (like pets), remind them again of the need for balance in remaining healthy.

Agenda

10 minutes — **Introduction**
1. Begin on time and welcome all participants.
2. Review the agenda for today's session.

20 minutes — **Group Activity: *What's Important?***
1. Divide the participants into three small groups.
2. Hang three sheets of flip chart paper around the room. At the top of each page, list the relationship to discuss (parenting, intimate partners and casual relationships).
3. Give each group a different color marker. Assign each one of the topics. (Using a different color marker keeps the activity flowing and will represent each group's ideas).
4. Give each group five minutes to list any ideas, suggestions or questions they have about the relationship.
5. Have the groups rotate every five minutes, adding new ideas.

20 minutes — **Group Discussion**
1. Review the comments for each relationship.
2. Pose any questions listed to the group for their response.
3. Lead a discussion using the following questions:
    a. Which section did you find the most challenging? Why?
    b. Are there ideas for how to nurture these relationships?

10 minutes — **Break**
Remind participants to return at the scheduled time.

10 minutes — **Fellow Community Members**
1. Read the folktale on p. 239.
2. Lead a discussion using the following questions:
    a. What do you think of the idea of *"ujima"*? Do you agree with the concept or not? Why?
    b. Can you name any examples of community building that, like the folktale, brought people together? How were you involved? How did you feel about participating in your community efforts?

10 minutes — **Spiritual Supporters**
1. Read pp. 240-241 (start at "Spiritual Supporters" and end at "Pets and Other Supports").
2. Lead a discussion using the following questions:
    a. Do you have a spiritual supporter? What form of support do they provide to you?

10 minutes   **Spiritual Supporters, cont.**
       b. What qualities do you find important in a spiritual supporter?
       c. What are some ways we can build on our spiritual support?

10 minutes   **Pets and Other Supports**
1. Read p. 241 (start at "Pets and Other Supports").
2. Lead a discussion using the following questions:
   a. Are pets important to you? Why or why not?
   b. Some people say their pets are more of a support to them than people. Do you agree with this statement? Why or why not?
   c. What makes the relationship with pets different than those we have with other people?

10 minutes   **Support from the Universe**
1. Read p. 242 (end at the exercise).
2. Lead a short discussion using the following questions:
   a. What support do you receive from the universe?
   b. Is this type of support important to you? Why or why not?

10 minutes   **Review the Day's Session**
1. Encourage participants to try the exercise on p. 242.
2. Provide the reading assignment for the next session.
3. Remind the group of the next session and thank them for coming.

Personal Notes

_____
_____
_____
_____
_____
_____
_____

Session #7
Exploring Our Relationships, cont.

Overview
Session #7 concludes the discussion and exploration of specific roles and relationships. Participants will learn how to nurture current relationships and practice using good communication skills.

Goals
During this session, participants will:
1. Discuss how to renew their social circle.
2. List three things they can do to nurture a current relationship.
3. Learn seven tips for good communication.

Readings
Chapter 7, pp. 243-246

Quote
"Only connect!" (E.M. Forster, *Pathways to Recovery*, p. 244)

Materials
- *Pathways to Recovery* text
- Flip chart or white board and markers
- Pens/pencils

Handouts
- Mixed-Up Messages, p. 372

Facilitator's Tip
Body language can be a very effective tool to encourage participation. As the facilitator, you might push your chair away from the table to essentially "turn over" the discussion to the group. A simple smile or nod of the head can be an encouragement to a shy group member. Likewise, a closed body stance (for example, frowning or crossing your arms) can hinder open participation.

Notes
The translation for the "Mixed-Up Messages" activity is: "Ants talk without saying a word! Did you know that when ants touch each other with their antennae, it is one way they talk or communicate?"

Agenda

10 minutes — **Introduction**
1. Begin on time and welcome all participants.
2. Review the agenda for today's session.

10 minutes — **Discussion of the Homework Assignment**
1. Review the homework assignment from Session #6 (the exercise on p. 242).
2. Lead a short discussion using the question from the exercise.

30 minutes — **Sharing Our Stories: *Julie***
1. Read Julie's story on p. 243.
2. Lead a discussion using the following questions:
    a. What things has Julie learned to help her create and nurture her relationships?
    b. In what ways would you like to nurture your current relationships? How would you like to rekindle old relationships?
    b. Does Julie's story give you hope for your own relationships? Why?
3. Finish by asking participants to complete the questions on pp. 243-244.

10 minutes — **Break**
Remind participants to return at the scheduled time.

20 minutes — **Small Group Activity: *Mixed-Up Messages***
1. Have participants pair up with one other person.
2. Hand out "Mixed-Up Messages."
3. Give the pairs 5 minutes to "un-mix" the message (see "Notes" for the correct translation).
4. Lead a discussion using the following questions:
    a. How is communication like this "mixed-up message?" (For example, we send mixed messages, it takes time to find the real meaning of a message, communication can be frustrating at times, results in our message not being heard, etc.).
    b. Have you experienced these types of communication mix-ups before? What ways did you use to make your message more clear to the one/s you were trying to communicate with?

30 minutes **How Well Are We Communicating?**
1. Read pp. 244-246 (start at "How Well Are We" and end at "Nourishing Our Circle").
2. Either as a group or individually, have participants complete the questions in the workbook.

10 minutes **Review the Day's Session**
1. Provide the reading assignment for the next session.
2. Remind the group of the next session and thank them for coming.

Personal Notes

Session #8
Nourishing Our Circle of Support

Overview
Session #8 examines the importance of nourishing personal relationships on an on-going basis. In addition to discussing how to be a good supporters, the group will also examine the need to change relationships and how to become a mentor to others.

Goals
During this session, participants will:
1. Identify at least three ways they can nurture their current relationships.
2. Learn six tips on how to become a good supporter to others.
3. Discuss the need to change their personal supports.
4. Examine the value of being a mentor to others on their recovery journey.

Readings
Chapter 7, pp. 246-250

Quote
"Treat people as if they were what they ought to be, and help them become what they are capable of being." (Goethe, *Pathways to Recovery*, p. 249)

Materials
- *Pathways to Recovery* text
- Flip chart or white board and markers
- Pens/pencils

Facilitator's Tip
If you find the need to talk with someone individually, do so outside of the group setting (during break or before/after the session). Most people respond best when they are given the respect of privacy.

Notes
Being a good supporter or mentor to others will also help participants with their own recovery journey. Group members should understand that whether they are the student or the teacher makes no difference; what matters is that we all learn something from the people we meet.

Agenda

10 minutes — **Introduction**
1. Begin on time and welcome all participants.
2. Review the agenda for today's session.

15 minutes — **Nourishing Our Circle**
1. Read p. 246 (start at "Nourishing Our Circle").
2. Lead a discussion using the following questions:
   a. What does it mean to "nourish" our support?
   b. Can you list two or three ideas for how you could do this?

25 minutes — **How Do We Become Good Supporters**
1. Read pp. 247-248 (end at "When We Must").
2. Discuss each tip, using the following questions as guides:
   a. Can you think of some specific examples of how to use these tips effectively?
   b. In what ways can these tips be helpful in our attempts to nourish our relationships?

10 minutes — **Break**
Remind participants to return at the scheduled time.

30 minutes — **Changing our Travel Companions**
1. Read pp. 248-249 (begin at "When We Must" and end at "Becoming a Mentor").
2. Lead a discussion using the questions in the workbook on p 249.

20 minutes — **Becoming a Mentor:** *Encouraging Another Person's Recovery*
If participants are interested in becoming a mentor, encourage them to read the tips on p. 250.
1. Read pp. 249 (begin at "Becoming a mentor").
2. Lead a short discussion using the following questions:
   a. Have you had a mentor in your recovery journey?
   b. What have they done to help you grow and become more resilient?
   c. Do you think you could be a mentor to someone else? Why or why not?

10 minutes — **Review the Day's Session**
1. Provide the reading assignment for the next session.
2. Remind the group of the next session and thank them for coming.

Personal Notes

Session #9
Supercharging Strategy: Gratitude

Overview
Session #9 looks at supercharging strategy #2—nurturing an "attitude of gratitude." Participants will define gratitude and develop strategies for incorporating thankfulness into their recovery journey.

Goals
During this session, participants will:
1. Discuss why gratitude is important.
2. Examine how they have already incorporated gratitude in their recovery journey.
3. Complete a "gratitude inventory."
4. Identify at least two ways they can personally use gratitude to feel better.

Readings
Chapter 11, pp. 346-355

Quote
"You cannot be grateful and bitter. You cannot be grateful and unhappy. You cannot be grateful and without hope. You cannot be grateful and unloving. So just be grateful." (Author Unknown, *Pathways to Recovery*, p. 353)

Materials
- *Pathways to Recovery* text
- Flip chart or white board and markers
- Pens/pencils

Handouts
- 101 Things to Be Thankful For, p. 373 (if needed)

Facilitator's Tip
It's just as important for you as a facilitator to embrace an "attitude of gratitude." You might want to think about keeping your own gratitude journal specific to your facilitation. Keep track of positive comments you receive, personal moments of learning or examples of how participants are incorporating their learning.

Notes

Gratitude is a tremendously powerful tool to use that can help overcome negative thought patterns and give participants the ability to embrace their inner power to change their life. Although not all the material in this supercharging strategy will be covered during this session, strongly encourage participants to begin noticing and keeping track of those things in their life for which they are grateful. The exercise on p. 350 is one good example of how to begin noticing the "new" things around us or the group might also want to create a list of "101 Things to Be Thankful For."

Agenda

10 minutes — **Introduction**
1. Begin on time and welcome all participants.
2. Review the agenda for today's session.

20 minutes — **What is Gratitude & Why is it Important?**
1. Read pp. 346-347.
2. Lead a discussion using the following questions:
    a. Why is it important to think about gratitude?
    b. Do you agree with the text that we can improve our quality of life by focusing on the things we "have" instead of what we "lack"?
    c. What positive effects have you experienced from using an "attitude of gratitude?"

20 minutes — **How to Develop an "Attitude of Gratitude"**
1. Read each topic on pp. 348-349 separately (do not include the story at this time).
2. For each topic, ask the following question and list responses on the flip chart or white board:
    a. Can you give a short example of how you (or someone you know) have used this gratitude tip?

10 minutes — **Pat's Story**
1. Read Pat's story on p. 349.
2. Lead a short discussion using the following questions:
    a. Can you identify with what Pat describes?
    b. In what ways do you consider yourself, as Pat describes, "gutsy?"
    c. Why do you think Pat can now say she is a "new person"?

10 minutes — **Break**
Remind participants to return at the scheduled time.

20 minutes	**Ways to Support our Sense of Gratitude**

One of the best ways to begin using gratitude is to take a gratitude inventory. This exercise will give participants the opportunity to start seeing the different areas of life in which they can be grateful.
1. Read p. 351 (start at "How Can We Support").
2. Individually, have the participants complete the gratitude inventory.
3. Conduct a short discussion using the following questions:
    a. How difficult did you find this exercise?
    b. In what way do you think this inventory will help you be more thankful?

20 minutes	**Supporting & Maintaining Gratitude**

1. Review the suggestions listed that can be helpful to encouraging a grateful attitude (including gratitude journals, times to be thankful, honoring others and daily rituals).
2. Lead a discussion using the following questions:
    a. Does anyone currently use any of these techniques for gratitude? If so, can you share an example?
    b. What is one thing you will begin to do that can support and maintain your efforts at being more grateful?

10 minutes	**Review the Day's Session**

1. Provide the reading assignment for the next session.
2. Remind the group of the next session and thank them for coming.

Personal Notes

_____

_____

_____

_____

_____

_____

_____

_____

Session #10
Reducing Stress

Overview
Session #10 provides an overview of the influence stress can have in one's life. The group will discuss how stress impacts them while learning new strategies for reducing stress. Participants will also meet in their small groups to continue planning their presentations.

Goals
During this session, participants will:
1. Examine the importance of incorporating "tune-ups and rest stops" in the recovery journey.
2. Discuss the impact of stress.
3. Practice at least two methods of reducing stress.
4. Make a list of potential activities that will help with stress management.
5. Meet with their small groups to continue planning their presentation.

Readings
Chapter 10, pp. 313-319

Quote
"If you take muddy water and still it, it gradually becomes clear. If you bring something to rest in order to move it, it gradually comes alive." (Lao-Tzu, *Pathways to Recovery*, p. 318)

Materials
- *Pathways to Recovery* text
- Flip chart or white board and markers
- Pens/pencils

Facilitator's Tip
Be sure to keep your own stress levels down. Don't be worried by people who are late, get up in the middle of the group or leave early. Learn to be more flexible and patient and you will be less stressed and worried.

Notes
Managing and reducing stress is a major factor in recovery and relapse prevention. Encourage the group to focus on positive, simple and convenient methods of monitoring their levels of stress. Also, remind them that it makes no difference if it is *good* stress or *bad* stress...it is STILL stress!

Agenda

10 minutes — **Introduction**
1. Begin on time and welcome all participants.
2. Review the agenda for today's session.

10 minutes — **The Need for Tune-Ups & Rest Stops**
1. Read p. 313 (end at "AHHHH...Letting Go").
2. Provide a short look at the topics to be covered in Chapter 10.

20 minutes — **Basics of Stress**
1. Read pp. 313-315 (begin at "AHHHH...Letting Go" end at "This section includes...").
2. Lead a discussion using the following questions:
    a. In what ways does stress impact you?
    b. Do you agree that stress can be motivating? How have you found that to be so?
    c. In what area/s of your body do you "feel" stress?

10 minutes — **Exercise: *Breath Work***
1. Choose one of the breathing exercises on pp. 316-317.
2. As you read the exercise, have the group try the technique.

10 minutes — **Exercise: *Muscle Relaxation Techniques***
1. Choose one of the muscle relaxation techniques on p. 318.
2. As you read one of the methods, have the group try the technique.

10 minutes — **Break**
Remind participants to return at the scheduled time.

20 minutes — **Activity: *Stress Words***
1. Choose a word that relates to reducing stress (such as *focus, rest, relax*). The words should not have duplicate letters.
2. On the flip chart or white board, write the word vertically down the side of the page.
3. Draw a line between each letter, forming the same number of rows as the number of letters in the chosen word.
4. For each letter in the word, have the group list ideas or examples of ways to reduce stress, using the first letter in the word to begin the suggestion (for example, if the letter is "r," the group could list reading, riding a bike, rowing, etc.).
5. If possible, make a copy of the list for each participant.

20 minutes   **Small Group Project Planning**
  1. Provide time for the small groups to work on their project.
  2. If they have not already done so, help the groups decide on the topic or activity they will present.

10 minutes   **Review the Day's Session**
  1. Provide the reading assignment for the next session.
  2. Remind the group of the next session and thank them for coming.

Personal Notes

Session #11
Rebalancing

Overview
This session will look at the need to incorporate a sense of balance in our lives. The group will examine why being balanced is important and create a plan for restructuring their time to better meet their goals.

Goals
During this session, participants will:
1. Examine being "out of alignment" and complete a self-assessment.
2. Identify at least three factors of why balance is necessary.
3. Complete a self-inventory of their current and preferred activities.

Readings
Chapter 10, pp. 319-323

Quote
"Be aware of wonder. Live a balanced life. Learn some and think some and draw and paint and sing and dance and play and work some every day some." (Robert Fulghum, *Pathways to Recovery*, p. 319)

Materials
- *Pathways to Recovery* text
- Flip chart or white board and markers
- Pens/pencils
- A variety of materials for the small group activity (paper, straws, balloons, tape, glue sticks, etc.)

Handouts
Finding Balance, p. 374

Facilitator's Tip
Be enthusiastic…but not overly so. While your energy can help motivate and encourage some individuals, it might feel intimidating to others.

Notes
Because recovery effects the mind, body and spirit, finding a balance between them is very important. In the same way, participants will need to find a balance within each of the life domains in order to keep their life on a steady path of recovery.

Agenda

10 minutes — **Introduction**
1. Begin on time and welcome all participants.
2. Review the agenda for today's session.

25 minutes — **When We are Out of Alignment**
1. Read p. 319-321, having the group complete the questions and self-assessment.
2. Finish by having the participants decide on one thing they will commit to doing to better care for themselves.

25 minutes — **Small Group Activity: *Finding a Balance***
1. Divide the participants into two groups.
2. Pass out a variety of materials to each group.
3. Provide the following directions:
    a. Each group will take 10 minutes to create any type of building or structure they choose.
    b. Group #1 will build their structure with the largest part at the bottom (similar to a triangle with the base at the bottom).
    c. Group #2 will build their structure with the largest part at the top (similar to an inverted triangle).
4. At the end of the activity, lead a discussion using the following questions:
    a. Which structure do you think will be able to stand or last longer? Why?
    b. What worked well in the building process? What didn't?
    c. In what ways do the different structures illustrate the need for balance?

10 minutes — **Break**
Remind participants to return at the scheduled time.

40 minutes — **Exercise: *Finding Balance***
For many individuals, this exercise is a good visual reminder of what they may be lacking in their lives. For others, the ability to see how much time is devoted to certain activities is an ideal motivator for change. This exercise is especially effective if each section of the "pie" is done in a different color or format.
1. Read the directions to the exercise on p. 322.
2. Using the handout or another piece of paper, help the participants determine what activities they do and how much time they spend on each.
3. Add each activity to the circle, dividing the time like a piece of pie (the "slices" will be different sizes depending on the amount of time devoted to each activity).

Cont.	**Exercise: *Finding Balance, cont.***
4. Once the circle for the current activities are completed, have the group review the drawings and answer the questions at the bottom of p. 322 and the top of p. 323.
5. Next, have the group complete a circle of how they would "prefer" to be spending their time.
6. As a group, discuss the changes made between the two circles. (What are the changes and why have they been made?)
7. Finally, have the group complete the questions at the bottom of p. 323.

10 minutes	**Review the Day's Session**
1. Provide the reading assignment for the next session.
2. Remind the group of the next session and thank them for coming.

Personal Notes

Session #12
Living "In the Moment"

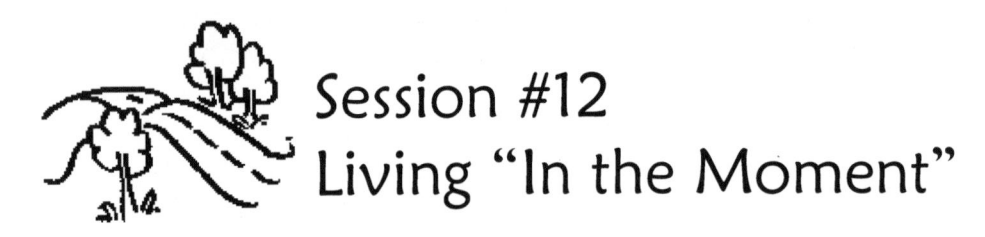

Overview
During session #12, participants will be introduced to the idea of seeing what is happening "now" or what it is like to live "in the moment." Participants will also have an opportunity to evaluate their experience in the group up to this point.

Goals
During this session, participants will:
1. Discuss the importance of living in the moment.
2. Practice observation skills.
3. Identify at least two ideas or activities to help bring more enjoyment in their lives.
3. Share their personal experience about using *Pathways to Recovery*.

Readings
Chapter 10, pp. 324-328

Quote
"Why are we here? We're here to feel the joy of life pulsing in us now." (Joyce Carol Oates, *Pathways to Recovery*, p. 324)

Materials
- *Pathways to Recovery* text
- Flip chart or white board and markers
- Pens/pencils

Handouts
These Things I Can.., p. 375
Mid-Session Satisfaction Survey, p. 344
Facilitator Self-Assessment, p. 345

Facilitator's Tip
Asking for—and receiving—feedback, especially when it appears negative, can be difficult for facilitators, especially when you are just starting out. But just as you would expect hard group interactions to be learning experiences for group members, the same is true of the evaluations you receive. Keep in mind that *all* feedback is necessary in order for you to become a better and more skillful facilitator.

Notes

Remember, evaluation is vital to becoming a better facilitator. Be prepared for compliments and criticisms. This is an opportunity for you to make changes to provide a greater learning experience for all group members. You may also want to invite someone to take notes or record participant's answers on the flip chart or white board. If you are uncomfortable or you would like to give the group an opportunity to be completely honest, consider asking someone who is not part of the group to conduct the evaluation. Finally, be sure to complete your own self-assessment.

Agenda

10 minutes   **Introduction**
1. Begin on time and welcome all participants.
2. Review the agenda for today's session.

20 minutes   **Enjoying the Present Moment**
1. Read p. 324.
2. Lead a discussion using the following questions:
   a. In what ways do you feel you are living in the present?
   b. In what ways do you get the message to either live in the past or in the future?
   c. What did Thornton Wilder mean when he wrote, "enjoy your ice cream while it is on your plate"?

15 minutes   **Group Activity: *Now You See It, Now You Don't!***
1. Have the group stand and pair up with one other person.
2. Give each pair 30 seconds to look at each other.
3. On the count of three, have the pair turn with their backs to each other.
4. Next, each person should change five things about themselves (for example, take their glasses off, remove their hat, switch their jewelry from one side to the other, etc.).
5. Have each pair see if they can notice the changes that have been made.
6. Lead a discussion using the following questions:
   a. How many of you were able to figure out all five changes?
   b. Why was it hard to find all the changes?
   c. What does this activity have to do with living in the present moment?

15 minutes   **Small Group Activity: *These Things I Can...***
One of the easiest ways to begin living in the moment is to begin paying attention to our senses — what we can see, hear, taste, touch and smell. This exercise will help the group start to become aware of what is around them.

Cont. **Small Group Activity: *These Things I Can...*, cont.**
1. Pass out the handout.
2. Give the group five minutes to look around the room, out the windows, etc. and write down as many things as possible that they can see, hear, taste, touch and smell.
3. Lead a discussion using the following questions:
    a. How many things were you able to name in each category?
    b. Did you list anything in more than one category? Why or why not?
    c. Did you notice anything new or different?
4. Encourage the group to complete the exercise on pp. 326-327 as homework.

10 minutes **Break**
Remind participants to return at the scheduled time.

30 minutes **Mid-Session Evaluation**
Evaluation can be a powerful tool in giving voice to participants. Encourage and respect open and honest comments.
1. Lead a discussion focusing on how the participants view the success of the sessions thus far. Use all or part of these questions:
    a. How has the experience of attending the sessions benefitted your recovery?
    b. What is your favorite part of the group? Why?
    c. What is your least favorite part of the group? Why?
    d. What do I (the facilitator or co-facilitators) do to help you learn?
    e. What suggestions can you offer to make the group better?
    f. What could I (the facilitator or co-facilitators) do to improve the group?
    g. As a group, do you feel we are staying true to the "Partnership Pact?"
    h. Do you feel you are able to uphold the "Recovery Pledge?" Why or why not?
    i. Does anyone have a need for support around his or her recovery efforts?

10 minutes **Written Evaluation**
1. Pass out "Mid-Session Satisfaction Survey."
2. Ask the group to complete the form and leave it with you. Be sure to let them know their comments are anonymous and will only be used to make changes in the group as needed.

10 minutes **<u>Review the Day's Session</u>**
1. Provide the reading assignment for the next session.
2. Remind the group of the next session and thank them for coming.

Personal Notes

Session #13
Travel Tips

Overview
Session #13 examines six common but necessary travel tips to help the recovery journey go more smoothly.

Goals
During this session, participants will:
1. Discuss six common travel tips for the recovery journey.
2. Identify at least one travel tip that is important to them.
3. List at least two more tips they have found helpful.

Readings
Chapter 10, pp. 329-332

Quote
"My fear of change caused me a lot of anguish and heartache until I learned to accept some simple facts of life: change is the only constant—the trick is to learn to see it as just another opportunity to grow, a chance to transform yourself from the person you are into the person you want to be. When you fear it, you fight it. And when you fight it, you block the blessing." (Patti Labelle, *Pathways to Recovery*, p. 330)

Materials
- *Pathways to Recovery* text
- Flip chart or white board and markers
- Pens/pencils

Handouts
- The Road Leads Home, 376

Facilitator's Tip
One thing most experienced facilitators have is a box or container of items that they *might* need. This could include things such as extra pens or markers, tape, paper clips, tissues, safety pins, mints, aspirin, scissors, extra paper or any item that you could need quickly. You might also want to include a screw driver or electrical cord and extra batteries. Be sure to check the container after sessions and replace any items used.

Notes

The opening activity for today's session is meant to be fun but will also get the participants traveling! In addition to the description given, you could also have individuals move two spaces forward or three steps back (remember "recovery whiplash"?).

Agenda

10 minutes **Introduction**
1. Begin on time and welcome all participants.
2. Review the agenda for today's session.

10 minutes **Activity: *The Road Leads Home***
1. Have participants form a circle.
2. As you read each of the questions from the handout, if individuals can answer "yes," have them take one step to the right. If they must answer "no," they will stay where they are (this will force some individuals to be "stacked" 2-3 or more at a time). The first person back to their original space wins.

30 minutes **Small Group Activity: *Enhancing the Travel Tips***
1. Divide participants into three small groups and ask them to choose one person to record their ideas.
2. Assign (or have the groups choose) two travel tips to discuss (don't duplicate the tips). Ask the small groups to do the following:
   a. Read each tip and discuss.
   b. As a group, develop at least five positive ways to use each tip (each small group will present their information to the larger group).

10 minutes **Break**
Remind participants to return at the scheduled time.

35 minutes **Group Discussion**
1. Ask each reporter to share highlights of their discussion.
2. List each group's suggestions on the flip chart or white board.
3. Add any suggestions from the rest of the participants.
4. Lead a discussion using the following questions:
   a. How do these travel tips apply to your everyday life?
   b. Are there other travel tips that you have found helpful or would recommend to others?
   c. Of all the tips, which one do you feel is most beneficial for you to follow? Why?

15 minutes   **Sharing Our Stories:** *Julie*
  1. Read Julie's story on p. 331.
  2. Lead a discussion using the following questions:
     a. How does Julie use the travel tips to keep her on course?
     b. In what ways can you follow Julie's example?

10 minutes   **Review the Day's Session**
  1. Provide the reading assignment for the next session.
  2. Remind the group of the next session and thank them for coming.

Personal Notes

Session #14
Supercharging Strategy: Affirmations

Overview
Session #14 examines the final supercharging strategy from Chapter 12 – affirmations. In addition to learning the basics of how to write an affirmation, the group will spend time developing their own.

Goals
During this session, participants will:
1. Examine why affirmations are important.
2. Create at least one personal affirmation in multiple life areas.
3. Discuss one person's experience of the power of using affirmations.

Readings
Chapter 11, pp. 358-364

Quote
"The past is over and done and has no power over me. I can begin to be free in this moment. Today's thoughts create my future. I am in charge. I now take my own power back. I am safe and I am free." (Louise L. Hay, *Pathways to Recovery*, p. 363)

Materials
- *Pathways to Recovery* text
- Flip chart or white board and markers
- Pens/pencils
- Index cards (see "Notes")

Facilitator's Tip
Many facilitator's use affirmations to help them relax before the session or even during a group to keep them focused. They can also be very helpful when you're feeling uncertain about your skills or if you receive a difficult evaluation.

Notes
A good homework assignment for this session would be to give each participant 5-6 index cards on which they could write their favorite affirmations. These could then be kept in a purse or backpack or posted in a place they will see them frequently.

Agenda

10 minutes

Introduction
1. Begin on time and welcome all participants.
2. Review the agenda for today's session.

10 minutes

Why Use Affirmations?
1. Read pp. 358-359 (start at "Supercharging Strategy #6" and end at "How Do We Create").
2. Lead a short discussion using the following questions:
    a. How does using affirmations relate to all we've been talking about?
    b. If it is true that affirmations "show us the amazing power of our words," in what ways do you consider your words powerful?

20 minutes

Creating Powerful Affirmations
1. Read the qualities of a good affirmation on pp. 359-360 (start at "How Do We Create" and end at "Creating Affirmations").
2. Ask for one of the group members to give an example of an affirmation. Write it on the flip chart or white board.
3. Using this example, walk through each of the affirmation tips to see if it fits the guidelines. Make changes as needed.

10 minutes

What Affirmations Have You Used?
1. Make a list of affirmations that the group members have used.
2. If time permits, ask for specific examples of how the affirmations have been beneficial.

10 minutes

Break
Remind participants to return at the scheduled time.

30 minutes

Creating Affirmations
In creating these affirmations, you can use the life areas listed or the life domains covered during Module Three.
1. Write each of the affirmation categories (pp. 360-362) at the top of a large piece of paper and hang around the room.
2. Ask participants to move around the room and add an affirmation to each category.
3. Have the group read through all the affirmations.
4. Finish by discussing ways to keep and use the affirmations (see examples on pp. 362-363 and ask for group suggestions). Encourage individuals to adopt at least one affirmation they will try to use.

20 minutes **Sharing Our Stories:** *Suzette*
Suzette's story, aptly entitled "The Power of Affirmations," is a great example of how one individual began using affirmations—even though she wasn't sure they would work. Her persistence paid off and allowed her to use these new "tools" to make her life better.
  1. Read Suzette's story on pp. 363-364.
  2. Lead a discussion using the following questions:
     a. Suzette talks of negative self-talk and being "tired of my depression." How did using affirmations help her overcome these feelings?
     b. Why do you think affirmations can compliment other practices?
     c. What is the "magical stillness" Suzette discovered?

10 minutes **Review the Day's Session**
  1. Provide the reading assignment for the next session.
  2. Remind the group of the next session and thank them for coming.

Personal Notes

Session #15
Why Tell Your Story?

Overview
Session #15 begins the exploration of why and how to tell a personal story of recovery. Participants will also meet in their small groups to continue planning their presentations

Goals
During this session, participants will:
1. Meet with their small groups to continue planning their presentation.
2. Examine the common features of one's story.
3. Discuss three of the six reasons why telling stories is important to recovery.

Readings
Chapter 12, pp. 375-384

Quote
"I haven't a clue as to how my story will end. But that's all right. When you set out on a journey and night covers the road, you don't conclude that the road has vanished. And how else could we discover the stars?" (Author Unknown, *Pathways to Recovery*, p. 377)

Materials
- *Pathways to Recovery* text
- Flip chart or white board and markers
- Pens/pencils

Facilitator's Tip
When individuals are reporting back from their small group activities, avoid adding your own thoughts and comments. If you share too much yourself, others may be hesitant to talk or may remain silent. Instead, let participants take ownership of their own ideas.

Notes
Telling one's story is the culmination of all that has been discussed during this and previous modules. The ability to tell our stories provides healing, understanding and connection to others.

You will probably find it difficult to facilitate a group on stories without everyone telling their story! While that may sound like a contradiction, most of us do have a need to share and make sense of our personal experiences. You will want to allow some time for sharing although each session on personal stories will provide specific time to do so. Be sure to remind the group to keep their stories focused and without specific details.

Notes, cont.
Get an update on the progress of the small group projects. If barriers or problems are present, schedule a brainstorming time to help them.

Agenda

10 minutes — **Introduction**
1. Begin on time and welcome all participants.
2. Review the agenda for today's session.

20 minutes — **Small Group Project Planning**
1. Provide time for the small groups to work on their project.
2. Assist them with planning as needed.

20 minutes — **The Importance of Telling Our Story**
1. Read p. 375.
2. Lead a discussion using the following questions:
    a. If it is true stories are everywhere, in what places or times do we tell our story?
    b. How does listening to the stories of others benefit you?
    c. Why is listening and telling of stories so important?

10 minutes — **Break**
Remind participants to return at the scheduled time.

20 minutes — **Small Group Activity: *Why Stories are Important***
This activity will begin during this session and continue during Session #16. The topics for today are: (1) (re)making history, (2) gaining perspective and meaning and (3) connecting with others.
1. Divide the participants into three groups and ask them to choose one person to record their ideas.
2. Assign each group one topic from pp. 376-378.
3. Ask the groups to do the following:
    a. Read their respective topics.
    b. Discuss the material and share personal examples.
    c. Finally, have the group decide on one example that best fits the topic that they will share with the larger group.

20 minutes — **Group Sharing**
1. Ask each reporter to give a brief description of their topic and share the group's chosen story.

10 minutes   **Sharing Our Stories:** *Pat*
  1. Read Pat's story on p. 379.
  2. Lead a short discussion using the following question:
     a. Why is Pat's statement important to you?

10 minutes   **Review the Day's Session**
  1. Provide the reading assignment for the next session.
  2. Remind the group of the next session and thank them for coming.

Personal Notes

_____
_____
_____
_____
_____
_____
_____
_____
_____
_____
_____
_____

Session #16
Why Tell Your Story?, cont.

Overview
Session #16 continues the discussion of the importance of telling one's story. The group will also take time to share their own stories within the format of a story circle.

Goals
During this session, participants will:
1. Continue the discussion of why telling stories is important to recovery.
2. Share parts of their personal stories within a small group format.

Readings
Chapter 12, pp. 385-389

Quote
"Seeing is of course very much a matter of verbalization. Unless I call attention to what passes before my eyes, I simply won't see...It's all a matter of keeping my eyes open." (Annie Dillard, *Pathways to Recovery*, p. 386)

Materials
- *Pathways to Recovery* text
- Flip chart or white board and markers
- Pens/pencils

Handouts
- Story Circle Questions, p. 377

Facilitator's Tip
Present activities and tasks in a clear and simple manner. If everyone understands what to do, there is a better chance they will do it well and be more willing to try the activity. It is also helpful to have tasks broken down and written on a flip chart or white board so everyone can see them as they are completing the activity.

Notes
As will be read and discussed, telling one's story to others can be a very healing activity. Many people are afraid to speak in front of others and that keeps them from sharing their story.

Notes, cont.
Sharing stories is also a wonderful way to reduce the stigma of mental illness. If the participants would like to publicly share their story, they may want to get some assistance with not only writing their story but to practice it and get feedback. Many agencies and organizations actively look for individuals to be part of a speaker's bureau.

Agenda

10 minutes — **Introduction**
1. Begin on time and welcome all participants.
2. Review the agenda for today's session.

20 minutes — **Small Group Activity: *Why Stories are Important***
This activity continues from Session #15. The topics for today are: (1) helping us heal, (2) learning to contend with challenges and (3) becoming role models to others.
1. Divide the participants into three groups and ask them to choose one person to record their ideas.
2. Assign each group one topic from pp. 379-383.
3. Ask the groups to do the following:
    a. Read their respective topics (groups do not necessarily need to answer the questions listed but may find them helpful in their discussions).
    b. Discuss the material and have the group share personal examples.
    c. Finally, have the group decide on one example that best fits the topic that they will share with the larger group.

20 minutes — **Group Sharing**
1. Ask each reporter to give a brief description of their topic and share the group's chosen story.

10 minutes — **Sharing Our Stories: *Janice***
1. Read Janice's story on p. 382.
2. Lead a short discussion using the following question:
    a. Janice talks of the "memories of people who have touched my life" and how she has touched theirs. Can you agree with this comment? Why or why not?

10 minutes — **Break**
Remind participants to return at the scheduled time.

30 minutes **Story Circle**
This activity simply gives participants an opportunity to share their story with others. While there is no discussion planned, encourage the groups to share, listen and have fun!
  1. Divide participants into small groups of 3-4 people.
  2. Ask the participants to do the following:
     a. Choose one of the questions from the handout and share their answer — their story — with the group.
     b. Be sure to keep the stories short so everyone has time to share and ask questions. Also remind the participants to limit details of difficult situations or challenges.

10 minutes **Sharing Our Stories: *Anonymous***
  1. Finish today's session by sharing the story on p. 384.
  2. Encourage participants to spend time thinking about and working on developing their own story.

10 minutes **Review the Day's Session**
  1. Provide the reading assignment for the next session.
  2. Remind the group of the next session and thank them for coming.

Personal Notes

Session #17
Beginning the Process

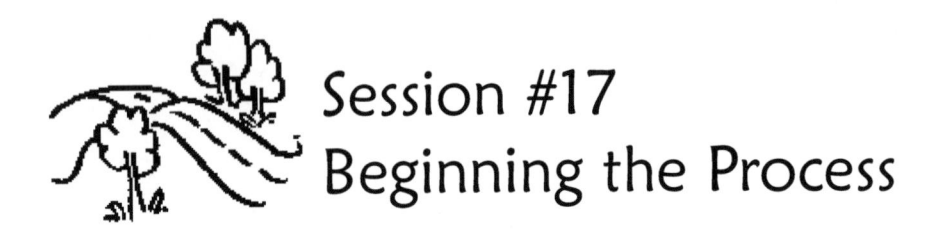

Overview
Session #17 gives participants the opportunity to begin developing their personal story.

Goals
During this session, participants will:
1. Learn at least three methods for designing a recovery story.
2. Develop a plan for making time to create their story.
3. Examine the seven stages of storytelling.
4. Practice using the stages to develop a personal story.

Readings
Chapter 12, pp. 385-389

Quote
"Each person's life is a story that is telling itself in the living." (William Bridges, *Pathways to Recovery*, p. 385)

Materials
- *Pathways to Recovery* text
- Flip chart or white board and markers
- Pens/pencils

Handouts
- Writing Your Story, p. 378

Facilitator's Tip
As they begin creating their story, participants may experience strong emotions; laughter, tears, anger and guilt are all common to the experience. Instead of discouraging such emotions, let the group know this is common. For most people, developing their story is as much about the process as it is about the ultimate product.

Notes
Telling your story doesn't mean you have to tell *everything*. Let participants know that others will only know what they choose to say. Remember that telling too much information (such as specific traumas, abuses or "gory" details) will only cause people to stop listening or to be triggered if they have been through similar experiences. Be sure to have group members follow these guidelines as they share their stories.

Agenda

10 minutes — **Introduction**
1. Begin on time and welcome all participants.
2. Review the agenda for today's session.

20 minutes — **How to Begin**
1. Read p. 385.
2. Lead a discussion using the following questions:
    a. Have you used any of these suggestions to begin telling your story? If so, how have they been helpful?
    b. Are there other ways you can think of that will help you develop your story?

20 minutes — **Writing Your Story**
1. Read p. 386.
2. Have the group complete the questions and share their responses.

10 minutes — **Break**
Remind participants to return at the scheduled time.

15 minutes — **Stages in Creating & Sharing Your Story**
1. One by one, read through the stages listed on pp. 387-388.
2. Answer questions as needed.

35 minutes — **Small Group Activity:** *Writing Your Story*
1. Read p. 389.
2. Divide participants into groups of 2-3 people.
3. Have them choose one of the questions from p. 389.
4. Using the handout, have the groups walk through each stage, listing ideas and activities they would use to develop a story.
5. Have groups share their ideas and experiences with the activity.

10 minutes — **Review the Day's Session**
1. Provide the reading assignment for the next session.
2. Remind the group of the next session and thank them for coming.

Personal Notes

_____

_____

_____

Session #18
How & Where to Share Your Story

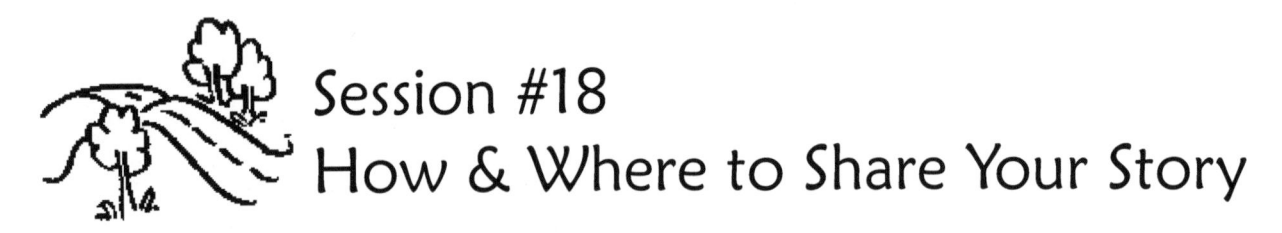

Overview
Session #18 looks at the options for how and where to publicly share one's story. In addition, participants will also meet in their small groups to finalize their small group presentations.

Goals
During this session, participants will:
1. Examine at least four ways to share their story with others.
2. List at least one or two ways to celebrate the creation of their story.
2. Meet with their small groups to finalize plans for their presentation.

Readings
Chapter 12, pp. 390-393

Quote
"To write about one's life is to live it twice, and the second living is both spiritual and historical, for a memoir reaches deep within the personality as it seeks its narrative form." (Patricia Hampl, *Pathways to Recovery*, p. 391)

Materials
- *Pathways to Recovery* text
- Flip chart or white board and markers
- Pens/pencils

Facilitator's Tip
The Internet is a great way to learn new techniques, fresh ideas for activities or find further information on a specific topic. Use trusted sites or recommendations from those you know to search for information (there are several sites listed in the "Resources" section on p. 385.

Notes
One tip that can help participants in writing their own story is that, if they have used journaling or art as part of their recovery, they can use it for inspiration to develop their story. If participants are wanting to try and publish their story, they can use notes from their journals, poetry they have written, drawing or paintings, etc. that reflect their thoughts &/or feelings at the time.

Agenda

10 minutes — **Introduction**
1. Begin on time and welcome all participants.
2. Review the agenda for today's session.

15 minutes — **Sharing Stories of Recovery**
1. Read p. 390.
2. Have the group complete the questions in the workbook.
3. Using the individual's responses, create a group list of the people who could benefit from hearing recovery stories.

10 minutes — **Sharing Our Stories: *Chris***
1. Read Chris's story on p. 391.
2. Lead a short discussion using the following question:
   a. How does this story encourage you to share your own?

15 minutes — **Sharing Stories of Recovery, cont.**
1. Read p. 391 (begin at "Put Your Story").
2. Lead a discussion using the following questions:
   a. Do you know of specific websites or publications that accept and publish recovery stories?
   b. What are the advantages of sharing your story in one of these places? What are the personal barriers?

10 minutes — **Break**
Remind participants to return at the scheduled time.

30 minutes — **Sharing Our Stories: *Shelly***
Shelly's story is an excellent example of someone who has incorporated many of the tools and skills that have been discussed during this and previous modules (for example, focusing on strengths, using affirmations, accepting change, using and revamping her social supports, etc.).
1. Read Shelly's story on pp. 392-393.
2. Lead a discussion using the following questions:
   a. What do you think about Shelly's story?
   b. In what ways can you relate to her journey?
   c. Of all we've discussed during our own group journey, what skills and tools has Shelly used?
   d. What do you think is the most important message in this recovery story?
3. Finish by reading p. 393 (after the story). Have group members identify one thing they will do to celebrate writing and sharing their story.

20 minutes **Small Group Project Planning**
This will be the last scheduled time for groups to meet.
1. Provide time for the small groups to work on their project.
2. Assist them with planning as needed.

10 minutes **Review the Day's Session**
1. Provide the reading assignment for the next session.
2. Remind the group of the next session and thank them for coming.

Personal Notes

Session #19
Where Do We Go From Here?

Overview
Session #19 provides an opportunity for participants to creatively explore where they have been and where they would like to go next on their recovery journey.

Goals
During this session, participants will:
1. Discuss the aspects of learning they will use as they continue their journey.
2. Create a visual representation of how they would like see their ongoing journey.
3. Share final questions and comments as they look toward the future.

Readings
Chapter 12, pp. 394-395

Quote
"Your trek ends at ocean's edge. You cannot go farther. Yet you build a boat to carry your dreams, to carry you across the water." (Michael King Gowdy, *Pathways to Recovery*, p. 394)

Materials
- *Pathways to Recovery* text
- Flip chart or white board and markers
- Pens/pencils
- Art supplies (paper, old greeting cards or magazines, ribbon, stickers, scissors, glue sticks, tape, etc.)

Facilitator's Tip
Good facilitators know how to effectively end each session. Be careful not to just stop; rather, let the group know you are concluding. Review the highlights of the session, answer any questions the group may have and finish with an inspirational thought or words of encouragement. By properly ending, you can reinforce the learning that took place during the session.

Notes
Although the group will be looking at how to continue their journey today, this is not a time to evaluate the sessions; rather, participants will take time to discover the many parts of themselves that have been impacted by what they have learned throughout the modules. This activity can help "bring it all together" and encourage individuals to develop a better sense of how to continue their journey.

Agenda

10 minutes — **Introduction**
1. Begin on time and welcome all participants.
2. Review the agenda for today's session.

20 minutes — **The Ongoing Journey**
1. Read p. 394-395 (leave Michael's poem for later).
2. Lead a discussion using the following questions:
   a. What are some of the important aspects of recovery that you want to be sure to incorporate into your life?
   b. How do you envision your ongoing journey?
   c. What will you need from yourself to see this happen? What will you need from others?

30 minutes — **My Self-Portrait**
1. Using the available art supplies, have participants create a visual image of where they would like to be as they continue their exploration of the recovery journey. Some ideas include:
   a. A collage that includes the important elements to remember for the journey to be successful;
   b. A travel map indicating the steps to take which would make the journey positive and forward-moving;
   c. A completed puzzle with each piece representing a different aspect of the recovery journey.
2. Let the group know they will take time after the break to share their work with the larger group.

10 minutes — **Break**
Remind participants to return at the scheduled time.

30 minutes — **Where Do We Go from Here?**
1. Ask individuals to share their creative work with the group.
2. Encourage questions and celebrations of each person's work.

10 minutes — **Sharing Our Stories: *Michael***
1. Read Michael's poem on p. 394.
2. Ask the group for final thoughts and comments.

10 minutes — **Review the Day's Session**
1. Provide the reading assignment for the next session.
2. Remind the group of the next session and thank them for coming.

Personal Notes

Personal Notes

Session 20
Facilitator's Choice

Overview
This session allows the group to further explore subjects of interest or to examine sections of the *Pathways to Recovery* text not covered.

Goals
During this session, participants will (*to be determined by the group &/or the subject chosen*). List your goals below:

1.

2.

3.

Readings
To be determined by the group &/or the subject chosen.

Quote
"Once in a while you can get shown the light in the strangest of places if you look at it right." (Jerry Garcia, *Pathways to Recovery*, p. 325)

Materials
- *Pathways to Recovery* text
- Flip chart or white board and markers
- Pens/pencils

Handouts
To be determined by the group &/or the subject chosen.

Facilitator's Tip
One of the things most facilitator's do in planning group sessions is to build in extra time for activities and discussion, especially if you are fairly certain your group members will enjoy or find the topic particularly useful. Including a planned session such as the "Facilitator's Choice" gives you the opportunity to make sure you have the time to cover all the information you want to provide.

Notes

There are a variety of options for this session, including:

1. Covering previous topics in which the group needed more time.
2. The group may choose a topic/s in which they would like more information. However remember that, as the facilitator, you may need to spend time preparing materials.
3. Arrange for a special speaker to share with the group. This might include a peer role model or a panel of individuals who can talk about their recovery.
4. You may have local sites or museums that the group would like to visit.

At the end of the session, talk with the group about the upcoming end of Module Four. Discuss how they would like to celebrate the completion of the sessions. Each group is different and they will come up with unique ideas that will fit the members of the group. Here are some of the ways other *Pathways to Recovery* groups have celebrated:

- Have a pizza party or potluck dinner.
- Coordinate a craft or activity day.
- Get a movie and a pizza.
- Have lunch or dinner at a restaurant.
- Spend the day at the park (with a picnic, nature walk or other park activities).
- Attend a free concert.
- Take a special hike.
- Volunteer in the community together.

Since this is the last module, you may want to consider a special celebration if the group is completing the entire book. These are just a few suggestions:

- Playing a specially created game such as *Jeopardy*, *Wheel of Fortune* or other popular game show (questions and answers would be created around material learned during the modules)
- Individualized memory or scrap books
- Any ceremony or group ritual that would mark this "rite of passage"
- A group mandala
- A time capsule

You will also want to make some decisions on activities to recognize the progress and outcomes of this group. Recognition and validation is extremely important! Be creative and have fun!

Agenda

10 minutes **Introduction**
1. Begin on time and welcome all participants.
2. Review the agenda for today's session.

Agenda, cont.

40 minutes **Group Activity, cont.**
To be determined by the group &/or the subject chosen.

10 minutes **Break**
Remind participants to return at the scheduled time.

30 minutes **Group Activity**
To be determined by the group &/or the subject chosen.

20 minutes **Celebration Planning**
1. Talk with the group about the celebration during Session #24.
2. Provide a list of possible activities (see "Notes" section).
3. Decide what activity most represents the group.
4. If possible, ask the group members to share in the planning and preparation for the celebration.

10 minutes **Review the Day's Session**
1. Provide the reading assignment for the next session.
2. Remind the group of the next session and thank them for coming.

Personal Notes

Session #21
Small Group Project Presentations

Overview
Session #21 allows participants—within a small group format—to share more in-depth information on a topic of recovery.

Goals
During this session, participants will:
1. Present recovery-oriented information to the other group members.
2. Identify at least four aspects of recovery from the small group assignment presentations.

Readings
Small group participants will provide their own readings if needed

Quote
"What do we live for, if not to make life less difficult for each other?" (George Eliot, *Pathways to Recovery*, p. 201)

Materials
Small group participants will provide their own materials as needed

Handouts
Small group participants will provide their own handouts if needed

Facilitator's Tip
What topic of recovery would you like to learn about? Before your next sessions begin, take time to research special interests you have or a particular facilitation skill that you would like to sharpen or improve.

Notes
Your role as facilitator is to keep the presentations moving and on time. Don't allow one group to take more time than allotted. Keeping the groups on time shows respect for the other groups who have spent time planning and preparing for their presentation.

Take time to review the presentations with the group. Be sure to celebrate and recognize the accomplishments of each group. Encourage members to talk with their group peers if they are interested in learning more about a specific topic.

Agenda

10 minutes — **Introduction**
1. Begin on time and welcome all participants.
2. Review the agenda for today's session.

40 minutes — **Small Group Presentations**
1. Allow a few extra minutes if a group needs to do any set up for their presentation.
2. Introduce each small group, their members and their project.
3. Validate each group's efforts in presenting information to the larger group.

10 minutes — **Break**
Remind participants to return at the scheduled time.

40 minutes — **Small Group Presentations, cont.**
1. Continue the presentations.

10 minutes — **Discussion and Thanks**
1. Briefly discuss what group members have learned from their peers in today's session.
2. Thank each group and acknowledge them for their efforts and courage in presenting to their peers.

10 minutes — **Review the Day's Session**
1. Provide the reading assignment for the next session.
2. Remind the group of the next session and thank them for coming.

Personal Notes

_____
_____
_____
_____
_____
_____
_____
_____
_____

Session #22
Small Group Project Presentations

Overview
Session #22 continues the small group presentations, allowing participants — within a small group format — to share more in-depth information on a topic of recovery.

Goals
During this session, participants will:
1. Present recovery-oriented information to the other group members.
2. Identify at least four aspects of recovery from the small group assignment presentations.

Readings
Small group participants will provide their own readings if needed

Quote
"The man who moved a mountain was the one who began by carrying away small stones." (Chinese Proverb, *Pathways to Recovery*, p. 307)

Materials
Small group participants will provide their own materials as needed

Handouts
Small group participants will provide their own handouts if needed

Facilitator's Tip
Are there current group members who you think would make good co-facilitators during your next *Pathways to Recovery* groups? Having identified peer facilitators or supporters is very helpful to the overall group process and one that most group participants will find both comforting and motivating. Talk with these individuals and support their leadership abilities.

Notes
Remember, your role as facilitator is to keep the presentations moving and on time. Don't allow one group to take more time than allotted. Keeping the groups on time shows respect for the other groups who have spent time planning and preparing for their presentation.

Notes, cont.

Take time to review the presentations with the group. Be sure to celebrate and recognize the accomplishments of each group. Encourage members to talk with their group peers if they are interested in learning more about a specific topic.

Agenda

10 minutes — **Introduction**
1. Begin on time and welcome all participants.
2. Review the agenda for today's session.

40 minutes — **Small Group Presentations**
1. Allow a few extra minutes if a group needs to do any set up for their presentation.
2. Introduce each small group, their members and their project.
3. Validate each group's efforts in presenting information to the larger group.

10 minutes — **Break**
Remind participants to return at the scheduled time.

40 minutes — **Small Group Presentations, cont.**
1. Continue the presentations.

10 minutes — **Discussion and Thanks**
1. Briefly discuss what group members have learned from their peers in today's session.
2. Thank each group and acknowledge them for their efforts and courage in presenting to their peers.

10 minutes — **Review the Day's Session**
1. Provide the reading assignment for the next session.
2. Remind the group of the next session and thank them for coming.

Personal Notes

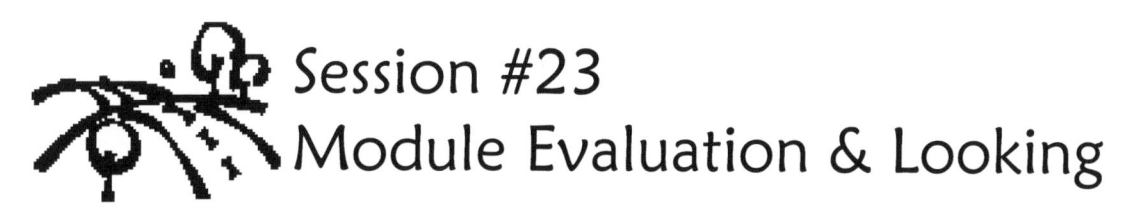

Session #23
Module Evaluation & Looking

Overview
Session #23 will allow participants to reflect on the past sessions and share any ideas or comments about what they have learned. It will also allow group members to formally evaluate their own experience.

Goals
During this session, participants will:
1. State at least three learning experiences from participating in Module Four of the
   Pathways to Recovery group.
2. State what they liked and disliked about the sessions.

Readings
None

Quote
"You must be the change you wish to see in the world." (Mahatma Ghandi, *Pathways to Recovery*, p. 19)

Materials
- *Pathways to Recovery* text
- Flip chart or white board and marker
- Pens/pencils

Handouts
- Final Session Satisfaction Survey, p. 350
- Facilitator Self-Assessment, p. 345

Facilitator's Tip
Now is a good time to begin thinking about what you will do differently the next time you facilitate a *Pathways to Recovery* group. Look for what went well and what you need to change. Did your publicity work? Were certain sessions more difficult for you to facilitate? What went right? The best time to ask these questions is when the group events are fresh in your experience. Review the notes, participant evaluations and your own self-evaluations as a way to revise future sessions.

Notes

Remember, evaluation is vital to becoming a better facilitator. Be prepared for compliments and criticisms. You may want to invite someone to take notes or record participant's answers on the flip chart or white board. If you are uncomfortable or you would like to give the group an opportunity to be completely honest, consider asking someone who is not part of the group to conduct the evaluation. If you are completing all four modules, consider completing an assessment of the entire *Pathways to Recovery* group. Finally, don't forget to complete your own self-assessment.

Agenda

10 minutes — **Introduction**
1. Begin on time and welcome all participants.
2. Review the agenda for today's session.

15 minutes — **Small Group Activity: *Review of Module Four***
1. Divide participants into small groups of 3-4 people and ask them to choose one person to record their ideas.
2. Ask the group to make a list of the things they have learned in the group.

25 minutes — **Group Discussion**
1. Ask each reporter to share highlights from their discussion.
2. On the flip chart or white board, list the ideas given in categories for the different topics discussed (for example, recovery, identifying strengths, things needed for the journey, etc.).
3. If possible, record the responses and make copies for everyone.

10 minutes — **Break**
Remind participants to return at the scheduled time.

30 minutes — **Final Session Evaluation**
While some may feel sad the sessions are ending, remind them of all the things they have learned from the earlier discussion. Encourage participants to share and support each other in this stage of change. Allow ample time to share their feelings about the group.
1. Explain the importance of evaluating the participant's experiences during Module Four.
2. Lead a discussion using the following questions:
   a. What did you like about this module? Not like?
   b. What was your favorite session?
   c. What was your least favorite session?

Cont. **Final Session Evaluation, cont.**
      d. What would you change about the group?
      e. Have any of you had problems or experienced anything negative around your recovery so far? If so, how have you dealt with it or how do you plan to make changes?
      f. Does anyone need help with anything related to recovery or with what we have discussed during the sessions?
      g. What will you do now that you have completed the *Pathways to Recovery* group?

10 minutes **Written Satisfaction Survey**
Let participants know that the written forms are anonymous and will be used only to improve the next sessions. Share your appreciation for their honesty.
1. Hand out the "Final Session Satisfaction Survey."
2. Have participants complete the evaluation.

10 minutes **Celebration Planning**
1. Take this time to finalize plans for the celebration activities during Session #24.
2. If needed, remind participants of any details for the celebration (for example, change of location, time, things to bring, etc.).

10 minutes **Review the Day's Session**
1. Provide the reading assignment for the next session.
2. Remind the group of the next session and thank them for coming.

Personal Notes

Session #24
Celebration!

Overview
Session #24 reviews Module Four, with participants reflecting on their experience and learning. It also provides all group members the opportunity to celebrate individual and group accomplishments.

Goals
During this session, participants will:
1. Identify accomplishments, individually and for each member.
2. Celebrate the completion of Module Four &/or the completion of all the modules.

Readings
To be decided by the facilitator or the group

Quote
"It if is a quiet day, trust the stillness. If it is a day of action, trust the activity. If it is a time to wait, trust the pause. If it is a time to receive that which we have been waiting for, trust that it will happen clearly and with power, and receive the gift in joy!" (Unknown, *Pathways to Recovery*, p. 332)

Materials
Supplies for today's session will depend on what the group decides to do

Handouts
- Certificates of Achievement (or similar recognition), p. 379
- A Recovery Pledge, p. 380 (if needed)

Facilitator's Tip
It's just as important for you to celebrate the accomplishments you have made in facilitating the sessions. What will you do to reward yourself for the hard work you have done?

Notes
The activities for this final session should be predetermined by the participants. The main goal for today is to celebrate the accomplishments of coming together as a group to work on the journey of recovery.

Notes, cont.
You should also recognize individual accomplishments made during the sessions. Some suggestions include:

- Certificates of attendance or accomplishment
- Small gifts individualized for each person
- The same gift for each person
- A card or note with your personal thanks

Since this is the last session and completes the work on the entire *Pathways* text, you may want to do something special. How about a framed copy of the "Recovery Pledge" or a quote or verse the group found particularly important? Above all, make sure that *each* person is recognized and celebrated.

Agenda

10 minutes — **Introduction**
1. Begin on time and welcome all participants.
2. Review the agenda for today's session.

20 minutes — **Highlights of Module Four & The Recovery Pledge**
For many groups, the "Recovery Pledge" is a very important element to connect individuals and keep the group focused.
1. Start by having the group recite the "Recovery Pledge" (p. 20).
2. Lead a discussion using the following questions:
    a. Is this pledge still important to you?
    b. Does it mean anything different to you now?
    c. How do you think you have done upholding the pledge?
    d. What will you do to continue using the pledge after our group is over?
3. Using the flip chart or white board, make a list of the highlights and outcomes for Module Four.

On Your Own — **Celebration!**
1. Conduct the celebration activities.
2. Be sure to recognize each individual and their accomplishments during the session.

10 minutes — **Review the Day's Session**
1. Invite participants to join in attending other groups that may be available at your site.
2. Encourage the group members to stay in touch with each other and to participate in other recovery-based activities.
3. Thank each group member for participating.

Personal Notes

Handouts

"The greatest achievement of the human spirit
is to live up to one's opportunities
and make the most of one's resources."
~ Marquis de Vauvenargues

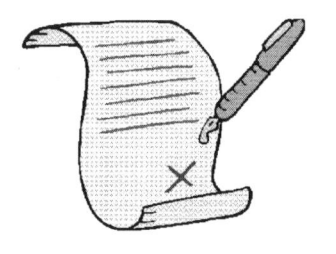

Reasons to Participate in the Pathways to Recovery Group

- You will create a **step-by-step plan** to guide you on the path of your recovery.

- You will **become more aware** of your values, cultural resources, talents, hopes, commitments and aspirations.

- You will determine what is **important to you** in many areas of your life.

- You will set **long-term and short-term goals** for your life — goals that truly reflect what is important to you.

- You will **plot a course** to move toward the kind of life you want.

- You will **discover resources** that you never knew were available to you which will help you reach your goals.

- You will **find ways to celebrate** every step that moves you closer to the life you want.

- You will find **companionship and support** from others as you attend the *Pathways to Recovery* group sessions.

Questions to Ask Yourself about Participating in the Pathways to Recovery Group

Please **DO NOT** put your name on this paper.
Give your answer to the facilitator when
you have finished answering the questions.

1. Why do you want to participate in this section of the *Pathways to Recovery* group?

2. What do you hope to get from attending the *Pathways to Recovery* sessions?

3. What unique thing about yourself can/will you contribute to the *Pathways to Recovery* sessions?

Pathways to Recovery
Handy Reminder for Group Members

The location of the group is _____

The day/s of the group are _____

The sessions will begin at _____ and end at _____

My group facilitator/s are _____

_____

I can call them at _____ or _____

Following are some **reminders** about participating in the *Pathways to Recovery* sessions:

- ☙ Please make sure that you bring your copy of *Pathways to Recovery* each session.

- ☙ There will be times during the sessions that, as a group, we will be making a variety of creative projects. Feel free to donate old magazines or art supplies as needed.

- ☙ To get the most out of the *Pathways to Recovery* sessions, we recommend that you be present at all sessions. If you do have to miss one, it's your responsibility to get in touch with the facilitator and find out what material you missed. It's also helpful to contact the facilitator to let them know you will not be attending.

- ☙ It's always good to have support. One of the ways to for this to happen within the group is for participants to exchange contact information (phone numbers, e-mail address, etc.). This way, if you need support or have questions between sessions, you can connect with someone. Please make sure that you do not share this information with others unless you have checked it out first with the individual.

- ☙ It's your responsibility to attend and actively participate in *Pathways to Recovery* group activities. Remember, you will only get out of the group what you put into it.

- ☙ It's your responsibility to uphold the "Partnership Pact" developed by group members.

- ☙ It's your responsibility to keep track of and not lose your copy of *Pathways to Recovery*.

- ☙ Be sure to ask your facilitator about bad weather policies or if there are any times when the group will not be meeting.

The Partnership Pact

The Partnership pact is the agreement made between our group members to insure a safe, supportive and strengths-based group based on each individual's unique values and needs.

I/we agree to abide by the following guidelines of the "Partnership Pact."

1. _____
2. _____
3. _____
4. _____
5. _____
6. _____
7. _____
8. _____
9. _____
10. _____
11. _____
12. _____
13. _____
14. _____
15. _____

Signatures of the group members:

Icebreaker Questions: Who Are You?

What is the best advice you have ever received?

What is your favorite time of day and why?

Whom do you respect the most and why?

What is your favorite food or meal?

After a busy day, how do you unwind?

What is one thing you've learned about yourself in the last 6 months?

For what in your life are you most grateful?

Which of your birthdays brings back the best memory and why?

What is the best thing that has happened to you during the last year?

What is a silly nickname someone has given you?

What is the best thing you have done for someone else this year?

What is the silliest thing you have ever done?

What is your favorite season of the year and why?

If you could meet one person dead or alive who would it be and why?

When you're feeling peaceful, where are you & what are you doing?

When you were a child what was your favorite toy?

What is your favorite holiday and why?

If money of were no object, where is the one place you'd go to visit & why?

Identifying My Strengths Worksheet

Your Name _____

*Please list below one strength you have seen in this person.
When finished, pass the list to the left until it reaches
the person whose name is listed above.*

Module One
Small Group Project Presentations
Instruction Sheet

This project is an opportunity for your small group to look at a recovery topic in which you are all interested. As a group, you will design your own project and then present it to the entire group during session #21 or 22.

Each presentation should be 10-15 minutes in length and focus on one topic related to Module One. Here are some examples of projects that can be done, however, your group is free to be creative and develop a new project!

1. Examine further ideas on how to use creativity in recovery.

2. Create a brochure for families or community members describing recovery. Discuss the brochure with the larger group.

3. Develop a skit to show a positive way of presenting recovery and mental illness in the media.

4. Read poetry or writings from famous individuals who have also ha symptoms of mental illness (such as William Styron, Virginia Wolff, Edgar Allan Poe, Emily Dickinson, etc.).

My group members are:

_____

_____

_____

_____

The topic we have chosen is_____

_____

_____

Our presentation will be given during this session_____

Great Movies that Inspire Hope

When you are in need of some hope, go to the movie rental store or your local public library and check out one of these titles. Or add your favorites to the list!

1. Lean on Me
2. Mr. Holland's Opus
3. It's a Wonderful Life
4. Milagro Bean Field War
5. Hope Floats
6. Benny & Joon
7. A Beautiful Mind
8. Erin Brokovich
9. October Sky
10. Fried Green Tomatoes
11. The Doctor
12. Lorenzo's Oil
13. Shawshank Redemption
14. Groundhog Day
15. Shine
16. Good Will Hunting
17. Dream Team
18. Radio
19. Stand & Deliver
20. Seabiscuit
21. Dead Poet's Society
22. Forrest Gump
23. _____
24. _____
25. _____
26. _____
27. _____
28. _____
29. _____
30. _____

Famous People with Mental Illness

Bette Midler
Entertainer
Charles Schultz
Cartoonist
Dick Clark
Entertainer
Irving Berlin
Composer
Rosemary Clooney
Singer
Burgess Merideth
Actor
Peter Tchaikovsky
Composer
Charlie Pride
Singer
Roseanne Barr
Comedian
Marlon Brando
Actor
Carrie Fischer
Actor
Lional Aldridge
Pro Football Player
Gaetano Donizetti
Composer
Buzz Aldrin
Astronaut
Margot Kidder
Actor
Vaslov Nijinsky
Dancer

Ricky Williams
Pro Football Player
Eugene O'Neill
Playwright
Abraham Lincoln
US President
Emily Dickinson
Poet
Ludwig van Beethoven
Composer
Vincent Van Gogh
Artist
Sir Isaac Newton
Scientist
Ernest Hemmingway
Write
Wolfgang Amadeus Mozart
Composer
Patty Duke
Actor
Charles Dickens
Writer
Benjamin Franklin
Inventor
Virginia Woolf
Writer
John Forbes Nash, Jr.
Scientist
Leo Tolstoy
Writer
Mike Wallace
Journalist

From the National Alliance for the Mentally Ill (NAMI)
www.nami.org

Pathways to Recovery
Mid-Session Satisfaction Survey

1. How **satisfied** are you so far with the entire group? Please circle your answer.

    Very Satisfied   Satisfied   Neutral   Somewhat Satisfied   Not Satisfied

2. What has been your **favorite part** of the sessions? Why?

3. What has been your **least favorite part** of the sessions? Why?

4. How would you rate the **skill of the facilitators** so far? Please circle your answer.

    Outstanding   Good   Average   Poor   Very Poor

    Please share any comments you may have about the facilitator/s.

5. What suggestions can your offer that would **improve upcoming sessions**?

6. Are there **any other comments** that you would like to share? Please feel free to use the back of the page if you need more room.

Thank you for sharing your ideas!

Facilitator Self-Assessment

On a scale of 1 to 10 (with 1 meaning *poor* and 10 meaning *excellent*), how would you rate your performance?

What did you do well? (*Give yourself credit!*)

What needs to be refined or adjusted?

Did anyone ask for extra help or resources? If so, what are they and how will you go about meeting the request/s?

Did you receive any compliments? What were they?

Is there anything you would like to do differently for the next session/module?

"STOP" Those Negative Thoughts!

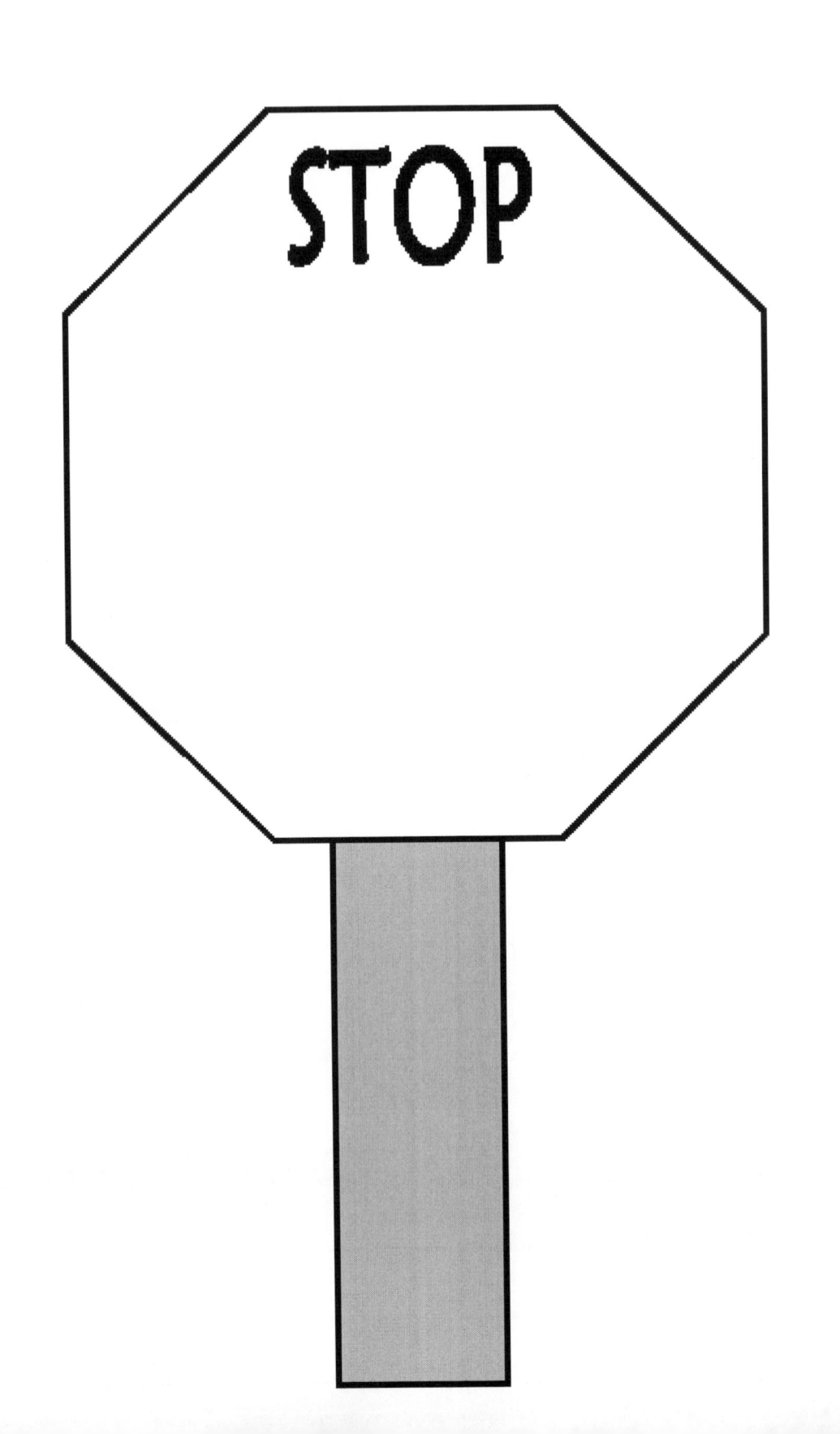

STOP

Positive/Negative Self-Talk Worksheet

Read each statement or question. Then write in your initial response in the column next to it. If your initial responses are more on the negative than positive side—take some time to come up with positive responses. Ask a friend for help if you are struggling with this. Take some time to feel the difference in how you feel when you answer with a negative response and then write down a positive response. PRACTICE responding to life positively!

Someone says this to you	Negative self-talking tells you this about yourself	Positive self-talking tells you this about yourself
"You have a wonderful life."		
"Look in this mirror. What do you see?"		
"Here, try on this new swimming suit!"		
"Will you go to a party with me? You probably won't know anyone there but me."		
"I need you to take this test please."		
"Will you sing/plan an instrument/read this poem at my wedding?"		
"Will you baby-sit (or pet-sit) for me?"		
"You are so creative! You've done such a wonderful job!"		

101 Ways to Celebrate!

*"The more you praise and celebrate your life,
the more there is in life to celebrate."*
~ *Oprah Winfrey*

1. _____	35. _____	69. _____
2. _____	36. _____	70. _____
3. _____	37. _____	71. _____
4. _____	38. _____	72. _____
5. _____	39. _____	73. _____
6. _____	40. _____	74. _____
7. _____	41. _____	75. _____
8. _____	42. _____	76. _____
9. _____	43. _____	77. _____
10. _____	44. _____	78. _____
11. _____	45. _____	79. _____
12. _____	46. _____	80. _____
13. _____	47. _____	81. _____
14. _____	48. _____	82. _____
15. _____	49. _____	83. _____
16. _____	50. _____	84. _____
17. _____	51. _____	85. _____
18. _____	52. _____	86. _____
19. _____	53. _____	87. _____
20. _____	54. _____	88. _____
21. _____	55. _____	89. _____
22. _____	56. _____	90. _____
23. _____	57. _____	91. _____
24. _____	58. _____	92. _____
25. _____	59. _____	93. _____
26. _____	60. _____	94. _____
27. _____	61. _____	95. _____
28. _____	62. _____	96. _____
29. _____	63. _____	97. _____
30. _____	64. _____	98. _____
31. _____	65. _____	99. _____
32. _____	66. _____	100. _____
33. _____	67. _____	101 _____
34. _____	68. _____	

Questions to Think About During the Movie

Does this movie feel "real" to you or "made up"? Why?

Does this movie have a hero/heroine? Who do you think it is? Why?

What about this movie motivates you?

What part of the story do you relate to the most?

What was your favorite part/scene of the movie?

Why do you think this movie was made?

What point is the movie trying to make?

Did the movie give you any ideas on how to increase your own motivation?

Are there any other movies you've seen that are like this movie?

Pathways to Recovery
Final Satisfaction Survey

1. How **satisfied** are you with the entire group? Please circle your answer.

    Very Satisfied   Satisfied   Neutral   Somewhat Satisfied   Not Satisfied

2. What was your **favorite part** of the sessions? Why?

3. What was your **least favorite part** of the sessions? Why?

4. How would you rate the **skill of the facilitators**? Please circle your answer.

    Outstanding   Good   Average   Poor   Very Poor

    Please share any comments you may have about the facilitator/s.

5. What suggestions can your offer that would **improve the group**?

6. Are there **any other comments** that you would like to share? Please feel free to use the back of the page if you need more room.

Thank you for sharing your ideas!

CERTIFICATE OF ACHIEVEMENT

presented to

_____

Pathways to Recovery: **MODULE ONE**

Name _____ Name _____

Date _____ Date _____

"To Live!"

"No matter what befalls me,
I feel commanded to
choose life.
You cannot give in to despair.
You may hit bottom,
but then you have a choice.
And to choose life
means an obligation
not merely to survive,
but to live."

~ Nessa Rapoport

Be a STAR!

For every session, print & cut out one square. Punch a hole in the top left-hand corner and use a ribbon or clip to hold the stars together. Participants will add a new star for each session covering the information from Chapter 9 on "Overcoming Detours & Roadblocks."

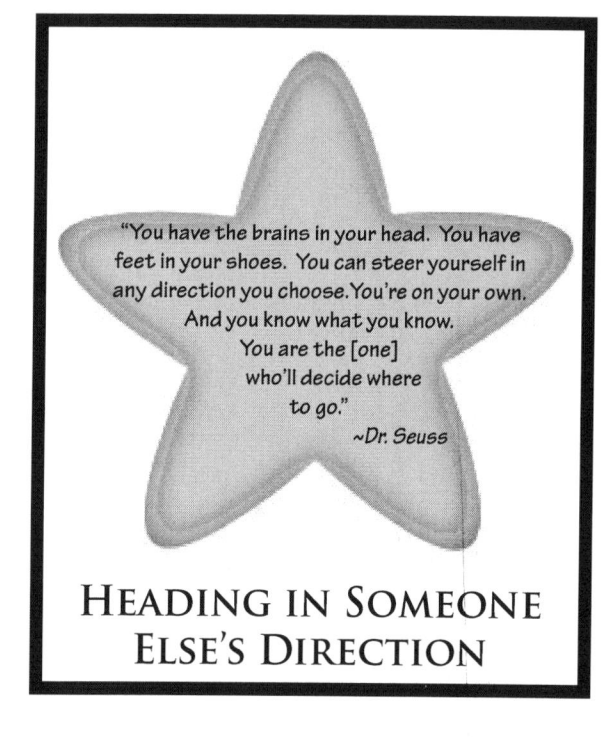

Be A STAR!

MOVING PAST DETOURS AND ROADBLOCKS

"What you need to know about the past is that no matter what has happened, it has all worked together to bring you to this very moment. And this is the moment you can choose to make everything new. Right now."
~Unknown

DRIVING USING THE REARVIEW MIRROR

"You have the brains in your head. You have feet in your shoes. You can steer yourself in any direction you choose. You're on your own. And you know what you know. You are the [one] who'll decide where to go."
~Dr. Seuss

HEADING IN SOMEONE ELSE'S DIRECTION

"Life just moves pretty fast. If you don't stop and look around sometimes you just might miss it."
~From Ferris Bueller's Day Off

DRIVING DAY AND NIGHT

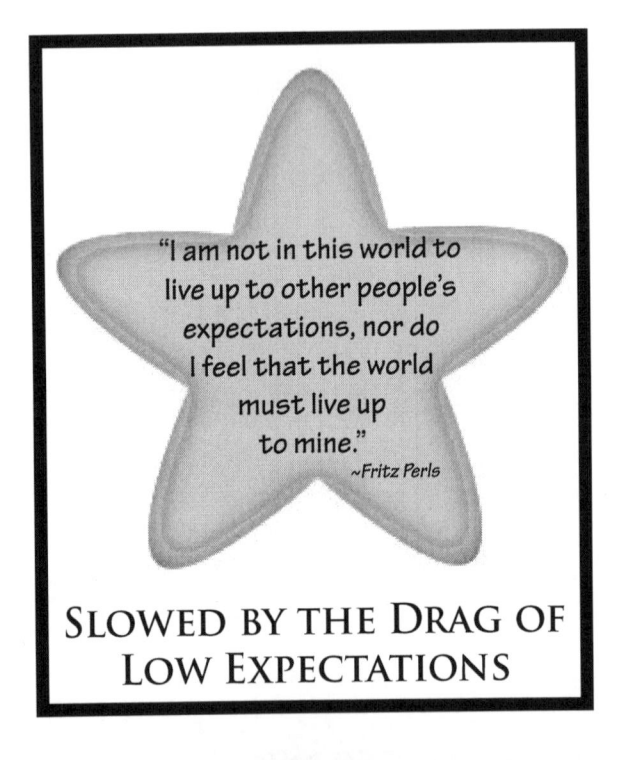

Be a STAR!, cont.

For every session, print & cut out one square. Punch a hole in the top left-hand corner and use a ribbon or clip to hold the stars together. Participants will add a new star for each session covering the information from Chapter 9 on "Overcoming Detours & Roadblocks."

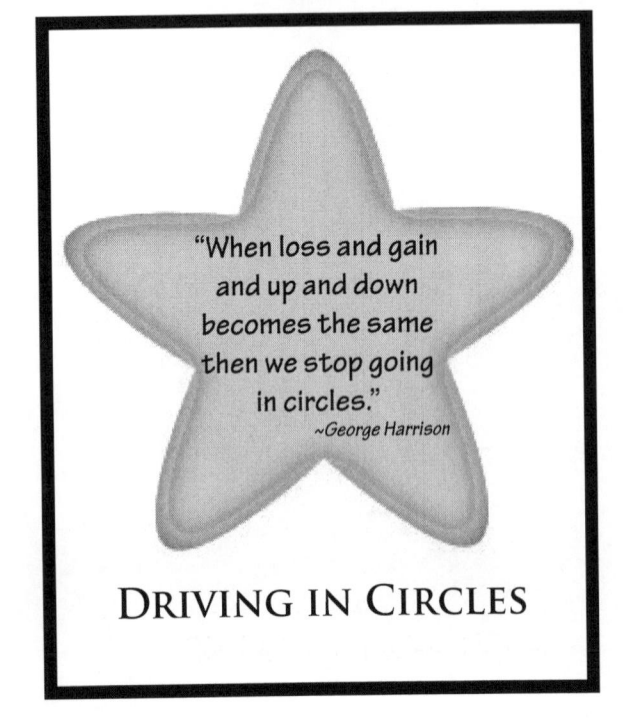

"I am not in this world to live up to other people's expectations, nor do I feel that the world must live up to mine."
~Fritz Perls

SLOWED BY THE DRAG OF LOW EXPECTATIONS

"When there is no enemy within, the enemies outside can not hurt you."
~African Proverb

HEALING SELF-STIGMA

"When loss and gain and up and down becomes the same then we stop going in circles."
~George Harrison

DRIVING IN CIRCLES

"Movement without direction will create a hole in the ground."
~Sophia Bedford-Pierce

FEELING LOST

Be a STAR!, cont.

For every session, print & cut out one square. Punch a hole in the top left-hand corner and use a ribbon or clip to hold the stars together. Participants will add a new star for each session covering the information from Chapter 9 on "Overcoming Detours & Roadblocks."

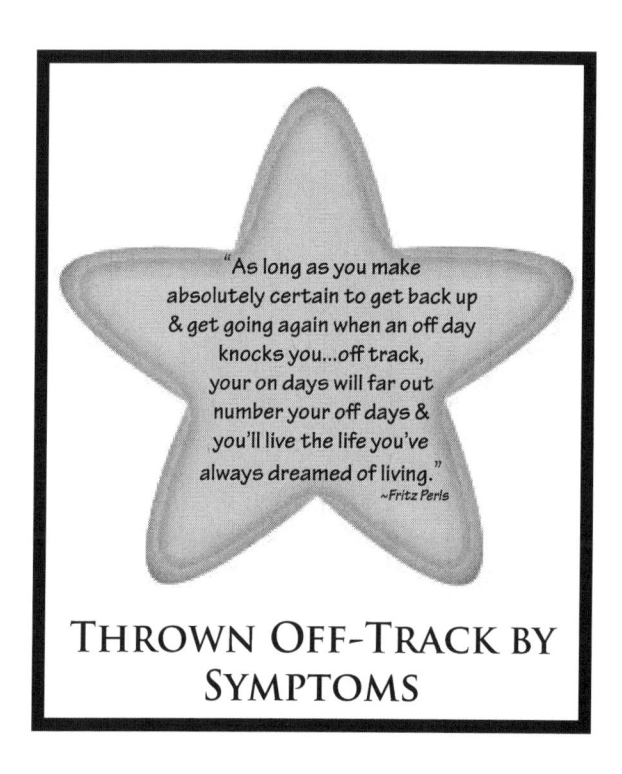

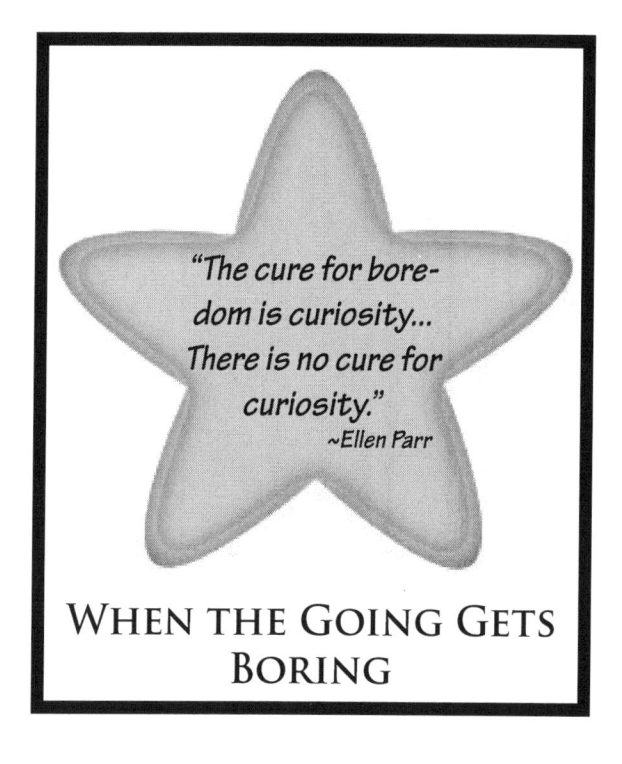

"As long as you make absolutely certain to get back up & get going again when an off day knocks you...off track, your on days will far out number your off days & you'll live the life you've always dreamed of living."
~Fritz Perls

THROWN OFF-TRACK BY SYMPTOMS

"It just so happened that I was riding the brake for so long -- it caught fire -- I lost my vision -- and that was all there was."
~Unknown

RIDING THE BRAKE PEDAL

"The cure for boredom is curiosity... There is no cure for curiosity."
~Ellen Parr

WHEN THE GOING GETS BORING

You are a STAR!

MOVING PAST DETOURS AND ROADBLOCKS

Module Two
Small Group Project Presentations
Instruction Sheet

This project is an opportunity for your small group to look at a recovery topic in which you are all interested. As a group, you will design your own project and then present it to the entire group during session #21 or 22.

Each presentation should be 10-15 minutes in length and focus on one topic related to Module Two. Here are some examples of projects that can be done, however, your group is free to be creative and develop a new project!

1. Other meditation or visualization exercises

2. Examining the life of someone who overcame roadblocks.

3. Creating a positive quotation booklet for everyone in the group.

4. Creating a game to play (like bingo or *Life*, etc.) focusing on the group member's strengths.

My group members are:

_____

_____

_____

_____

The topic we have chosen is_____

_____

_____

Our presentation will be given during this session_____

Arrivals & Departures

"Working on yourself is one thing; working yourself over is something else."
~ Victoria Moran

Healing self-stigma requires a lot of effort and time to change negative thoughts and behaviors. In the spaces below, list those things you would like to keep—your "arrivals" and those things you would like to rid yourself of—your "departures."

ARRIVALS *Behaviors to Keep*	DEPARTURES *Behaviors to Let Go*

"Re-Frame" Relapse

"[In my recovery] progress did not come easy, by any means. Often it was a matter of reminding myself that three steps forward and two steps back, is still progress. Other times, it has been necessary to try to conceive of the fact that three steps forward and five steps back, is still progress...Relapse is part of recovery. It is not a failure."
~ *Donna Orrin*

Self-Nurture Calendar

*"If you nurture your mind, body, and spirit, your time will expand.
You will gain a new perspective that will allow you to accomplish much more."*
~ Brian Koslow

Day of the Week	How I will Nurture Myself

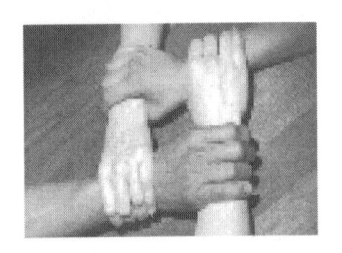

Strengths Encounters

The purpose of this exercise is to give everyone in the group a chance to explore and explain their strengths in a comfortable and fun manner. Change or adapt the questions if your current partner is having difficulty answering the question/s.

What is one thing you've done in your life to make a difference?	For what would you like to be remembered?	Name one way that you help others around you.	What poem, song or quotation can you recite from memory?
What is one physical feat that you can perform?	Who inspires you? What is one quality that they possess?	Name one way that you consider yourself to be creative.	What meal do you prepare well?
What skill or talent would you most like to learn how to do?	What experience has taught you the most about life?	What is one way you have learned to adapt to your symptoms?	What community resource do you use on a regular basis?
Name one tool or machine that you can operate well.	What is one place that gives you strength & encouragement?	What one item in your home is important to you? Why?	Do you collect anything? What & why?
Name one strength you have gained by being a "survivor."	What subject were you best at in school?	Name one thing you have recently learned from someone else.	What do you most enjoy doing during your spare time?

STRENGTHS YOU SEE IN ME

I appreciate the time that you are willing to take to identify some of my strengths. The following are just a few categories that you may want to consider in listing strengths that you see in me.

What I Know/Knowledge I Have/Things I Have Learned
People are constantly learning and experiencing life. This learning can occur in a formalized setting (schools, textbooks and classes). However, the majority of learning occurs in informal settings (from family, the workplace or from the culture), especially from first hand experience. For example, a person may understand computers, know how to take care of a baby, know how to grow geraniums, have knowledge about relaxation techniques or know how to navigate through the mental health system.

Please list below some of the knowledge you know I have:

Please list things that you believe I have an interest in learning:

STRENGTHS YOU SEE IN ME, cont.

The Talents and Skills I Have
Examples might include being able to sing on key, solving problems, sketching and drawing, getting along well with people, gardening, reciting poetry, long distance runner, crafts, baking bread, etc.

Please list below some of the gifts, talents and skills you see in me:

My Cultural Identity and Resources
A person's cultural identity can strongly influence his or her lifestyle and behavior. Cultural strengths may include rituals, styles of communication, geographic influences, generational identity (such as being a "baby boomer"), celebrations, sources of pride or cultural resources.

Please list below some of the strengths you see that I can draw from my cultural identity:

STRENGTHS YOU SEE IN ME, cont.

My Personal Qualities
Examples might include a sense of humor, staying calm in an emergency, enthusiastic, reliable, energetic, caring, organized, free-spirited, friendly, loyal, etc..

Please list below some of the personal qualities you see as strengths in me:

Things I Can Take Pride in
People have things to be proud of, such as attainments. One source of pride is "survivors pride" that people develop through getting through great difficulties or barriers.

Please list below some of the things you think I can take pride in:

Are there any other strengths that you see in me?

Thank You for Taking the Time to Help Me to Identify my Strengths!

CERTIFICATE OF ACHIEVEMENT

presented to

Pathways to Recovery: MODULE TWO

_____
Name

_____
Date

My Favorite Things

"When the dog bites, when the bee stings, when I'm feeling sad, I simply remember my favorite things, and then I don't fee so bad."
~ *Oscar Hammerstein, II*

On Saturday afternoons, I like to _____
_____.

The best place I ever lived was _____.

These are two things that always make me laugh— _____
_____and
_____.

One thing I do to stay healthy is _____
_____.

_____is my favorite holiday.

My silliest friend is _____.

My dream job would be as a _____.

If I got a million dollars today, the first thing I would buy would be_____
_____.

I've always wanted to learn how to _____
_____.

The person I've learned the most from in life has to be_____
_____.

If I could go anywhere to relax, that place would be _____
_____.

My favorite place to eat at is _____.

Module Three
Small Group Project Presentations
Instruction Sheet

This project is an opportunity for your small group to look at a recovery topic in which you are all interested. As a group, you will design your own project and then present it to the entire group during session #21 or 22.

Each presentation should be 10-15 minutes in length and focus on one topic related to Module Three. Here are some examples of projects that can be done, however, your group is free to be creative and develop a new project!

1. Presenting a humorous skit

2. Exploring any of the domains further.

3. Developing a handbook of local community resources.

4. Further exploring any aspect of the domains (such as job accommodations, alternative health practices, etc.)

My group members are:

_____

_____

_____

_____

The topic we have chosen is_____

_____

_____

Our presentation will be given during this session_____

The Benefits of Exercise

The benefits of exercise are well known. It helps us relax and feel better. It can help with anxiety and levels of stress. It can also reduce feelings of depression, lessen the risk of certain diseases and promote good health.

Here's a list of reasons to exercise. Which of the following are important to you?

- ❏ Improve my concentration
- ❏ Reduce my weight
- ❏ Improve my muscle strength
- ❏ Reduce my stress
- ❏ Help me focus
- ❏ Reduce my symptoms of depression
- ❏ Enhance my flexibility
- ❏ Help me sleep better
- ❏ Make me feel better
- ❏ Give me more energy
- ❏ Reduce my pain
- ❏ Give me a break from my daily routine

- ❏ Reduce the risk of disease
- ❏ Increase my stamina
- ❏ Get together with friends
- ❏ Improve how I look
- ❏ Strengthen my muscles and bones
- ❏ Help me feel stronger
- ❏ Make my daily activities easier
- ❏ Help me feel younger
- ❏ Help me feel more productive
- ❏ Give me greater mobility
- ❏ Improve my self-esteem
- ❏ Other? _____
- ❏ Other? _____

What are one or two types of exercise that you would like to try?

- ❏ Walking
- ❏ Yoga
- ❏ Take an aerobics class
- ❏ Bicycle
- ❏ Team Sport _____
- ❏ Swimming

- ❏ Jogging
- ❏ Lifting weights
- ❏ Skating/rollerblading
- ❏ Dancing
- ❏ Go to a gym or fitness center
- ❏ Jumping rope
- ❏ Other? _____
- ❏ Other? _____

Here are my exercise goals:

Type of Exercise	Goal	Benefit/s I Expect	Barrier/s I Expect

101 Things to Do to Create Humor

"A person without a sense of humor is like a wagon without springs."
It's jolted by every pebble on the road."
~ Henry Ward Beecher

1. _____
2. _____
3. _____
4. _____
5. _____
6. _____
7. _____
8. _____
9. _____
10. _____
11. _____
12. _____
13. _____
14. _____
15. _____
16. _____
17. _____
18. _____
19. _____
20. _____
21. _____
22. _____
23. _____
24. _____
25. _____
26. _____
27. _____
28. _____
29. _____
30. _____
31. _____
32. _____
33. _____
34. _____
35. _____
36. _____
37. _____
38. _____
39. _____
40. _____
41. _____
42. _____
43. _____
44. _____
45. _____
46. _____
47. _____
48. _____
49. _____
50. _____
51. _____
52. _____
53. _____
54. _____
55. _____
56. _____
57. _____
58. _____
59. _____
60. _____
61. _____
62. _____
63. _____
64. _____
65. _____
66. _____
67. _____
68. _____
69. _____
70. _____
71. _____
72. _____
73. _____
74. _____
75. _____
76. _____
77. _____
78. _____
79. _____
80. _____
81. _____
82. _____
83. _____
84. _____
85. _____
86. _____
87. _____
88. _____
89. _____
90. _____
91. _____
92. _____
93. _____
94. _____
95. _____
96. _____
97. _____
98. _____
99. _____
100. _____
101. _____

CERTIFICATE OF ACHIEVEMENT

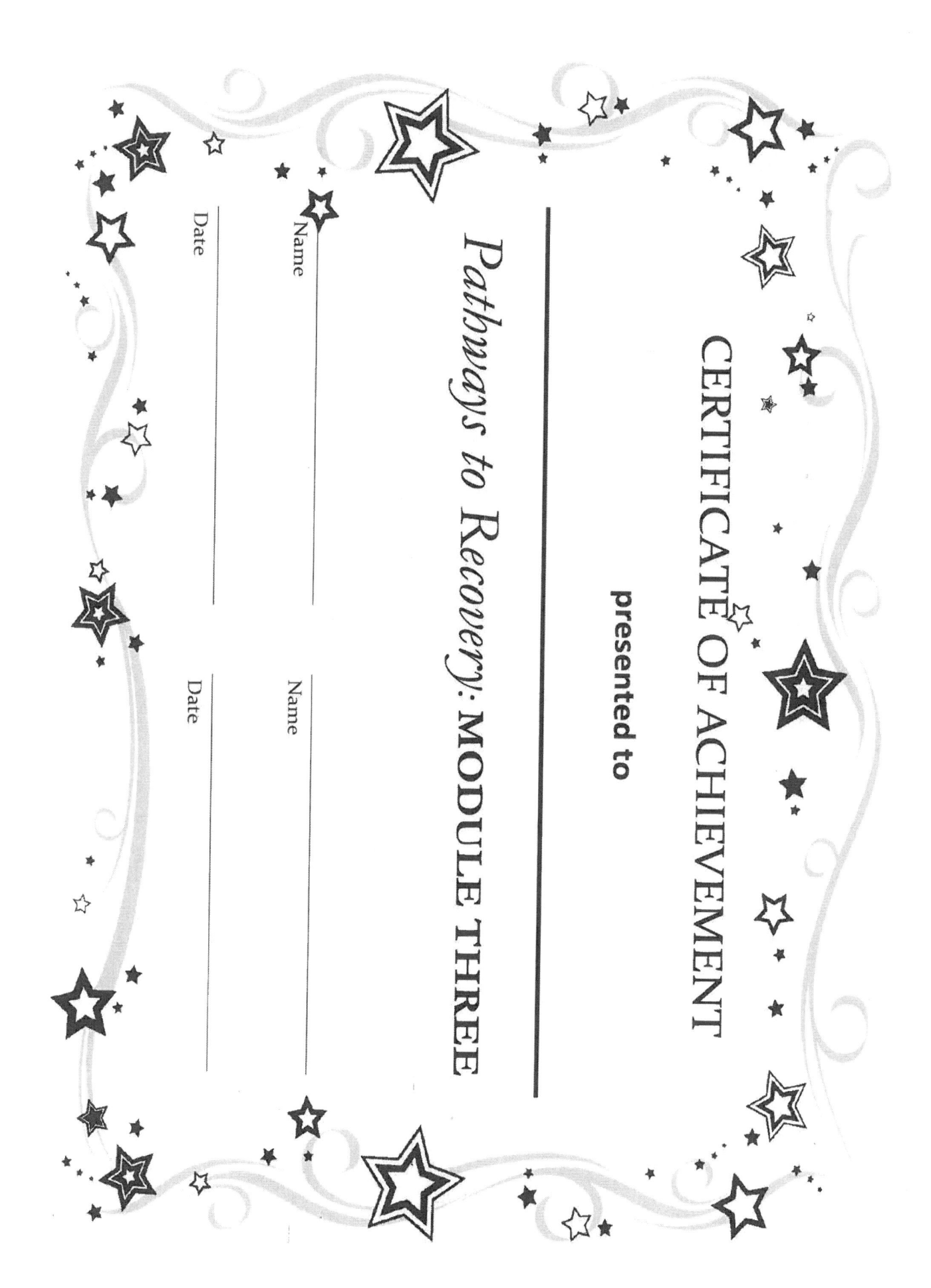

presented to

_____

Pathways to Recovery: MODULE THREE

Name _____

Date _____

Name _____

Date _____

This or That?
Which will you choose?

For each question below, circle your favorite answer.

Gold or Silver?

Winter or Summer?

Mountains or Ocean?

Roses or Daisies?

Left or Right?

Music or Reading?

Cat or Dog?

Morning or Evening?

Write a Letter or E-mail?

Comedy or Drama?

Roller Coaster or Ferris Wheel?

Apple or Banana?

Thick or Thin?

Rain or Snow?

Stop or Go?

Shower or Bath?

Good or Bad?

Candy Bar or Potato Chips?

Before or After?

North or South?

East or West?

Lead or Follow?

Rock & Roll or Country?

Healthy or Wealthy?

Pen or Pencil?

Like or Love?

Heads or Tails?

Bicycle or Motorcycle?

Red or Blue?

Light or Dark?

Inside or Outside?

Solitare or Dominoes?

Black & White or Color?

_____ or _____ ?

_____ or _____ ?

_____ or _____ ?

Module Four
Small Group Project Presentations
Instruction Sheet

This project is an opportunity for your small group to look at a recovery topic in which you are all interested. As a group, you will design your own project and then present it to the entire group during session #21 or 22.

Each presentation should be 10-15 minutes in length and focus on one topic related to Module Four. Here are some examples of projects that can be done, however, your group is free to be creative and develop a new project!

1. Developing a list of "101 Ways to Reduce Stress."

2. Further exploring the concept of gratitude (why it's helpful, why it works, etc.).

3. Creating a short skit on how to meet someone new.

4. Preparing a resource list of places to submit recovery stories for publication (for example, specific websites, addresses of publishers, etc.

5. Designing all or part of the final celebration activity.

My group members are:

_____

_____

_____

_____

The topic we have chosen is_____

_____

_____

Our presentation will be given during this session_____

Mixed-Up Messages

Can you figure out what this message is saying?

Stna klat without gniyas a drow! Did you know that hwen stna outch each ohter with their eannetna, it is one yaw they klat or etacinummoc?

What do you think this message says? _____

_____

Adapted from http://www.letsfindout.com

101 Things to Be Thankful For!

"Feeling gratitude and not expressing it is like wrapping a present and not giving it."
~ *William Arthur Ward*

1. _____
2. _____
3. _____
4. _____
5. _____
6. _____
7. _____
8. _____
9. _____
10. _____
11. _____
12. _____
13. _____
14. _____
15. _____
16. _____
17. _____
18. _____
19. _____
20. _____
21. _____
22. _____
23. _____
24. _____
25. _____
26. _____
27. _____
28. _____
29. _____
30. _____
31. _____
32. _____
33. _____
34. _____
35. _____
36. _____
37. _____
38. _____
39. _____
40. _____
41. _____
42. _____
43. _____
44. _____
45. _____
46. _____
47. _____
48. _____
49. _____
50. _____
51. _____
52. _____
53. _____
54. _____
55. _____
56. _____
57. _____
58. _____
59. _____
60. _____
61. _____
62. _____
63. _____
64. _____
65. _____
66. _____
67. _____
68. _____
69. _____
70. _____
71. _____
72. _____
73. _____
74. _____
75. _____
76. _____
77. _____
78. _____
79. _____
80. _____
81. _____
82. _____
83. _____
84. _____
85. _____
86. _____
87. _____
88. _____
89. _____
90. _____
91. _____
92. _____
93. _____
94. _____
95. _____
96. _____
97. _____
98. _____
99. _____
100. _____
101. _____

Finding Balance

"The older I get, the more wisdom I find in the ancient rule of taking first things first—a process which often reduces the most complex human problems to manageable proportions."
~ Dwight David Eisenhower

Current Time & Tasks

What activities do you do on a daily or weekly basis? How much time do you spend on each task? Add these to the "pie" at left.

_____
_____
_____
_____
_____
_____
_____

Preferred Time & Tasks

What activities do you want to continue doing on a daily or weekly basis? How much time would you like to spend on each? Add these to the "pie" at right.

_____
_____
_____
_____
_____
_____
_____

In what ways are the two "pies" the same? _____
_____

How are they different? _____
_____

What will you have to change to move from the first "pie" to the second? _____
_____

These Things I Can...

"How good is...life, the mere living! How fit to employ all the heart and the soul and the senses forever in joy!"

~ *Robert Browning*

See_____

Hear_____

Taste_____

Touch_____

The Road Leads Home

Do you like the color red?

Do you own a car?

Do you own a radio?

Would you drink goat's milk?

Do you have two sisters?

Do you like rain?

Can you wiggle your ears?

Can you ride a bicycle?

Were you born in a country other than this one?

Is your birthday in October?

Have you had a pet named Muffin?

Do you eat breakfast every day?

Would you eat in a restaurant by yourself?

Do you have a grandson?

Do you own a green chair?

Have you ever seen a bear (but not in the zoo)?

Do you like to clean your home?

Would you buy an orange tablecloth?

Can you play a guitar?

Have you ever been in a hot air balloon?

Can you cross all your fingers and toes at the same time?

Story Circle Questions

*"Stories move in circles. They don't move in straight lines. So it helps if you listen in circles. There are stories inside stories and stories between stories, and find you way through them is as easy and as hard as finding your way home. And part of the finding is the getting lost.
And when you're lost, you start to look around and to listen."*
~ Corey Fischer, Albert Greenberg & Naomi Newman

Was there a specific person who inspired you on your road to recovery? Perhaps it was ... a friend, a family member or a peer.

Take 3-5 minutes to talk about what it was they did & how this sparked your recovery journey.

What risks have you had to take in your recovery? What kind of challenges have you faced?

Take 3-5 minutes to talk about how you have taken risks to help you on your recovery journey.

What was it that "sparked" your recovery journey? Did you have a ... Slow awakening? A dramatic turnaround? An "aha" moment? A eureka experience?

Take 3-5 minutes to share how you knew you were on a recovery journey and what it was that allowed you to grab hold of your own life.

What wellness or comfort tool or strategy has helped you in your recovery journey?

Take 3-5 minutes to share with others the one tool or strategy you have used most to help you maintain balance & focus in your life.

Writing Your Story

My recovery question is _____

_____

Stage #1: *Preparation*
What things can you do that will help you explore your story?

Stage #2: *Germination*
What images or ideas will you gather to help you?

Stage #3: *Working*
What method/s can you use to build your story?

Stage #4: *Deepening*
What questions can you ask that will help you decide what your story is really about?

Stage #5: *Shaping*
In what form would you like your story to be?

Stage #6: *Completion*
What can you do that will help you reach this stage?

Stage #7: *Going public*
In what ways could you share your story publicly?

CERTIFICATE OF ACHIEVEMENT

presented to

_____

Pathways to Recovery: **MODULE FOUR**

Name _____

Date _____

Name _____

Date _____

A RECOVERY PLEDGE

I acknowledge that I am in recovery.

I believe that all people are made up of more than just their mental illness.

I believe in the principles of recovery...that the journey is unique for each person, it requires the will to recovery, it is a self-directed process of discovery, it is nonlinear with unexpected set backs and it requires self-effort, endurance and courage.

I believe in the essence of recovery that all individuals can live a full life and participate as citizens of our community.

I understand that education and self-advocacy are keys to my recovery.

I believe that it is important for family, friends, professionals and my peers to join together as partners to build a community of hope.

I will strive to support others on their journey of recovery.

I believe that I have a tomorrow and that I can shape my future by enjoying life to the fullest and sharing my own story of hope with others.

~Pathways to Recovery, p. 20

References

"The moment one gives close attention to any thing, even a blade of grass, it becomes a mysterious, awesome, indescribably magnificent world in itself."
~ Henry Miller

Bachel, B.K. (2001). *What do you really want?: how to set a goal and go for it.* Minneapolis, MN: Free Spirit Publishing.

Belknap, M. (1997). *Mind, body, magic: creativities for any audience.* Duluth, MN: Whole Person Associates.

Booth, N. (1996). *Meeting room games.* St. Paul, MN: Brighton Publications, Inc.

Hopkins, E., Woods, Z., Kelley, R., Bentley, K., & Murphy, J. (1995). *Working with groups on spiritual themes: structured exercises in healing.* Duluth, MN: Whole Person Associates.

Capacchione, L. (2000). *Visioning: ten steps to designing the life of your dreams.* New York: Penguin Putman, Inc.

Carpenter, Jenneth (2002). Mental health recovery paradigm: Implications for social work. *Health & Social Work, 27,* 86-94

Copeland, M.E. (1997). *Wellness recovery action plan.* Brattleboro, VT: Peach Press.

Copeland, M.E. (1999). *Winning against relapse.* Oakland, CA: New Harbinger Publications.

Deegan, P.E. (1990). Spirit breaking: when the helping professions hurt. *The Humanistic Psychologist, 18*(3), 301-313.

de Mello, Anthony. (1984). *Wellsprings.* New York, NY: Doubleday.

Dynes, R. (1988). *Creative writing in groupwork.* Bicester, Oxon, UK: Winslow Press Ltd.

Eastman, J. (1999). *Simple indulgence: easy, everyday things to do for me.* Kansas City, MO: Andrews McMeel Publishing.

Gawain, S. (1991). *Meditations, creative visualization and meditation exercises to enrich your life.* San Rafael, CA: New World Library.

Gesell, I. (1997). *Playing along: 37 group learning activities borrowed from improvisational theater.* Duluth, MN: Whole Person Associates

Grout, P. (2000). *Heart and soul: 156 ways to free your creative spirit.* Kansas City, MO: Andrews, McMeel Publishing.

Grout, P. (2001). *Living big.* Berkeley: Conari Press.

Hendricks, G. & Hendricks, K. (1999). The conscious heart. New York, NY: Bantam.

Hopkins, E., Woods, Z., Kelley, R., Bentley, K., & Murphy, J. (1995). *Working with groups on spiritual themes: structured exercises in healing.* Duluth, MN: Whole Person Associates.

Jennings, S. (1986). *Creative drama in groupwork.* Bicester, Oxon, UK: Winslow Press Ltd.

Louden, J. (1992). *The woman's comfort book.* San Francisco: Harper.

Louden, J. (1994). *The couple's comfort book.* San Francisco: Harper.

Moran, V. (1999). *Creating a charmed life.* San Francisco: Harper.

Newstrom, J., & Scannell, E. (1996). *The big book of business games: icebreakers, creativity exercises, and meeting energizers.* New York: McGraw-Hill.

Newstrom, J., & Scannell, E. (1998). *The big book of team building games.* New York: McGraw-Hill.

Nilson, C. (1993). *Team games for trainers.* New York: McGraw-Hill.

Perry, M. (2004). *Confidence booster workout: 10 steps to beating self-doubt.* San Diego, CA: Thunder Bay Press.

Pollack, R. (2000). *The power of ritual.* New York: Dell Publishing.

Potamkin, L.B. (1999). *Messages from the heart.* Carlsbad, CA: Hay House.

Rice, W., & Yaconelli, M. (Eds.). (1993). *Play it again!: more great games for groups.* Grand Rapids, MI: Zondervan Publishing House.

Ridgway, P., McDiarmid, D., Davidson, L., Bayes, J. & Ratzlaff, S. (2003). *Pathways to Recovery: A Strengths Recovery Self-Help Workbook.* Lawrence, KS: University of Kansas School of Social Welfare.

Race, P., & Smith, B. (1996). *500 tips for trainers.* Houston, TX: Gulf Publishing Company.

Rapp, C.A. (1998) *The strengths model: Case management with people suffering from severe and persistent mental illness.* New York: Oxford University Press.

Ryan, M.J. (2000). *365 health and happiness boosters.* Berkeley: Conari Press.

Self-Help 101, (n.d.). Retrieved May 17, 2006, from http://www.selfhelp.on.ca/shaw2002Factsheet.pdf

Simpkins, A., & Simpkins, A.M. (1996). *Principles of meditation: eastern wisdom for the western mind.* Boston: Charles E. Tuttle Company.

Syx, C. (1995). The mental health service system: how we've created a make-believe world. *Psychiatric Rehabilitation Journal, 19(1),* 83-85.

West, E. (1997). *201 icebreakers: group mixers, warm-ups, energizers, and playful activities.* New York: McGraw-Hill.

Resources

"I've learned that the resources we need to turn our dreams into reality are within us, merely waiting for the day when we decide to wake up and claim our birthright." ~ Anthony Robbins

For topical resources on module topics (motivation, goal-setting, spirituality, stress, etc.), check the "Resources" sections at the end of each chapter in *Pathways to Recovery*.

You can find numerous resources for facilitators at your local library or bookstore. Some recommended publications include:

- Art of Facilitation: How to Create Group Synergy by Dale Hunter, Anne Bailey & Bill Taylor

- The Big Book of Business Games, Icebreakers, Creativity Exercises and Meeting Energizers by John Newstom & Edward Scannel

- The Big Book of Team Building Games by John Newstom & Edward Scannel

- Creative Art in Groupwork by Jean Campbell

- Creative Drama in Groupwork by Sue Jennings

- Creative Games in Groupwork by Robin Dynes

- Creative Movement & Dance in Groupwork by Helen Payne

- Creative Music in Groupwork by Christopher Achenbach

- Creative Relaxation in Groupwork by Irene Tubbs

- Creative Writing in Groupwork by Robin Dynes

- A Facilitator's Fieldbook: Step-by-Step Procedures by Thomas Justice and David Jamieson

- 500 Tips for Trainers by Phil Race & Brenda Smith

- Getting Together: Icebreakers and Group Energizers by Lorraine L. Ukens

- Hot Tips for Facilitators: Strategies to Make Life Easier for Anyone Who Leads, Guides, Teaches or Trains Groups by Rob Abernathy & Mark Reardon

- Moving Beyond Icebreakers by Stanley Pollack & Mary Fasoni

- <u>Tips for Self-Help Group Leaders</u> (Available from www.selfhelpconnection.ca)

- <u>201 Icebreakers: Group Mixers, Warm-Ups, Energizers and Playful Activities</u> by Edie West

- <u>Working with Groups on Spiritual Themes: Structured Exercises in Healing</u> by Elaine Hopkins, Russell Kelley, Katrina Bentley & James Murphy

The Internet also offers a multitude of sites that provide specific tips to enhance your skills. Trying a simple search for facilitation, training or teaching will give you lots of links. Here are some good ones to begin:

- http://school.discovery.com/teachingtools/teachingtools.html (teaching tools)

- http://osa.stanford.edu/Resources/icebreakers.htm (free icebreakers)

- www.guilamuir.com (free articles and on-line newsletter)

- www.iaf-world.org (International Association of Facilitators)

- www.masterfacilitatorjournal.com (weekly facilitation tips)

- www.selfhelpnetwork.wichita.edu (provides tips on self-help groups)

- www.thiagi.com (free resources and online newsletter)

- www.wilderdom.com/games/ (sample activities, games and exercises)

Meet the Authors of the Group Facilitator's Guide

Lori Davidson is one of the original authors of *Pathways to Recovery*. As a social worker, Lori has worked in a variety of mental health settings for over twenty years, using her own experience with depression as a means of understanding and supporting others to take risks in their own journey. As a storyteller and sometimes artist, Lori is particularly interested in using creativity as a way of healing. She loves lilacs & playing with "her kids."

Diane McDiarmid is also one of the original authors of *Pathways to Recovery*. She has served as past Director of Supported Education for The University of Kansas School of Social Welfare/Office of Mental Health Research & Training. Along with *Pathways to Recovery*, Diane's current work centered on emerging best practices in supported education, including research, training and consultation. She was a trainer for the Strengths Perspective across the United States and internationally. Beyond spending time with her family and friends, you will often find Diane on the water as a competitive rower.

Jean M. Higbee has extensive personal experience with recovery from her mental illness and is a frequent wellness and recovery trainer across Kansas. She is also the assistant director of Project Independence, Inc., a consumer-run organization in Wichita and is active in the CRO Network of Kansas. She is a frequent volunteer and speaker at workshops, local schools, a botanical garden and with emergency first responders. Jean is a published poet and enjoys reading, collecting antique books and hanging out with her cat, "Smudge." She is currently writing her life story.

Notes:

Printed in Great Britain
by Amazon